Learning Disabilities and Life Stories

EDITED BY

Pano Rodis

Upper Valley Associates in
Psychology & Education
and
Dartmouth College

Andrew Garrod

Dartmouth College

Mary Lynn Boscardin

University of Massachusetts

Allyn and Bacon

Boston • London • Toronto • Sydney • Tokyo • Singapore

Vice President, Editor in Chief, Education: Paul A. Smith
Senior Editor: Virginia C. Lanigan
Editorial Assistant: Jennifer Connors
Marketing Manager: Brad Parkins
Editorial-Production Administrator: Annette Joseph
Editorial-Production Coordinator: Holly Crawford
Composition Buyer: Linda Cox
Electronic Composition: Karen Mason
Manufacturing Buyer: Suzanne Lareau
Cover Administrator: Jenny Hart
Cover Designer: Michael J. Kase of Blumlein Associates, Inc.

Copyright © 2001 by Allyn & Bacon
A Pearson Education Company
160 Gould Street
Needham Heights, MA 02494

Internet: www.abacon.com

Library of Congress Cataloging-in-Publication Data
Learning disabilities and life stories / edited by Pano Rodis, Andrew Garrod, Mary Lynn Boscardin.
    p. cm.
   Includes bibliographical references and index.
   ISBN 0-205-32010-4
    1. Learning disabled—Education (Higher)—United States—Case studies. 2. Learning disabilities—United States—Case studies. 3. Learning disabled—United States—Biography. I. Rodis, Pano. II. Garrod, Andrew. III. Boscardin, Mary Lynn.

LC4818.38 .L42 2000
362.4—dc21   99-087271

Printed in the United States of America
10 9 8 7 6   05

Photo Credits: pp. 51 and 73, Will Hart

Text Credit: p. 165, "Hands of the Day" from *Late and Posthumous Poems: 1968–1974* by Pablo Neruda, translated by Ben Belitt. Copyright © 1988 by Ben Belitt. Used by permission of Grove/Atlantic, Inc.

W

*To Karen Sophia, Leda Maria, and Maria Dionyssa,
my companions in the effort to learn
justice, generosity, and boisterous joyfulness.*

—P. R.

*To Felicity, Vanessa, Katie, Fenella, Misha,
Katya, and Sasha with love.*

—A. G.

*To Marco, Tristan, and Adriane for their
love, support, and encouragement
throughout another
long-term, time intensive project.*

—M. L. B.

Learning disabilities is a general term that refers to a heterogeneous group of disorders manifested by significant difficulties in the acquisition and use of listening, speaking, reading, writing, reasoning, or mathematical abilities. These disorders are intrinsic to the individual, presumed to be due to central nervous system dysfunction, and may occur across the life span. Problems in self-regulatory behaviors, social perception, and social interaction may exist with learning disabilities but do not by themselves constitute a learning disability. Although learning disabilities may occur concomitantly with other handicapping conditions (for example, sensory impairment, mental retardation, serious emotional disturbance) or with extrinsic influences (such as cultural differences, insufficient or inappropriate instruction), they are not the result of those conditions or influences.

—National Joint Committee on Learning Disabilities (1988)

Contents

Preface

This book is intended as an honest, critical, and yet affirmative study of the lives of persons who have learning disabilities. It is not our aim to offer a book that contributes further to the *disabling* of persons whom we regard as rich in abilities and capacities of many sorts. On the contrary, it is our hope to contribute positively to the lives and reputations of persons with learning disabilities. We aim to do this by attempting to articulate and solve authentic problems, evaluating existing professional practices, and proposing ways that educators, psychologists, family members, and friends can respond more productively to persons of every age who learn in a manner different from most others.

The editors embarked on this project with the hope of answering the long-standing needs of at least three significant groups of readers.

First of all, *Learning Disabilities and Life Stories* is designed to fill the need in college-level education and psychology courses for a text that makes vivid and concrete the many significant issues raised by learning disabilities. Our review of existing textbooks suggests that *Learning Disabilities and Life Stories* is unique. Although there is a small handful of earlier efforts that rely on interviews with persons who have learning disabilities, these are scholarly works intended for a professional audience and hence not appropriate for most undergraduate and graduate courses. Moreover, the autobiographical essay is a much more riveting, original, and deeply textured piece of writing than the interview. The autobiographical essays in this collection do more than complement the professional discourse on learning disabilities; rather, they vitally reframe, challenge, and dramatize that discourse, bringing students in education and psychology face-to-face with questions that will surely arise in the course of their future professional lives.

Secondly, *Learning Disabilities and Life Stories* responds to the immediate need to offer practitioners and researchers in education and psychology a *phenomenological* perspective—which is to say a perspective that conveys the ways that learning disabilities are experienced by those who have them. Such a perspective is essential to authentic success in fields that exist primarily to provide direct service to others.

Thirdly and most importantly, the book fills a critical need on the part of persons with learning disabilities and their families to hear from others like themselves. While it can be tremendously helpful to read an "expert's" view on learning disabilities, such experts are also outsiders; they have not, in most cases, lived the things they write about. Accordingly, such experts usually employ a language and a stance that is impersonal. For persons with learning disabilities, a valuable understanding and comfort can come from reading the deeply personal narratives of others like themselves, particularly when these others have managed to enter college and succeed there despite their difficulties in learning.

It is worth noting here that virtually all of the students who contributed essays to this collection reported that writing their autobiographies was among the most transformative and positive experiences of their lives. This feeling is palpable in their essays, giving them exceptional quality and fullness. For this reason and for the many others cited above, these essays are deeply worth reading.

All the same, to view these 13 narratives as the final word on the experience of living with learning disabilities would be quite mistaken. It is, in fact, of urgent importance that all persons who have learning disabilities be given—or that they assertively seize—the opportunity to express their unique minds and their own wills, thus directly shaping the particular worlds in which they live.

After three years of work on this project, we are indebted to many persons for their skillful, energetic, and thoughtful contributions. This project would not have been possible without the invaluable assistance of these tutors and researchers: Kregg Strehorn, Patricia Pier, Tom Daughton, Gabrielle Glorioso, Lydia Greene, Belinda Corteza, Denise Manning, Karen Sopper, and Melanie Smith. Frank Dufresne and Gary Stoner, research supervisors at the University of Massachusetts, Amherst, are owed a special debt, as are our administrative allies at Landmark College, Dan Toomey and Tom Trenchard. Friends whose close reading and editorial suggestions improved the manuscript as it was in process were Karen Blumlein, Erwin Stunkel, Larry Clifford, Dody Riggs, Bill Levin, and Karen Maloney. Valued administrative assistants include Dartmouth College students Megan Cummins, Matthew K. Nelson, and Pete Fritz. For encouragement and advice in the early stages of the project, we are grateful to Carl Thum and Nancy Pompian. We are especially thankful to Christie Jackson for her role in the editorial process and her gracious and able support in the time-consuming work of preparing the manuscript for final submission.

We particularly want to recognize and thank all the persons who composed autobiographical essays. Those whose essays are not printed here gave no less generously of themselves, and they contributed inestimably to the total endeavor: We are in their debt. Finally, we acknowledge the courage and acumen of the autobiographers whose essays comprise the heart of this volume.

Introduction

I invite you into my world for two reasons. One is the hope that you will gain some insight, understanding, compassion, or even strength. I also write for myself in the hope that this process will help me to love myself for who I am and all that I can be.

—Lynn Pelkey

I am a prisoner, a survivor, a target, and a struggler, continuously defending, negating, and recreating myself. My disability? My disability is that I have been disabled, as well as discouraged and discounted by a temporarily able-minded, able-bodied general public.

—Aaron Piziali

I.

Many researchers—including educators, neurologists, and psychologists—have worked productively over the last 35 years to advance our understanding of learning disabilities. Although there continues to be a need for more discovery—as well as more debate—in almost every specific area of inquiry, it is possible to find in the published literature a meaningful working knowledge of what learning disabilities are, how they have an impact on educational success, and what procedures might be used in schools to help students with learning disabilities learn more efficiently.

What there is much less of is an understanding and appreciation of the *persons* who live with learning disabilities. It is not possible to make "persons" a topic of research in the same way that one can the neuropsychology of dyslexia. Our humanity is much too complex, various, and dynamic for that, as are the contexts in which persons are situated. But the questions sparked by the notion that there is a *person* to go along with every learning disability, and that we err in imagining that we have understood the person if we have described his or her learning disability, are not to be casually dismissed. In fact, it should be apparent that the central reason we even bother with learning disabilities is for the sake of the persons affected by them. Moreover, most of us know from experience that neglecting persons in order to "treat" or otherwise focus on their difficulties rarely leads to success. Why do fewer than half of students with learning disabilities graduate from high school (Vogel & Reder, 1998)? Why does there appear to be a correlation between having a learning disability and depression (Brumback & Weinberg, 1990)? Could it be that our failure to consider persons who have learning disabilities in their totality—which is to say as complete social, psychological, cultural, spiritual, and political beings—has something to do with these persons' all-too-frequent failure to thrive?

This book has its origins in exactly this set of problems and meditations. It started, in other words, with the question: How might it be possible to understand the complex persons behind their learning disability diagnoses?

The basic answer to this question is very simple and direct: Give these persons the floor. Invite them to speak for themselves. Make it possible for *them* to say who they are.

Accordingly, during the years 1996 and 1997, young adults (ages 20–35) attending four very different higher educational institutions in the northeastern United States were invited to write autobiographical essays about their experiences of living with learning disabilities. Within the context of a one- to two-semester independent study course in writing, 30 students at the University of Massachusetts, Amherst; Greenfield Community College; Landmark College; and Dartmouth College explored their own lives, meeting weekly in one-on-one sessions with a researcher/instructor. As a group, these students possessed diagnoses of a wide range of specific learning disabilities, including Attention-Deficit/Hyperactivity Disorder (ADHD), some of which were detected early in life, others undiagnosed until college. In working with these students, the researchers/instructors followed no set agenda nor did they direct the writing process, rather, they assumed a posture of open, respectful curiosity. They did, however, ask frequent and very direct questions about learning disabilities, some of which were written out and offered to the students as potential writing prompts. These questions wandered within and beyond the margins of the established, professional discourse on learning disabilities, treating matters as diverse as the observable manifestations of an individual's learning disability, positive and negative educational experiences, the formation of a sense of self, the degree of support offered by family members, and so on. The thrust of our common work was to focus on the writers in their human totality and complexity, not on learning disabilities per se as a kind of malady or cluster of problems. We wished to be attentive to negative processes and life problems, as well to how typical academic challenges were or were not met, but we were most interested in the ways that the writers' lives had been constructed, both from within (i.e., how the writers thought and felt about themselves) and from without (i.e., how they have been seen, treated, and valued or devalued by other individuals and institutions). We wished, in other words, for the writers to consider their learning disabilities as facets of (a) their total selves and (b) their total social, cultural, and political existences.

This was a sound starting place. But, as those of us involved in the making of this book quickly discovered, it was just not enough—in fact, it was far from enough—to support the writing of these essays merely with the objective of "revealing" or "illuminating" or otherwise "making visible" persons who have learning disabilities. In fact, such a notion runs very close to asking persons to put themselves on display as specimens to be studied. Moreover, we were forced to ask ourselves if it were legitimate to speak of persons with learning disabilities as "them"? Does group identity exist once inquiry has moved beyond the level of diagnosis to the level of the person? Or, once we have come to the matter of personhood, do we find only an awesomely heterogeneous scattering of individuals, too dissimilar for science—or its applications in education and psychology—to grasp?

What we needed to realize was a fundamental renaming of our purpose. We needed, in other words, to grasp that the primary rationale for creating a forum for persons with learning disabilities was not to *show* them to others, but rather so that they could *act* on their own behalf and on the behalf of other persons facing similar life circumstances. Rather than encouraging the writing of essays that function only like windows that let others peer in, we wanted these essays actively and deliberately to guide the seeing of their readers, much as any film, novel, or other piece of conscious art might do. We wanted a creative process that acknowledged that what it means to "see" a person is to see *with* them, to join somehow in the movements of their consciousness, sensitive to the subtle and broad activity of their wills, open to their experiences. We also wanted a process attuned to the possibility that "seeing" others requires that we understand how they see *us*, allowing their seeing in some fashion to reshape our beliefs and actions, to organize our relations with them. For, we reasoned, neither "seeing" nor "being seen" ultimately means much unless each results in a positive remaking of the worlds in which we together live.

Accordingly, as the autobiographers wrote, displaying their unique and impressive forms of expertise, the researchers/instructors operated less as viewers (*voyeurs*) and more as collaborators in the process of bringing a "many-voiced" book into being. Following the natural impulses of the autobiographers to pose problems, render critiques, and take positions on issues, the researchers came to understand that one essential purpose of the book was to support persons with learning disabilities in further assuming an *active* stance toward their own lives, past and present. Thus, if the autobiographers identified a past problem or unhappiness, the researchers asked them how they managed to overcome or at least survive it, suggesting that they place these solutions into their narratives. Rather than merely working at the production of retrospectives or memoirs (i.e., writings that are oriented strictly to the past), the writers were encouraged to be goal oriented, concretely envisioning the ways that their values and ambitions might be realized here-and-now and tomorrow. Additionally, the researchers promoted a certain level of audience-awareness; that is, the writers were asked to imagine their essays being read by others, particularly other persons who have learning disabilities and their families, but also educators and mental health practitioners. If the writers could have a direct influence on the attitudes and actions of others, what would they like that influence to be? All in all, we sought to create a writing process oriented toward positive, responsible dialogue with self and world. Moreover, we sought to produce a final work in which all included voices possessed equal authority and legitimacy, as well as a common agenda: the will to meaningfully improve the circumstances and fortunes of persons who have learning disabilities.

The accomplishment of our transition in purpose was gradual, perhaps in part because it required a significant transformation in identity, both for the so-called "researchers" and the so-called "research subjects." What was required, in other words, was that we challenge from the ground up the old problem in scientific cultures of the division between the knowing, speaking, active "scientist" and the unknowing, silenced, passive "subject." When these two groups enter into collaborative, mutually supportive relationships, they break from established scientific protocol, as well as from the established social hierarchy in schools, be they elementary schools or universities. While such relationships—and the shifts in identity they create—are on the way to becoming standard in disciplines such as anthropology, they are rarer in psychology, and even rarer in the field of learning disabilities research. As the anthropologist Renato Rosaldo (1993) suggests, traditionally when research is done: "Disciplinary norms . . . require that a cultural gap separate analysts from their subjects. My argument, of course, is that . . . analysts should work from one position and try to imagine (or consult with others who occupy) the other" (188–189). Rosaldo's last sentence asserts the vital possibility of a two-way relationship between "analysts" and their "subjects"; a relationship in which each party not only actively studies the other, but also actively informs the other about its own identity. In this model, the "researched subject" resists being defined and delimited by the "researching subject"; and the methods and constructs of the "researching subject" can become topics of analysis for the probing of the "researched subject."

This is quite a shift for the learning disability field. Given the preoccupation of the field with cognitive differences as *disabling*, it has implicitly embraced—or at least not widely challenged—the notion of the person with a learning disability as a "disabled seer," or as one *unable* to play the role of the analyst. Clearly, this notion must change. And equally clearly—as the narratives in this book so eloquently establish—there is every reason to believe that this notion *can* be responsibly discarded, giving way to a conception of the person who must live with a learning disability as a viable thinker, speaker, co-researcher, political analyst, and problem solver.

II.

In its published form, *Learning Disabilities and Life Stories* can be described most simply as an anthology—or collection of voices—with two major components.

The first component consists of 13 autobiographical essays written by the students at the four colleges. Speaking in terms alternately intimate and analytical, these essays each tell of a sustained personal encounter with the challenges and mysteries of living with a learning disability. These writers do not mince words—their stories are told frankly and with the clear ambition of revealing not only what they have experienced, but also what they have felt. They are moving pieces, and it is hard to imagine a reader who will not respond to them emotionally. Indeed, because of the great intimacy of their accounts, a few of the autobiographers chose to publish under pseudonyms and to be represented by photos of children other than themselves. All the same, these autobiographies are by no stretch of the imagination merely personal, which is to say concerned solely with their writers' private lives. Rather, they are all in various ways consciously analytical, offering astute critical readings of culture and society. To have lived with a learning disability, the writers tell us, means to have directly confronted a variety of cultures (e.g., educational, familial, and political) that are generally ill prepared to respond positively to them. In the process of narrating what they have lived, the autobiographers also move to assert what should *change* so that the lives of persons with learning disabilities can be qualitatively improved. Combining impulses toward social justice with specific proposals for institutional change, they ask for reform characterized by a recognition of the potentialities of persons with learning disabilities, an acknowledgment of their strengths, and a realignment of the ways that the worth of their (and all other) persons is calculated. Our hope is that the reader will comprehend the essays in this collection not as tales of disability but as tales about persons intent on confronting the social construction of disability.

As is the rule with written material that goes to press, these essays have been taken through several drafts by their authors, and they have also been edited in order to condense them from their original length of 35 to 100 pages to a publishable length of 9 to 16 pages. In making cuts, the editors have kept a number of factors in mind, including an interest in capturing the shape and "feel" of the writers' life stories, as well as a focused desire to include the writers' most penetrating critiques of culture and society. The editors have also made requisite corrections in spelling and grammar, as well as an occasional stylistic change. We have, however, done nothing to alter, disguise, or rework these essays in ways inconsistent with their original forms. These essays are fully representative of their writers, preserving their writers' voice, diction, values, modes of emplotment, conceptual styles, and thought processes. Summaries of each writer's piece can be found just under the title of their essays, where they may be most useful to the reader.

The second component of this book consists of five analytical chapters written by scholars in the fields of education and psychology. The scholarly sections may be best conceptualized as (a) empathic responses to and (b) critical amplifications of the autobiographical essays. Drawing from their own professional and personal experiences and from other research literatures, the scholars attempt to grasp and then to converse with the autobiographers' messages, producing from these reflections specific suggestions for reform in the ways educators and psychologists work with persons who have learning disabilities. Although keyed to the autobiographies that comprise the first part of the book, these scholarly essays stand on their own as lucid contributions to the literature on learning disabilities.

Very briefly summarized, the scholars develop the following theses:

In "'Skin-Deep' Learning," Lisa Delpit offers a radical challenge to the widespread practice in U.S. education and society of categorizing persons according to their presumed (dis)abilities. Such a tendency, she suggests, not only leads to specific discriminatory practices against those labeled as "incompetent, inadequate, damaged," but also dovetails with forms of discrimination that have long oppressed children who are poor and/or African American. Instead, she argues, educators should embrace the position that learning styles "are not separate entities to be 'fixed,' but an integral part of the essential nature of any human being."

In "'Shimmers of Delight and Intellect': Building Learning Communities of Promise and Possibility," Carol Witherell and Pano Rodis outline a comprehensive moral and strategic vision of how general education teachers can support students with learning disabilities. Calling for a positive recognition of "intellectual diversity" among students, they suggest that "Students with learning disabilities are most likely to thrive educationally when teachers meaningfully recognize the talents and interests they already possess *and*, at the same time, seriously address their need to develop strength and fluency in primary academic discourses, including the discourses rendered most difficult by their learning disabilities."

In "The Educational Lives of Students with Learning Disabilities," Harold McGrady, Janet Lerner, and Mary Lynn Boscardin conduct a detailed, practical discussion of "what might be considered best practice in the education of students who have learning disabilities." Designed for both special and general educators, administrators, and parents, this chapter models a reflective approach to ascertaining which instructional practices are likely to be of benefit to students with learning disabilities.

In "Easing a World of Pain: Learning Disabilities and the Psychology of Self-Understanding," Robert Kegan articulates the reasons why a "'psychology of self-understanding' may be as (or more) important to the consideration of learning disabilities as a 'psychology of dysfunctional learning.'" According to Dr. Kegan, what a learning disability means to the person who has it is not static, but rather changes as that person passes through different universal stages of psychological development. By utilizing these wider frames of reference, teachers, psychologists, and parents may be empowered to develop both "detoxifying" and "anti-toxic" forms of support for young persons with learning disabilities.

In "Forging Identities, Tackling Problems, and Arguing with Culture: Psychotherapy with Persons Who Have Learning Disabilities," Pano Rodis describes three psychotherapeutic modalities particularly appropriate for both children and adults who have learning disabilities. Resting upon a meta-analysis of the 30 autobiographical narratives written by the participants in the *Learning Disabilities and Life Stories* project, this chapter offers a seven-stage model of identity formation for persons with learning disabilities, as well as specific techniques for supporting their psychological well-being.

As a whole, the autobiographical and the scholarly essays collaborate in offering grounded, original perspectives on learning disabilities. Although the writers do not always agree in their specific claims, they share in bringing to bear an unusual sensitivity to the psychological, cultural, and social forces that contribute to the experience of having a learning disability. Equally as important, they take responsibility for outlining clear, practical models for honoring the potentialities of persons living with learning disabilities.

III.

Having briefly described the making and the contents of this book, we wish to devote the remainder of this introduction to a discussion of the autobiographical essays, commenting on what these essays—through the very fact of their existence—say about established concepts and practices in the learning disabilities fields. In so doing, we hope to provide a prelude to the essays themselves.

As suggested, the autobiographical essays gathered here are, first of all, remarkable for their clarity and eloquence, their thoughtfulness, and their depth of insight. But these essays are also remarkable for their *rarity,* a fact deserving not of celebration but consternation. How is it possible that over the last 30-plus years of steadily mounting activity in the learning disabilities field so few persons with learning disabilities have found a significant public forum? Does it seem sensible that persons so able to make contributions—and whose welfare is so much at stake—should be excluded from the discourses that directly concern them?

The double fact of the richness and the rarity of these voices compels us to consider the possibility that far-reaching changes are necessary in many of the contexts wherein persons with learning disabilities are situated or their needs discussed. If we add in a third fact—the intensity of pain transmitted by these voices—we should be even more persuaded of the imperative for change. At heart, the changes required have to do with an end to the silencing of persons with learning disabilities, and the creation of an active, empowered role for them in the communities of which they are members. More specifically, these changes include a need for the active inclusion of persons with learning disabilities in professional discourses and research activities, a movement in education toward giving students active roles in determining the course and content of their educational programs, and a shift in U.S. culture at the broadest level away from a "disabling" view of persons with learning disabilities to a view that dignifies diverse approaches to knowing and learning.

These goals are reachable so long as professionals in the human service disciplines concerned with learning disabilities create collaborative, dialogic relationships with the persons they are ostensibly committed to serving. Such a sea-change is neither impractical nor difficult to sustain. Indeed, the making of this book stands as one strand of evidence in support of this claim. If professionals were to begin simply by seeking out and cultivating the active use of first-person voice—whether in conversation and writing or on audiotape, videotape, or some other media—by persons who have learning disabilities, much could change.

Unfortunately, at present the human service disciplines do not emphasize such dialogic practices, and as a result they seem to fall short of the goal of acknowledging the full, complex humanity of the persons to whom they are devoted. It seems unlikely that this state of affairs exists by design. Perhaps it is a circumstance created primarily by a kind of miasma: That is, unaware that persons with learning disabilities can collaborate meaningfully in programming and research, professionals do not think to encourage them to do so. Additionally, practitioners are constantly subject to external pressures that hinder collaborative, dialogic enterprises. Teachers, for example, may be under pressure to show that their students can pass statewide tests of basic skills and so choose to exclude activities that focus on the cultivation of thoughtful self-expression. Therapists may be confined by managed-care restrictions to only five sessions with their clients and so may adopt a program engineered to treat only the most problematic symptoms, neglecting to have the kinds of rich interaction that stimulate self-discovery and self-determination. But whatever the causes, the consequences of these inherently silencing practices can be severe, resulting both in the squandering of human potential and the lowering of professionals' true usefulness and efficacy.

A recent film that depicted these dynamics in the field of medicine was *Doctor* (1991), with the lead role played by William Hurt. In this story, a physician who had traveled quite far along the road to professional success by applying a strictly clinical—which is to say impersonal—approach to the treatment of cancer was suddenly himself struck by the dreaded disease. In the months that followed, compelled to walk in the footsteps of his patients, this doctor changed his tune. He learned the importance of paying attention not only to the disease and how "it" might be treated, but also to the living, feeling persons whom the disease had visited. From this new, foundational mode of attention, a wealth of new or altered practices sprung. He still sought to heal, but he understood that healing was a comprehensive process, only a part of which had to do with the malady itself. Clinical expertise remained important, but creating and sustaining a human dialogue—which is to say, a two-way conversation—with his patients came to define the spirit of his work, for when both parties are enabled to speak, far deeper and more varied potentialities are tapped. Solutions formerly unimagined develop. It is as if being allowed to speak is elementally strengthening for the speaker, regardless of whether the speaker is the healer or the one seeking to be healed. Better yet, to speak *and* to be listened to leads to the evolution of true working relationships, of persons actively partnered in the pursuit of life's betterment.

As has been suggested, the two human service fields that are most frequently and directly called into action when a person is suspected of having a learning disability are psychology and education. Psychologists and special educators typically are assigned the major role in diagnosing learning disabilities, as well as in aiding in the design of responsive interventions, be they educational, behavioral, or therapeutic. Teachers, of course, traditionally play the larger and more enduring roles, charged with instructing students in the ways that they can and do learn. If one were to take the number of programs and publications generated by practitioners in these two fields as proof of their commitment to persons who have learning disabilities, the unavoidable conclusion would be that there is a very high level of it. Since the date of the enactment of the Education for All Handicapped Children Act of 1975 (Public Law 94-142), services for students with learning disabilities have continuously expanded. Currently, approximately 6 million children in the United States are coded with specific learning disabilities, a more than twofold increase from the years 1994–1995, when only about 2.5 million children had this coding (U.S. Department of Education, 1997). As for the published discourse on learning disabilities, an informal review of any database discloses a steady proliferation and diversification.

Despite this prodigious growth in the learning disabilities industry, those of us who are teachers, special educators, psychologists, school administrators, counselors, and so forth, must be willing to ask hard questions about our practices. Such questions may lead to at least one striking and unhappy discovery: Much like the protagonist in *Doctor* during his early career, we have invested very little in the practice of entering into open, candid dialogue with persons who have learning disabilities. We have not often and liberally asked them to articulate what they want, what they need, and what they think and feel. Moreover, we have not asked them questions such as, How do you learn best? How would you teach if you were the teacher? How should special education programs be designed so as to avoid giving you the feeling that you are being excluded? What are the areas of research and inquiry that would most benefit you? Would you like to instigate this research or to join with others in its execution? Because we have not commonly asked such questions, our understanding of the lives of persons with learning disabilities is primarily stated in *our* words and *our* terms, not theirs. Consequently, we may have a much poorer understanding of their lives than we think. The proof of this is legion.

First of all, we rarely find in the education of persons who have learning disabilities an emphasis on encouraging and cultivating their capacities for self-expression. Much more commonly, educational interventions are designed to be directive, flowing from the teacher to the student. While these methods have genuine value for instruction in certain key areas (e.g., the acquisition of basic reading skills), we are remiss if these methods become definitive of students' *total* education, especially that part of education that has to do with the evolution and expression of a student's self. The self is not a thing, but an active, mysterious creator, marvelously able to experience and to articulate its existence in an untold variety of ways. Indeed, the signature of the self is *agency*, or the possession of the capacity for authorship in living. To "receive" instruction is, in balance with other forms of interaction, good. But to "receive" at the expense of being able to speak, articulate, compose, and make our own meaning is to be silenced. And through silence—if that is all there is—we cannot learn. As Paolo Freire (1992) argued, "[Persons] are not built in silence, but in word, in work, in action-reflection" (76). Learning in the fullest sense is a give-and-take, a matter of listening and speaking, a two-way conversation. Persons trapped in educational systems wherein they are not from the outset legitimized as speakers generally find themselves alienated from and opposed to those systems.

And then again, there is the stark scarcity of pieces written by persons who have learning disabilities in the published discourse on learning disabilities. An ethnographic perspective would suggest that any testimonial by a person who has lived with a learning disability is a valuable report by a knowledgeable—if not expert—informant. Indeed, if it is *expertise* that is valued, what of the expertise that comes from firsthand experience? Should you wish to understand, for example, what it is like to have dyslexia, would you not wish to consult a person who has lived with it? If you wanted to design a successful educational program for persons with difficulties in math, would it not be of great help to begin with how these persons experience their learning disabilities, both in the cognitive and the emotional dimensions? And should you wish to know how to make it through college even with difficulties in writing, wouldn't you want to hear from someone who has done just that? The fact is that the absence of a deep and wide literature created by persons who have learning disabilities is an impoverishment of the entire field. So much that has been learned firsthand has not been shared. So much earned wisdom that might have provided guidance for other individuals, for families, for schools, and for teachers and psychologists has not found its audience. Worst of all, this impoverishment strikes hardest those persons who have learning disabilities, for they ultimately pay the price of others' misunderstanding and of programs' lack of efficacy.

We may speculate about why this state of affairs exists. On the one hand, it is common in all the disciplines to wish to control, professionalize, and make orthodox their discourse. The competition is ever ongoing regarding the "right" way to talk about matters, especially in fields that have sought to define themselves as "sciences." This emphasis is rarely ill intentioned. More typically, practitioners in the fields of education and psychology have believed that a vigorous utilization of their most precise clinical tools is the fastest pathway to true, useful solutions for persons who have learning disabilities and suffer their effects.

On the other hand, the exclusion of persons with learning disabilities from the discourse on learning disabilities may be partly due to certain deeply embedded—yet generally unspoken and unchallenged—beliefs about the *incapacities* of persons with learning disabilities to articulate their knowledge, to help others, and to collaborate in the making of better, healthier systems of education. As discussed, the majority of professional educators and psychologists have long understood our primary mission to be that of transmitting *our* knowledge, of asserting *ourselves* as the experts. Could it be that by failing to engage in dialogic practices, we have been left with immature, unsound concepts about the persons we have been attempting to serve? Could it be that we have terribly underestimated them, and that this underestimation is a palpable wrong?

It is embarrassing and painful to recount, but it is also impossible to forget, the occasion when a number of the student writers gathered in this volume joined the editors in presenting at a professional conference on education. At the end of the session, a member of the audience and a professor of education began to ask questions about how much "help" some of the students had in composing their portions of the presentation. Apparently disbelieving the answers we gave him, the questioner finally blurted out, "No way could students with learning disabilities at my college have written anything like that." To his credit, he later came forward and spoke with many of us, expressing his desire to know how he could change his methods of teaching writing. We could not help but wonder about his students over the years and how much they and others like them have been affected by the dogma of low expectation and limited esteem.

The essays collected here should serve as an unambiguous exposé and refutation of this dogma. Read properly, these essays should prompt wide-ranging reconsideration of how much each of us is subtly or not so subtly affected by this dogma, and how this dogma influences our practices as educators, psychologists, researchers, or parents. Read with genuine attention, these essays should lead us to reground our interactions with persons with disabilities—regardless of their ages—in generously dialogic activities.

But the first step in any of these processes is simply to listen.

Life Stories

1

Blake Academy and the Green Arrow

Oliver Queen

Oliver is a 34-year-old, white, working-class man, who is currently in his senior year at a major state university, where he has been studying history. Diagnosed with dyslexia in 1976 at age 13, Oliver was sent to "Blake Academy," a special school for children with learning disabilities (LDs). In describing his first days at Blake Academy, Oliver focuses his narrative on issues of racism, segregation, and social marginalization. These issues were brought into view by the school system's efforts to separate children with learning problems, most of whom were white, from children with emotional and behavioral problems, most of whom were black.

Oliver's study of the fear, violence, and moments of friendship between the white and black children transported by the city's special education buses is given special depth by Oliver's admission that he, too, had severe emotional problems. In the second half of this essay, Oliver focuses in on these problems, telling in frank detail how his emotional survival depended for many years on his secret imaginary play with plastic toy action figures. When Oliver destroys all of his action figures (except his "beloved Green Arrow") in an effort to renounce his childhood habits and embrace adolescence, he succeeds only in exposing how emotionally frail he really is. In exploring his psychological difficulties, Oliver returns again and again to the role that his learning disabilities played in his lack of a secure social identity.

In 1976, when I was 13 years old, the Springfield school system determined I had a learning disability. Furthermore, they also found themselves in a quagmire: The school system was not adequately prepared or staffed to meet the needs of an LD student, but by law they were required to provide LD students with the specialized attention they required.

The answer to this dilemma presented itself in a most unexpected place. My best friend, Karl, who lived across Eastern Avenue from me, had been diagnosed LD a couple of years earlier. His family made no secret of his condition, and everyone on the block knew about it. He had been attending Farm Hill Academy, a prestigious prep school, when his LD was first identified. The school's advisors recommended Blake Academy as the school best suited to provide for Karl's academic needs. Karl had already been attending Blake for over a year when it was decided that I was to attend classes there the following year.

The school district was decidedly unhappy at having to pay my tuition to Blake, a hefty sum in excess of my mother's annual salary, but in the fall, off I went. In later years, I learned that Mom had been forced to sue the school district so they'd cough up my tuition. The school district had been happy to have me around and collect the federal money my presence represented so long as I was easy to care for. Once I demonstrated special needs, they were happy to be rid of me, but they didn't want to pay for my absence.

Sending me off to a private school was, in the opinion of the bean counters, not an equitable use of the school district's money. It was proposed that I could have my educational needs met easily, and much less expensively, in-house, by lumping me in with the lowest track students. Their logic was simple enough—in an environment of idiots I would quickly blend in (they reasoned that LD was a synonym for stupid) and no longer be victim to the oppression of the mainstream. Once assimilated in the shallow end of the grade pool, I would come to represent the mean of the lower track instead of the low end of the mainstream. Best of all, no one would be the wiser. This seemed to be standard practice for the district, locking their embarrassing students away so as not to be embarrassed by them and tossing enough food down so they'd survive, but not so much that they might grow and thrive.

Thankfully, my mother saw through their facade and demanded better for me. I have many issues with my mother, ones that make our relationship strained and distant, but she possesses one trait I have always sought to emulate: a powerful sense of justice in matters of family. Coming from a family of educators, she understood the necessity of a good education and dedicated her energies toward ensuring that I would not be shortchanged.

By this time, however, my relationship with Mom was in a serious downturn and had been for some time. My parents had divorced several years earlier, and the trauma of their disunion left me deeply scarred. I carried enough anger and frustration over the divorce for several people. The anger I hoarded was always manifested toward my family, at Mom and my sister, Kristen, especially. Emotional outbursts, triggered by any number of things, ranging from understandable to totally benign, occurred with even greater frequency during the transition from public to private school.

While the protracted legal battle raged over payment of my tuition, I was lost in the chaos of adjusting to a new school. Switching schools was not new to me. In the seven years of my academic career, Blake was to be my fourth school, so I saw myself as a veteran of the stand-up-in-front-of-the-class-and-tell-us-about-yourself exercise. Nonetheless, due to my supercharged levels of anxiety, making new friends was a most difficult process, one I rarely attempted. I had been so shy in the first grade that the other kids saw me as a freak and avoided contact with me. I was socially blackballed from the get-go. When my father, a man without many friends, heard of my social problems he passed along some less than sage advice. He said, "If they don't like you, dazzle them with bullshit." Once I was clear on what bullshit was, I embarked on a destructive path that ruined my prospects for making true friends. In order to keep people interested in maintaining a friendship, I jazzed myself up. When given the opportunity to advance my image in someone else's eyes, I leapt on it, no matter how outrageous the lie. After the divorce, my father's absence lent itself to a plethora of lies, everything from his being an astronaut or a super-spy to being the president of the United States. No lie, so long as it led to some measure of social acceptance, was too great, and I told them all.

All too soon, the practice began to backfire as my peers, not nearly as stupid as I believed, began to challenge my lies. For a while, I stood by my stories, unable to address why I told them or the effect they might have on others. But time and the constant doubt of my classmates eventually wore me down. By the third grade, I was beaten, defenseless, and had nowhere to retreat, so I publicly recanted. After that, word of my confession spread like pink eye through the school yard, and I was left alone. No one at school would befriend the known liar, the boy who could not tell the truth. As my peers rolled down the path of socialization, I was left standing in their dust. Early on, I had tried being myself and it had gotten me alienated. I tried being everything to everyone, and it cost me any hope of social acceptance. I was left with nothing, both socially and emotionally.

In the neighborhood I couldn't lie to the same extent as at school, because those kids saw how I lived and their parents knew my mother. The few friendships I managed were based more on convenience and lack of other playmates; most of the neighborhood gang didn't have similar interests until puberty set in.

I hoped, as some small part of each of us always hopes, that Blake would prove different and that being surrounded by peers, true peers, would make the process of friendship easier, but I doubted it. Too many years of disappointments had soured me on the likelihood of ever fitting in.

The bus ride my first day at Blake proved enlightening as to what exactly constitutes a peer. While the Springfield district hated doing it, they were required by law to provide students with transport to all the schools in the district, be they public or private. Most private schools had their own buses, but Blake had no fleet of its own, so Springfield provided it with its own van. There were six of us on the bus that day: Karl, me, a quiet, gawky kid named Gates who attended Blake's sister school, Greenfield, and the three Dixon Valley students.

The Dixon students scared the hell out of me from the word go. Dixon Valley, a state-run, mostly self-contained juvenile correction facility, had been in the township since the Eisenhower administration, and no one had paid it any mind until the population turned decidedly black in the late 1960s. The thought of a black jail in the heart of white suburbia terrified the racist element in the community. Contempt and hostility toward Dixon Valley was as much a factor in my development as television, comic books, and action figures. I had been surrounded, although not at home, by the notion that Dixon was a malignant tumor on the otherwise healthy, happy Springfield body. In the early 1970s, the state government decided Springfield's public schools were unable to supply the specialized attention Dixon's LD students needed, so it was arranged to send them to Greenfield.

I had never interacted with a black peer before transferring to Blake, but thanks to the prevailing racism of my youth, my perspective was already tainted. I felt an internal battle raging as I tried to make sense of the mixed messages of my upbringing. The community espoused that all blacks were trouble and brought only disease and chaos wherever they went. Yet, my family had marched on Washington with Dr. Martin Luther King Jr. in 1963, and the message taught at home was one of tolerance and compassion. These two views struggled within me for dominance as I watched the Dixon students board the bus and take seats toward the front. Part of me wanted to extend a hand in friendship, while the other wanted to run for cover.

I don't remember the names of the three Dixon kids, but I do remember the rage in their eyes. There wasn't a rational basis for this, but I felt as though they hated me from the outset just because I was white.

It's funny, but I always thought I had been given the short end of the stick. My family was poor, surrounded by the upper middle class. My parents divorced in a town where that was most uncommon, and I was LD. These were all weights hanging from my neck, preventing me from getting ahead. The Dixon kids had so much more going against them! They were poor and a minority, living in a correctional institution, and were LD. It's a wonder they were able to function at all. Understanding the reasons for their anger and extending the hand of kindness are two very different things, so we sat quietly for the remainder of the bus ride, avoiding eye contact with them.

An eternity later, the bus dropped us off at Greenfield, about 200 yards from Blake. There was a mob of students milling about outside, smoking cigarettes and taunting the security guards who did not yet have jurisdiction over them. Once the

Dixon kids were out of sight, Karl and Gates bolted for the door and disembarked. We bobbed and wove through the sea of teenagers and, once we penetrated the outer edge, darted for the woods that separated the two schools. "All this to get off the bus," I thought, "Lunch must be murder." It seemed more akin to breaking out of prison than going to school.

After we had caught our breath, we started at an ambling pace toward Blake. On the way, Karl explained the difference between the two schools. Greenfield, he explained, was a specialized version of Blake, which I found awfully funny since Blake itself is a specialized school. All the students who were in need of LD schooling, but dangerously violent, controlled by mood-altering medication, or had known discipline problems, were pulled out of the LD mainstream at Blake and put in Greenfield.

Gates, who had been in Greenfield since the second grade because of a serious violent disorder that required heavy medication, had told Karl more than a few war stories of life at Greenfield. He said that students were locked in their classrooms with their teachers, and their desks were bolted to the floor so they couldn't be used as weapons. Most disturbing of all, the beautiful huge picture windows that dominated the out-facing wall of every classroom were three inches thick: Any less and students might be able to hurl themselves through it.

The September morning air was brisk, and the leaves vibrant. As Karl relayed one horror story after another about Greenfield, his manner was frighteningly calm, like a death camp resident inmate deadened to the insanity around him. He told me of the student who threw himself against the window of his third floor classroom so many times that he broke his elbow and collarbone, and it still took three security guards to restrain him. Karl went on to tell of a student who beat his teacher so severely that he was taken away in a straightjacket and never heard from again.

Less than 200 yards from where I was going to try to get back on the education highway—or, at the very least, off the shoulder—sat a powder keg, primed to explode. I felt all my hopes of finding a home among my peers fading.

As Karl and I entered the double doors of Blake's main foyer, I expected to find "Abandon all hope ye who enter here" painted in blood over the receptionist's desk, so I averted my eyes as we queued up to find our room assignments. All morning, fear of the unknown had been pushing my blood pressure through the roof. Now, it was crushing it into the ionosphere. Terror seized me, and my world went red.

This had been happening to me for several years now. In high stress situations or when I felt totally out of control, a wave of anger would wash over me. While adrift in the sea of red, I did many things, terrible things, in an effort to stay afloat. I smashed objects, screamed uncontrollably, attacked others with no reason: anything to purge the helplessness that was overcoming me.

Attacks could come at any time and without warning. My heart would pound, my eyes would lose focus. Finally, once the adrenal gland decided to join the party, my entire body would shake from a surplus of energy surging though it. My perception of the visible light spectrum would shift, narrowing down to one color: red. The world would assume a blood-red hue as every ounce of hate, anger, self-loathing, and confusion stored within me simultaneously looked for an exit. My world, once colored for battle, then collapsed inward for an endless moment before, like a phoenix rising, it exploded outward, spreading chaos and violence.

"Maybe," I thought in a lucid moment, "they're sending me to the wrong school."

What started my descent into a freak-out was fear of the unknown. Being both physically small and LD made me a desirable target for bullies all my academic life. The painful lessons of the school yard—that being different was to be a target—had been pounded home time and again over the years. Bullies want public attention, using the weak to showcase their physical superiority. If you never surrender, no matter how often they hurl slanders or strike when the teacher's not looking, they eventually lose interest in you. I had never been in a knock-down, drag-out brawl, but I had been forced to throw a few lame punches to warn off the vultures. By never capitulating, I had, despite being prone after every attempt to defend myself, beaten the bullies. It earned me the distinction of being regarded—in addition to a liar and a turnip-head—as crazy. The label warded off bullies but also widened the chasm between me and my peers.

As I stood there that first day at Blake, surrounded by dozens of LD peers, I tried to picture the new playing field that awaited me. Up to the bus ride earlier that morning, I had assumed that Blake would share the dynamic of public schools. The bullies would still prowl, the cliques would form, but there would be lots of kids like me. I believed sharing LDs would band us together against the bullies. With everyone on equally shaky ground there was no bonding, only mutual distrust and terror.

Suddenly, the person before me in line bumped into me. As the world came back into focus, I received my room assignment. Before Karl and I parted company, he pointed out the way for me. Blake was divided into four sections, each representing three years of the twelve-year public school system. As Karl was two years younger than me, he was in the intermediate level, while I was in the junior.

I found my classroom easily enough and was pleasantly surprised to find that the entire class was comprised of only five students. No one spoke to each other as the teacher, Ms. Crowell, did her best to help us vault the awkward hurdle of introductions. Karl said he'd never been forced to stand up and introduce himself to the class, but there I was, standing before five strangers, answering a round of questions posed by Ms. Crowell. If we voiced a like or dislike, a hobby or sport we fancied, she went down that path gently trying to dismantle the various protective barriers we had erected around ourselves. After years of scorn and abuse, it was not easy for any of us to open up, and she was trying, slowly, with a surgeon's skill, to get us to trust her.

She went on and explained the routine of our day and Blake's educational goals. We were to be quite busy as, all totaled, we had four academic classes, an art class, and study hall, every day. Unlike elementary school, we had different teachers for each class and moved from room to room throughout the day. So, the five of us traveled as a pack, going to each class together, eating lunch at the same table, even wandering about the playground in loosely knit circles. We were far from opening up to each other, however.

As I looked around the playground, I noticed what an odd student body we were. Out of the sixty some students of the junior level, there were only six girls and two blacks. The sea of students outside Greenfield that morning had been prominently black, but at Blake the few blacks stood out. "Could the townies be right?" I wondered, as I gazed around the school yard of alabaster. "Why are there so many black kids over at Greenfield and so few at Blake? Are blacks more violent than whites?" The question was ripped away, unresolved, as the lunch bell sounded and the cafe monitor summoned us back inside.

The remainder of the day proved equally uninteresting. We went from room to room, class to class, listening to teachers tell us we were "special" and how Blake would have us up our grade levels in no time. Most of the teachers were indiscernible from those I'd had in public school, with the exception of Ms. Crowell, who I had for homeroom and English, and Mr. Hoffman, who was the social studies teacher. Mr. Hoffman was the most unique teacher I've ever known. Over the course of a year, he pushed all of us, myself especially, to broaden our minds and cast aside the notion that being LD in some way limited our capacity to experience life to its fullest. He played Beatles records while talking about the 1960s and he taught us how people danced back then. We went on nature walks. He had us construct an adobe hut in the spring so we'd better understand living conditions in Africa. He even taught us how to shout "a-wop-bob-a-do-wop-a-wop-bam-boom" with conviction and without a hint of embarrassment. I was never bored in Mr. Hoffman's class, and everyday I learned something new. That did not happen again until I went to college thirteen years later.

By the end of that first day, I was happy to pack up my books and go home. Karl and I convened at the bus stop. Since the bus carried students from two schools, it was decided, to be fair, that the bus drop us off at Greenfield and pick us up at Blake. We were the only Blake students, so we arrived first and immediately began exchanging stories about our day. After a few minutes had passed, the Greenfield group began arriving. They emerged from the woods, with Gates leading the way by a narrow margin. He had the same terrified look on his face that we'd had in the morning. After a moment the reason why became apparent. The taunts of the Dixon Valley students, directed for the moment solely at Gates, became audible before they broke the threshold of the woods.

Karl looked at me, and in his eyes I saw the same terror I felt. We tensed, but soon his motions became frantic. He looked desperately over the hill for our van as the Dixon trio broke through the edge of the trees and switched targets with their verbal barrage. Gates dashed by us in his flight to escape their abuse. He came to rest on the edge of the sidewalk, right where the bus would eventually come to stop and provide us with a sanctuary.

When the Dixon kids were close enough, they focused all the attacks on Karl, combining verbal insults with random shoving to keep him off balance mentally and physically. I believed the confrontation was similar to the shoulder-pushing "Oh, Yea!" matches I'd seen hundreds of times in the Oz-like world of suburbia and could be resolved easily enough. If I stood by Karl, showing the Dixon kids that the fight would be a bit more even, they would back down and the conflict would fizzle out. I summoned up all my courage, for this was the first time I had ever joined in a conflict to help someone out. Karl was my best friend, and when your best friend is threatened, you're expected to do something about it.

I managed only a weak "Hey!" before the kid closest hit me in the side of my face. It wasn't the impact that stunned me, for I had been hit before, or the pain, which would come later, but the idea that someone would violate the established rules of school yard fighting. Karl and I had watched lots of John Wayne movies together, and I had come to understand that there were rules to combat. Number one among them was you never hit someone without calling them out first.

Before I had the time to decide what to do next, the bus came into view. Until the bus actually stopped and its doors opened, the Dixon trio continued to taunt us with promises of violence to come. We boarded the bus quickly and fled for the safety of the rear. The ride home was shrouded in cowardly silence.

The bus dropped Karl and me off at the bottom of our street, and we set out slowly up the hill toward home. I wanted desperately to talk to Karl about what had happened, especially now that my face was starting to swell, but the words wouldn't come. We were trapped in a juvenile, stupid silence, shamed by our victimization. Kids don't open their hearts to each other easily, not after losing a fight and especially when they're LD. It is almost impossible to imagine open honesty, since we were on constant guard against the ridicule of others. It is a common trait among the LD to know how to endure hardship and keep dark secrets.

In one respect, it did seem like old times, for now I had bullies back in my life. These were *überbullies,* and they didn't subscribe to the norms of the school yard despots I'd known, but they were bullies, a known quantity. The bullies of public school were focused on power and harvesting attention from their peers. The Dixon Valley bullies had a different agenda, and I couldn't quite figure out what it was at first. Their only audience was each other, for Gates, Karl, and I were unwilling to sell each other out in a bid for acceptance and never gave them any sort of approval. Even more puzzling, the bullies never basked in their victory; when they pushed one of us around, they still seemed angry afterward. They were our physical superiors, but that was the extent of their power.

Once I understood the limits of their power, I began to examine their motivations. Every day of the school year, Monday through Friday, they boarded the bus with an air of aggression surrounding them. Our reaction was one of fear for the first few months, but over time, that shifted to acceptance. We couldn't change how they acted, so we modified our behavior. There came to pass, after half the school year was gone, days of détente. These occurred mostly when the usual dynamic was altered by an absence on either side. When one of the Dixon kids was out sick, the other two might sit in the back with us and laugh or kick about the lighthearted banter of friends. Likewise, if Karl, Gates, or I were sick, the Dixon trio tended to be more open. It never occurred if everyone was present, but there were days of peace.

It became apparent that there were two sides to the racism I'd grown up with. On the days when we all got along, the only difference between us was skin color. The fact that we did have détente most days did not cover up the violence, nor did it excuse it. The Dixon Valley students came from a violent world, one unknown to "white breads" like me. What's more, they all had some sort of major mental problem. This didn't justify their behavior, but it helped in my understanding of them. They were not typical blacks any more than Karl, Gates, and I were normal whites. We all exhibited atypical behavior and were in no way representative of our racial groups. What continued to baffle me was their outright unwillingness to accept us. Weren't we all LD after all?

It was the same with my peers at Blake. Despite sharing the pain of alienation and ridicule that went with being LD, we were not drawn together and made stronger—quite the opposite was the case. No one reached out and dared to speak of the pain that went with being LD. No one opened the debate on how it felt being the objects of scorn and jest. No one during my tenure at Blake dared to show how deep their scars ran. I don't remember which philosopher said these words, but they apply to Blake and doubly so to Greenfield: If you have one person, you have utopia. With two, they will argue. If three gather, two will alienate the third. With four people, they will reinvent prejudice. And if five people come together, they will have war.

At Blake and Greenfield, we were all of common stock, yet that did not unite us. The models of mass society were applied to our microcosm and all too quickly we were choosing up sides, closing our hearts, and checking hope at the door. In both public and private school, the division into cliques follows a frighteningly familiar evolution. People look for attributes that separate them from others, be it athletic prowess or academic acumen, and these differences are the basis for social stratification. Being surrounded by like-afflicted people, the differences are less pronounced, but they exist and only compound the alienation the LD student already feels.

In the end, it wasn't the color differences that separated Blake and Greenfield. To be certain, they compounded the tensions that already existed, and while prejudice certainly didn't help matters, we were already at sixes and sevens with each other. We'd spent so many years digging a moat around ourselves to shut out the unforgiving world that we'd forgotten how to let others get close. Racism, gender roles, sexuality: These were secondary and tertiary modifiers. I would have feared the Dixon kids, just as I feared Gates, no matter what color they had been. Being black only served to ignite the fires planted by the bigots who populated the community of my youth. I feared the Dixon kids first because they were like me, carrying the badge LD, not because of the confusion coming from my upbringing.

In the end, I carried from Blake the same emotional baggage I'd arrived with, but I had grown in a few respects. Academically, while no genius, I reached a place where learning was no longer anathema to me. I was up to a normal reading level, and while the quest to learn how to spell would plague me to this day, I finally pulled off the shoulder and reentered the educational highway. I wasn't going anywhere near 65 mph yet, but for the first time in my life the desire to learn began to drive me onward instead of frightening me. More importantly, I discovered some basic social skills. I still swam in a sea of retarded socialization, yet now I was adept at spotting those in a similar state, and I could make overtures of friendship.

Throughout all of this, Karl and I remained close. In some ways, our daily running of the bus gauntlet brought us closer together. We never discussed it, but the common secret added a dimension to our friendship and helped deepen the bond between us. During those two years we played more together, had almost weekly sleep-overs—especially in summer when we could pitch a tent outside—and crossed the threshold from a childhood friendship to an adolescent one.

I left Blake under less than desirable terms in the fall of 1978. I had a series of emotional outbursts in the early fall, shortly after school began, and Mom decided after the most volatile of our conflicts to send me away.

There was an underlying catalyst to the final confrontation, one that was truly at the heart of my recent difficult behavior. Two weeks prior, I had burned my action figures. All of them, that is, save my beloved Green Arrow, for I could never part with him. For as long as I could remember I had relied on my action figures to work through frustration and anger. Through them I had staved off total immersion into the real world. I used my action figures to create a world where being different was no big deal, where I set the social norms and created an environment where different people could fit in and be accepted. Karl and I had spent countless hours role playing through the action figures. In the years before I went to Blake, these games were the center of our relationship.

The problem reared its head when I couldn't stop playing with them. As I grew older, I tried to put my action figures away, but each time they beckoned from the closet, begging for one more adventure, one final epic to keep them warm during the long nights that awaited them in the Hall of Forgotten Toys. They had been the center of my world, the faithful ones, the unwavering allies against all who mocked, chided, or otherwise sought to damage me. United, we had stood against the outside world and in my room we had created our own universe.

Then along came puberty. Karl's fancy turned to sports and John Wayne movies, and it became apparent that everyone—friends and family—expected me to put aside my childhood toys and seek out adult ones. So, I packaged up my figures, wrapping each in its own burial shroud of tissue paper, careful to match each figure with its accessories—Captain America with his shield, Thor with his hammer, and so forth—and gently placed them in their new home, my closet. My tears had mixed like oil and water with promises to resurrect them for my children someday. I closed the door and with hollow resolve set out to find adult pursuits.

I found myself needing the action figures almost immediately. In school, during meals, while playing with friends, I felt the need to reenter the world I created with them, to feel the safety and acceptance that came only from their presence. They called to me most powerfully in dreams.

After days of this, my resolve began falling apart. Finally it all proved too much, and I liberated my plastic comrades. I spent the following weekend reenacting favorite adventures and leaving the real world far behind. A curious new feeling fell over me come Monday morning: shame. Never before had I felt anything but joy after two days of intense fantasy, but this Monday my face itched as if "loser" or "toy boy" had been tattooed on my face for all to see. The entire week became a long debate between rationalization and the reality of my psychological weakness. I knew it was necessary to grow up, but could I leave behind that which brought me the greatest joy? What is life, if not the pursuit of pleasure?

Back and forth the debate raged, until I had a moment of clarity. My epiphany was this: That which bestows both pleasure and shame is a Judas. To expunge the Judas, drastic measures were needed. I knew I couldn't leap across the chasm to adolescence by myself, for the six inch, brightly outfitted plastic wonders had too strong a grip on me. If I was going to break free of their power, I needed help. Asking Karl was out of the question; he'd just think I was being a child and laugh about it. So I called Gary, a friend seven years my junior. We had a synergy, Gary and me, so I knew he'd understand. Plus, Gary was seven years my junior and close to his inner child.

Together we set out on Saturday afternoon and massacred my entire population of action figures. Their deaths were unimaginably horrible. Caligula, Robespierre, Stalin: They were mere boys standing in my man-sized shadow when it came to devising gruesome means of execution. We burned, drew and quartered, mutilated, and dismembered our way through the Avengers and the Justice League. In the end only my beloved, most favorite superhero, Green Arrow, survived.

The Bob Dylan lyric "when you ain't got nothin', you got nothin' to lose" resounded through my head during the frenzied killing. The ends were desperately trying to justify the awful means as I stayed the course and saw each figure perish. As the sun set, a wave of emancipation washed over me with the darkness. The remains were buried, the fires put out, and I felt like I had finally severed the mooring that kept me docked to childhood.

There was one flaw in my plan: It was "bollocks." I had nothing to replace the void the sudden departure of my figures created. I'd been venting all my anger with action figure role play since I opened my first one, an Action Jackson, on Christmas day, 1972. With them gone, my emotional coffers were filling, and I had no means of draining them. A blowout was inevitable, and it came a week later.

Kristen and I started fighting the moment we got home from school on that fateful day. In the afternoon, we fought over the division of play space in our sunporch playroom; over dinner we quarreled about which TV program to watch. Before bed we clashed again over something equally trivial. We argued over the ownership of a toy neither of us truly wanted until Mom finally had her fill of our bickering and came out of her room to end it.

What made this night different from the hundreds of identical ones that preceded it was the sense of something dangerous hanging over me. While Mom confronted us, I saw, just for a moment as I looked beyond my own hurt and ire, something new in her eyes. The divorce had hit everyone, but I never really knew before that night just how hard it had impacted her.

A voice I'd never heard before issued from Mom's lips ordering Kristen upstairs. Mom's voice no longer had the sweet, gentle lilt to it. Kristen ran upstairs without looking back. Once she was gone, Mom turned toward me, her face inflamed with rage and crying, and asked, "Why do you do this? You're just like your father!"

Her words, fired with such force, stunned me. We'd verbally fenced countless times before, so I recovered quickly and launched my own verbal attack. My retort was cut off midsentence as Mom introduced a new element to our dueling: She hit me!

Corporal punishment was not new to our household. Mom had spanked me before. Typically, the punishment more than fit the crime, but this time was different. She had struck me open palmed and with enough force to push me back a few steps. The world around me began to go red. I was on the verge of a total freak-out, when Mom beat me to the finish line. Rage, so familiar a companion to me, had consumed her. Suddenly, she began to flail her arms wildly at me, trying clumsily to strike me again. She sobbed out a cadence, and as each blow fell, there flew out a soft, rhetorical "Why?"

In her desperation to hit me, Mom stopped using her arms and started kicking at me. Her legs moved even slower then her arms, so I tried to end the conflict by grabbing her foot. I held on to her foot and she quickly lost her balance. With a cry of both anger and embarrassment, she hit the floor, bottom first. Dumbfounded and uncertain as what to do next, I stood there, holding on to her foot.

Two things happened in rapid, sudden succession. First, I let go of her foot. It hit the floor with a dramatic thump. Next, Mom stood up, and the look on her face told me the fight was over. After a moment, she turned to walk upstairs. Before mounting the stairs, Mom turned to look back at me, with the look of a parent standing over the grave of her child. The vacuum in her eyes pierced my heart, bringing home the message I might as well be dead to her.

Watching Mom, the one emotional constant in my life, snap had a dramatic effect on me. Mom had been able to withstand any challenge, take on anything: She was Supermom. I had disagreed with almost every parenting decision she had made and fought her authority at every turn, but I always admired her strength and conviction. She seemed unscathed by all the pain life had inflicted, and she'd been the emotional grounding of my life. Now the model for all my perceptions of personal strength and fortitude turned out to be flawed. This, coupled with the loss of my means of venting rage, proved too much to cope with.

The half hour that followed is a blur of violence and mayhem. I went into my room and surrendered to the rage. My room became the epicenter as my stored anger exploded outward. The anger remained after my energy reserves were long gone. Exhausted, but still seething on the inside, I tried to imagine if this was to be the pattern of my life.

A rap on the door brought me out of my funk. It was soft in tone, but there was an undeniable firmness to it. Mom opened the door and calmly entered my room. The only light in the room came from the hall as during my cyclone of destruction I had broken my only lamp.

"I think it would be best for you to go away for a time," she began, matter-of-factly, as if discussing something frivolous. "Your Uncle George has agreed to let you stay with him and his family down in Maryland. It will be good for you to . . . ," she paused thoughtfully, as if her word choice would make me more receptive to the idea, "distance yourself from this. So you can reflect on tonight and resolve whatever it is that's tearing you apart."

She went on and on, trying to rationalize her decision, but it all came down to this—she was throwing me out. I imagined her sending me off, bouncing me from family member to family member, treating me like public school wanted to: hiding the psycho kid so he didn't ruin the family name. In a heated row, we went back and forth, stating and restating our positions, but in the end Mom won and I packed my bags. With a few days' change of clothes and my collection of Beatles records, I boarded a train for Baltimore the following morning.

In one quick stroke, I was withdrawn from Blake and cut off from my friends. Without the benefit of a phone call, I was tried, convicted, and exiled. I worried incessantly about what Karl, Gary, and the few others who actually cared about me would think about my sudden disappearance. Would Mom tell them I ran away or that I joined a band of drug smugglers operating out of Madagascar? In the long run, I supposed that it didn't really matter, but I didn't want anyone wondering what happened to me.

For the first few months following my arrival in Maryland, I didn't attend school and spent all my time in an emotional jumble. The aftereffects of the confrontation with Mom had left me without an emotional center. For the first time, I felt truly alone in the world. My uncle and his family were helpful in providing me with the canvas on which to begin painting the rest of my life, but the paints had to come from within me and I found my palette empty.

I spent much of the time in Maryland alone, walking in the woods around the apartment development. In solitude, I was finally able to recognize my emotional shortcomings and, for the first time, address the pain my parents' divorce left within me. Total self-therapy proved beyond my abilities, but for the first time I recognized that there were problems and found that deep within me dwelled the desire to address them. Although I was hardly a stable, mature, well-rounded individual when I went home, almost a year after my arrival, the foundation for healing had been laid.

The summer of my return, in 1979, was one of the best of my life. I returned home and caught up with all my friends. Karl had also left Blake that year and gone off to a boarding school in Boston. We spent much of that summer farting around, just as we had so many summers before, but this year we were on the brink of young adulthood: high school. In little more than a year, I had gone from a groundless, emotionally retarded kid to being four years away from the independence a high school diploma brings.

What occupied my thoughts more than anything else that summer was Blake. In the two years I was there, some harsh lessons went along with my attempts at academic catch-up. I saw that having an LD is much akin to being blind or losing the use of an appendage; it affects all aspects of your life. In dealing with this, you have two choices. One, you can acknowledge the parasitic relationship the LD has with you and consciously strive to excel despite its presence. That was the path Mr. Hoffman advocated and the one most appealing to me. The other path let the LD slowly dominate you and become the scapegoat for all your failings. Can't find a good job? Must be the LD. Relationships always fail? It's the LD. If you follow this destructive path, you spend the remainder of your life being controlled by your LD.

The best way to combat the self-destructive path is to wear your LD badge proudly, to show it off like the Congressional Medal of Honor. Make it work for you, not against you. In Blake, I saw both types of people, but most students fell into the latter category. They were young, but their LD had already made them socially maladjusted shells rather than fully realized people.

The time I spent surrounded by my own ilk at Blake afforded me the time to develop the ability to spot not just another LD student, but kindred spirits. Outside the mass body of school, once the jocks, nerds, squares, brains, aesthetically challenged, and LD students are removed, there exists a group that defies labeling. This faceless congregation is the comrade of the LD student. It is almost impossible for the LD to find sanctuary among the elusive popular castes. To belong among their ilk, one has to deny who and what one is and conform to the norms of others. But within the faceless mass, the body that doesn't allow the cliques to label them, there is a home for the LD. These students simply *are:* They are the majority who remain silent and faceless to the minority, yet grow beyond their anonymity to become fully realized people long before the social elite. Within the social fringes, people can show-off the qualities that make them who they are, all without fear of reprisal.

In high school, I found it easier to break the ice and take the plunge into mature friendships. Sure, the risk of betrayal was still there, but I'd be damned if my LD was going to control my actions and keep me bottled up any longer. Blake had shown me the dark side of LDs. My breakdown after Blake showed me how fragile I was and the dangers that came from keeping too much stored inside. It didn't happen overnight (hell, it still goes on today), but I've been moving forward, never stopping to dwell on or bemoan my LD.

Along the way I've gotten sidetracked more than once. Sex, drugs, and rock-'n'roll kept me from college and a future for many years, but I'm finally back on track. As I write this, I'm entering my senior year at a major state university in the northeast, I'm married, quite happily, to the woman of my dreams. We have a wonderful daughter and another baby on the way. It's hardly the conventional way of doing things, but then there is very little that is orthodox about having and overcoming an LD.

2

In the LD Bubble

Lynn Pelkey

Lynn is a 35-year-old, working-class, white woman, who was working toward a bachelor's degree in hotel management at a large northeastern state university when she wrote this essay. Although Lynn was in special classrooms for students with learning disabilities (LDs) from early elementary school to her graduation from a public high school, she had little understanding of her own specific disabilities until her late 20s, when she sought an evaluation from a psychologist. This evaluation confirmed that Lynn met criteria for dyslexia.

In this essay, Lynn focuses on the isolation and separateness from "normals" created by her learning disabilities. The "LD bubble" is her metaphor for this separateness, and her essay is devoted to articulating a moral, social, and psychological argument for the necessity of altering the conditions in which such separateness—and its crushing effects—forms. Describing a lifetime of struggle against the private conviction that she was "stupid," and thus unworthy of the esteem of herself or others, Lynn explores how reentering college in her early 30s brought about positive change.

As much as I want to find the perfect words to express what it is like to be dyslexic, I cannot. I can no more make you understand what it is like to be dyslexic than you can make me understand what it is like not to be. I can only guess and imagine. For years, I have looked out, wanting to be normal, to shed the skin that limits me, that holds me back. All the while, others have looked upon me, as well. There were those who have pitied me and those who have just given up on me, those who stood by, supporting me and believing in me, and those who looked at me as if I were an exhibit at the zoo. But, in general, people have shown a desire to understand what dyslexia is and how to teach those afflicted with it. Each side, it seems, longs to understand the other.

My dyslexia is like a bubble. I am enclosed in an invisible sheath that allows me to come excitingly close to being "normal" but never completely there. It is flexible yet confining. I can move within it but never outside of it. You cannot see it, but I can feel it. It has thick walls that are impossible to break free from. Sometimes, I hardly know it is there at all, and other times I have felt as if it were suffocating me, killing me.

I invite you into my world for two reasons. One is the hope that you will gain some insight, understanding, compassion, or even strength. I also write for myself in the hope that this process will help me to love myself for who I am and all that I can be. For, you see, I believe I was taught to hate myself.

"Dyslexia" is a label and only a label, but it carries so much negative weight. Had I been described as "gifted and talented," this, too, would have meant dealing with a label, but a positive one. Why must LD categories be classified around negative attributes? Can we not focus on strengths or positive attributes? As a child, my foundation for hating myself grew out of my much noted shortcomings and a lack of any abilities deemed positive.

I cannot remember my infancy, but I doubt very much that I hated myself then. My memories of my early years of childhood are happy. I was loved, and I felt loved. It was during my elementary school years that I started to feel different from the other children. It was discovered that reading and writing were difficult for me. I began some special programs designed to assist in my learning process. On the playground, in gym and art classes, or playing games, I was the same as any other child, but academically I could not achieve what other children could. As academics took on a more important role in my daily life, being with my playmates became less than pleasurable. We were no longer equal. At times, I was physically separated from my classmates. During these times, I was brought to the "special" room where I would receive help with my school work in hopes of bringing me "up to my class level." No one ever said this to me directly; it was what I overheard: "She is not doing as well as the other children," "She is having difficulty," "Scoring low," "Not trying," "Lazy." I knew the latter two were not true, but they certainly did not make me feel good about myself. It was in these ways that I became *less than.*

I do not know when I was labeled as learning disabled. It was not until junior high and maybe even into high school that the term LD started to surface with frequency. For years, my fellow LDers and I wondered what LD meant. No one ever told us. We did know that it set us apart from others and that we were different. Being LD was not something we received awards for. It was secretive and suspicious. It was something talked about in hushed tones. It was discussed at secret parent/teacher meetings. It was the reason I had to go to summer school. Is it any surprise that, even before I knew what LD meant, I felt ashamed about being LD? It was obviously something that was not good, and I had it.

I am not really sure how the school set about grouping us into the LD category, but I always had a feeling that it had something to do with the "state tests," the kind where you had to fill in circles with a number two pencil. While I was in early grammar school, I do not recall the tests bothering me, but when I started to realize that I didn't do as well as others, they bothered me greatly. The teacher always told us not to worry, but I did. I dreaded those tests. I would break into a sweat the moment the teacher would announce her plan. I could feel my face change color, first red hot with fear and embarrassment, followed by a pale, colorless sense of utter hopelessness. There was no way around it; I would have to take the test. We would each receive a booklet, face down, and a brand new, freshly sharpened, number two pencil. The teacher would give us some brief instructions on how to properly record our answers and take the test. We were to turn our booklets over and start when she said, "Begin!" and lay our pencils down and stop when she said, "Stop!"

The room would be unbearably quiet. The teacher would look at a stop watch, which I suspected the state must have provided with the testing package, because those were the only times I ever saw it. *Begin!* would echo through the room. My ears would absorb the word and send the painful message to my brain, my malfunctioning brain. At this point, just filling in my name was a challenge. I would be off by one column or fill in too many circles in another. Reality would kick in. Time was passing. My heart would be pounding as I frantically erased, rechecked, and colored in circles until my name was right. A great amount of time had already passed since *Begin!* had violated my brain, and now I couldn't remember the instructions the teacher had given us. I would have to read and reread the directions, using more valuable time. *Focus, focus, don't panic! Keep cool. I don't want other students to know I can't do this.* I hated the teacher. *How could she do this? She must know something is wrong with me. She always had those meetings with my parents. She must hate me as much as I hate her or she wouldn't be putting me through this. Maybe I should just leave, but then everyone would know that I can't do this and my parents will be called. Oh God, what am I going to do?* By this time, my nerves would be shot. I couldn't even sit still. I would glance around the room to see my classmates systematically filling in circles and working their way through the booklet. They seemed to have a look of deep concentration on their faces. That would be it, my body would betray me, giving me away to the whole class. My eyes would puddle up, my body temperature would rise so high that my ears would be on fire, and my hands would be so sweaty that my test booklet would start to warp beneath them. The lump in my throat made it difficult to breathe. I felt like the whole class was staring at me.

It felt like an eternity before I heard the word *Stop!* What a great relief! I would relax into my chair and start to feel better. As I brought my head up, my red-rimmed eyes met Chrissy Watson's. She sat at her desk, upright and proper, with her hands on her lap, her pencil positioned approximately four inches from the top of her desk. Her test booklet centered on the desk top just two inches below her pencil. Her answers right there in perfect sight, displayed so that the whole class could see. Her little black circles looked as if they had been printed with a laser printer. My test booklet was wrinkled and worn looking, except for the pages that I never got to. Big black smudges streaked my answer sheet and some spots I had erased so much that the print was coming off. I had to turn my booklet over so that no one could see. My pencil was worn to a dull point, and during the test, I had bitten down on the other end to maximize my erasing ability. I would put my head down on my desk pretending to be bored so that I could cover my booklet until the teacher collected them. As I lay there trying to give the other kids the impression that the test had simply bored me to death, panic was beginning to build. Who would be collecting the tests? Would it be the teacher or one of her pets? Probably Chrissy.

At first, the gap between me and my classmates was small. However, it was not long before I was ashamed of myself. I would compare myself to those around me. My performance was always less, the lowest, the bottom of the class. As the years passed, the gap grew, and the shame turned to deep-rooted self-hate. The gap, the shame, and the self-hate were not just my doing. Others, too, perceived me as "less than," and they taught me to accept their perceptions. Other students did not have any trouble telling me what was wrong with me, "Stupid," "Mental," "Idiot." I had to go to the "Retard Room" for a lot of my classes. This classroom was different from all the other classrooms. The doors were metal, and they had a long, thin window, which made it difficult to see in or out of the room. This had some advantages, because once you were inside, people in the hallways could not see you. The trick was getting into the room. I would usually hang out across the hall, by the entrance to the library, until after the second bell, waiting for a chance when the coast was clear. Then, quick as a dart, I would run into the room. In an arc printed across the top of the door in big black letters was "Remedial Reading." RR. The Retard Room.

The normal class had neat little rows of wooden-topped desks with metal blue legs facing the front of the classroom. The teacher's desk and the blackboard looked back at them. Above the blackboards were rolled up maps of far-off places that would snap up like the shades in my bedroom. The rooms were quiet in color. I always wanted to be in one of those rooms.

The RR was different. We had one large room about the size of two normal rooms. This space could be divided by a curtain that hung from the ceiling, like the kind they have in hospital rooms. We did not have individual desks but large rectangular tables. Our tables did not face the front of the room but were randomly placed throughout the room. Our blackboard was on wheels, and it was mostly used as a partition to separate us from each other. We did not have any maps; I guess they felt there was not a need to teach us that kind of stuff because we wouldn't need it for the types of lives that we would lead. It was during a humiliating episode with my cousin that I learned that Massachusetts was a state and not a country. The RR was cheerfully decorated, the bulletin boards were covered with construction paper in bright and happy colors. The decorations and colors would change to correspond with the seasons. The curtain that divided the room had been embroidered with a sort of spring scene. It was all very cute, like kindergarten. This room only fortified my feelings that I was dumb. Something was very wrong. All the other kids my age were growing up, but I was still in kindergarten. I felt humiliated going in and out of that room.

The teachers were very kind, but I believe now that they underestimated me. I would do what they told me to do, recite what they told me to recite, but I was rarely asked to really *think*, and I almost never experienced those moments when something I was learning came together and made sense. I think I did a lot of memorizing, but not much understanding.

However, I do recall one unique experience in junior high school when I did learn. This was outside the Retard Room and away from any "special" programs. I had made some friends on the outside. I would walk to their classes with them, and then at the very last moment I would hurry off to my class. As I lingered at the door of my friends' algebra class, waiting for the bell and fooling around, Paul, their teacher, would talk to us. Paul was really cool. He got to know me even though I was not in his class. One day, I was hanging out particularly late after the second bell had already rung. Getting though the halls was going to be tricky. Paul asked if I wanted to join the class. I said, "Yes," and grabbed a seat next to my friend. I did not have any paper or a book, I just sat and listened. I was in a "real" class with normal students. It was great. I just started skipping whatever class I was supposed to be in during that period and started attending Paul's algebra class on a regular basis.

As I sat in that class, something magical happened to me. I could understand what he was teaching. I was learning. I even started participating in the class, raising my hand and answering questions. I was LD. But then again I wasn't. I still couldn't multiply or divide very well, and I had to use elaborate ways to come up with the answer. But I wasn't memorizing, I was thinking, and I was figuring out the answer. I was learning. This was one of the first experiences that shot a pinhole in the bubble that trapped me in my LDness.

Sometime during the seventh grade, it was discovered that I would need corrective surgery for a birth defect that had gone undetected as a child. I would need a total of four operations in all, and I would miss a significant amount of school. During my first homebound sentence, I had a tutor. You would think that with the one-on-one attention I would have made great leaps and bounds, but it turned out to be a bust. My tutor just wanted me to read the textbook and do the problems, and she would check them on her visits. Of course, I was supposed to get them all right and never have a question, because then she would have to know the material and teach it to me. I had never been a self-directed learner, and trying to teach myself these lessons was no exception.

The next phase was to send me off to school for a reduced amount of time. I would meet with a tutor in a small, quiet room in the library. As much as I would like to say that my success with this tutor was all my doing, I can't. She is the unsung heroine of my junior high learning process. We really connected. It was there in that little room that I wrote my first paper, learned to solve for "x", and much more. But the most effective information that this tutor gave to me was information about myself. She talked directly to me about my disability. She explained it like this, "Lynn, you are part of a minority, a small portion of the population that has a learning disability. You and others like you learn a certain way. The rest of the people learn another way. Kind of like putting a round peg in a square hole. It can be done, but not as fast as putting the matching shape in the matching hole. I am sorry that you have to learn like this. You are truly special because you have stretched your brain and learned beyond and outside your abilities, and this is something the majority have not had to do."

She treated me as normal, and her expectations were normal. We were there to do work, and that is what we did. She was very patient, and she took me through my learning very systematically, step by step. We would not move ahead until I clearly understood what she had taught. We did a lot of repetition, but the learning moved quickly. I never became bored or idle. She was right there, moving me along. In this instance, the one-on-one attention was successful, and I was able to keep up with my class even though I had missed a lot of school.

During junior high, I did have a few regular classes such as science, art, and gym, but the rest of my time was spent in the Retard Room. I do not recall exactly the first day that I entered the remedial reading room at the junior high school, but I do remember an assortment of feelings associated with being there: fear, anxiety, uncertainty, and many more. I did not have one positive feeling about going into that room. Just me and the guys. What a group! Maybe about ten of us, ranging in types and degrees of disabilities. One girl (me) and the rest boys. That's right, I was the only girl in the whole school that was stupid, and it remained that way until I graduated.

Some of the boys frightened me, others annoyed me, and a few seemed tolerable. But as odd as it may seem, I developed a friendship so special and dear to me that nothing has ever compared to it. I think he knew how afraid I was. Maybe he was afraid, too. It was never a girlfriend/boyfriend thing or even a crush. I just needed a friend, and Brian was there. We were kind of the same in that you couldn't tell from looking at us that something was wrong. I think that we both played the same game with others. There was this unspoken and unwritten law that we both abided by. A code of silence. We never talked about our LDness with anyone except each other or other LDs. We would say "hi" to each other when we passed in the halls, and if any of my friends asked how I knew him, I would just say he is in one of my classes and leave it at that. And I am sure he did the same. We didn't really hang out together, but he kind of watched out for me. A lot of times, the other boys in the class would bother me, but Brian always seemed to come from nowhere and tell them to knock it off, and they would. There was such a comfort and ease being with Brian. I could be myself with him. He knew I was LD, and that was OK with him. As the years passed, we became better and better friends, and we made friends with other LDs. Brian even introduced me to my first real boyfriend.

I believe that being LD affected my adolescent dating experiences in numerous ways. As I mentioned earlier, I was the only girl in the LD class, and I think I was more concerned with survival than with thoughts of romance. Secondly, because of the separation between LD students and normal students, I did not spend much time with my female peers, so I did not have peer pressure to date. Third, I was not attracted to the boys that I spent a majority of my time with, and I did not have much exposure to the male population that I did find attractive. And finally, when I was with my normal peers, I felt out of place. I always felt like the new kid. They all spent so much time together, sharing the same classes, the same teachers, and the same assignments. I also think that it was less than desirable to date someone from the RR room.

In high school, things changed. Brian introduced me to Rich, one of my crushes. It turned out to be perfect for me. Rich was LD also. He was a junior, and I was a sophomore, so we did not have any classes together, but our routine was the same: some regular classes with normal students and the rest were LD classes. As I got to know Rich, I met his group of LD friends and their LD friends and so on. There was a whole underground network of LDs and I was part of it. It was like being part of a fraternity, a brotherhood, and we all lived by the code of silence. I experienced an additional thrill, because, while I found strength in numbers, I also felt special to be the only female with entrance. It was not uncommon for us to make jokes about being LD or to tease each other. This was OK for us to do because we all based our friendships on so much more. "Normal" students would judge us as stupid and worthless because our handwriting was similar to that of second graders. Our friendships and bonds went beyond these superficial judgments. What was important was that we were kind, supportive, and nonjudgmental of each other. Therefore, the teasing and jokes were harmless and really just a way for us to laugh while loving each other.

During my adolescence, I never got involved in sports, although I always wanted to. It appeared to me that only the smart kids got to play sports. Instead, I found my satisfaction in working. I always was proud to work. It was wonderful to experience praise and positive reinforcement. I took my jobs seriously. The harder I worked, the more praise and responsibility I received. The more I received, the more I wanted. My bosses seemed impressed with me and would rave about my maturity toward work. My friends at work would goof off, call in sick, and not show up, but I was always there, and I did my job. On the job, I got to prove myself, I didn't have to be the dummy. I pulled my own weight. Had I known at that point in my life that you could drop out of school, I think I would have. I am glad that I didn't, though, because I would probably still be stocking shelves at a toy store, and I'd probably be miserable. But there were times when I would think "I can do this. I should stay here. This could be my job." I would feel this sense of urgency to find my place in life and stick with it, because I knew I would never be able to get a college education, and I had to function within my limits.

I think another reason that I worked so hard was because it gave me a sense of freedom from being so needy. I couldn't make it in school on my own. I was so dependent on everyone: my parents, my teachers, the whole stinking system. But at work, it was up to me to prove myself, and again and again, I did. My bosses were always nice to me, and I worked very hard to please them. It was all very affirming for me.

Until one day, CRASH!!!! Bob, my boss at the time, was doing inventory. He asked me to help him, which I willingly agreed to. We started working on art supplies. I would tell him the product and count while he recorded. This all went along very smoothly until we got to the paints. Have you ever read the names on the tubes of oil paint? It was like a foreign language. I panicked. My face got red, I was sweating, and I didn't know what to do. I stumbled across a couple of the names and then with every bit of nerve that I had I told my boss, whom I respected and trusted, that I couldn't read them. He looked at me in disbelief and said, "Why? What's wrong?" I think he thought that maybe the writing had been unclear, or maybe I couldn't see. But when I repeated myself, saying, "I can't read it, I don't know what it says," he understood exactly what I meant. He snatched the tube of paint out of my hand and spoke to me in a loud disgusted tone, "BURNT UMBER." He said it maybe two or three times, his voice getting louder each time. I couldn't believe it. I was so embarrassed. But that wasn't enough for him. He started in on me. "You can't read this? How old are you? What the hell is wrong with you? You'll never go to college! You'll never be anything!" He may have continued his outburst, but that was all that I could take in. My ears hurt, and his words just melted together as I turned and walked off.

As I walked toward the front of the store, the whole incident replayed itself in my head, his words ripping me apart. It was difficult to breathe. Even now, I can see his ugly face, all distorted, yelling insults at me, treating me like I didn't have any feelings at all. All my fears were being screamed at me. He confirmed what I secretly had feared: I was stupid, I would never be anything to be proud of, and I'd never make it to college.

I worked the rest of my shift in silence as I thought about what kind of future was in store for me. He didn't speak to me either. Sue, a friend of mine and a fellow worker, had helped him finish the inventory. The night seemed to drag on. I was so relieved when 9:30 finally arrived, and I could leave. I waited outside the mall for my father to pick me up. It felt so good to get into the car and be driving away from that place. I started telling my father what had happened. When I got home, my mother joined my father and me, and they both listened to my story. They really listened. Neither one of them overreacted or told me that it was not a big deal. They were both very supportive and acknowledged my feelings of sadness, hurt, anger, embarrassment, and whatever else I was feeling. I felt much better after telling them, and they agreed that his behavior was out of line.

I took some time off, and when I returned to work, my boss asked to speak with me in his office. I was scared to death, and now I hated him, but working meant so much to me. The idea of quitting never entered my mind. I also felt thankful that I had a job, and I did not think I would ever be able to get another one. At this point, I had my walls so built up that I was determined that he couldn't hurt me. I wouldn't let him. He apologized and offered to help me if I ever needed it. I wish I could have accepted it and left it at that, but I couldn't. I could not forgive him. I knew he thought I was stupid, and his apology felt like pity. I was not about to feed his ego and ask him for help. No thank you. I told him it was no big deal and went back to work.

Being LD must be similar to how some gay people feel. You spend so much time and energy trying to hide who you really are. You are ashamed of what you are, and at times you long to be like others, but you are who you are, and so you lead this double life. Some know you as LD, and others know you as one of them, but you are not one of them. You are just pretending. You hate yourself for being LD, and you hate yourself for being a fake. And in the end, who are you? It is all very confusing. All the while you really just want to be you, without any fears. We LDs live a life of deceit—pretending to be like others—and shame—not wanting to be who we are.

My self-efficacy, my belief about my competence, fell into the category of failure-accepting. I expected to fail, so I set no goals, believing my ability was set (I had none). Thus, I learned helplessness. Everything was black and white, with no grey areas. There was good and evil, positive and negative, and, of course, smart and dumb. As I grew, I started to believe the negative stereotypes associated with my academic abilities. I was stupid! I couldn't do it! I accepted these stereotypes and let them define me. I erased myself. I hid who I was out of shame. I also had a growing fear of the unknown. What was really wrong with me? There had to be a reason and an explanation for why I was the way I was. Would it get worse as I got older? Was this it? Was I retarded? I was not sure that I wanted the answers to these questions. Eventually, I turned my back on academics.

I am the middle child among five children: four girls and one boy. Having two siblings that are not LD and two that are may have caused a heightened level of sibling rivalry in my family. It must have been very difficult for my parents to find a parenting style that would not be damaging to any of their children. Because home was a safe spot for me to be who I was, my parents and siblings usually had to bear the brunt of any frustrations school created for me. I am sure that my mother and father didn't have time to analyze my every mood to see if anything had upset me at school, and even if they had asked me, I don't know if I could have verbalized an answer for them. Sometimes life just sucked.

My sister, Carol, the oldest of the five, is suspected to be LD, but she has never been officially diagnosed. Our relationship was that of two strangers living in the same house. She did her thing, I did mine. Let's face it, I was her little sister, and I annoyed her. Carol could be a hostile, violent, and angry child. She was like a pressure cooker ready to blow. She would attack anyone at anytime for just about any reason. She would physically go after my father, which was truly frightening. I believe that she felt safe taking out her frustrations at home, because she knew deep down that we loved her and knew that she was good, no matter what others made her feel like. At the time, her anger confused me. I could not understand why she was so mad. Now it is painfully clear. From day one of her schooling, she was identified as a troublemaker. Not performing up to standards meant that she was not trying, and that made her a "bad girl." She knew she was not bad, but that is what others saw her as, and that's how they labeled her. Is it any wonder that she developed stomach ulcers by her early teens? To this day, I believe that she is fighting to find the child that got lost when she entered school.

My next oldest sister, Patty, was a tough act to follow. She was popular, smart, beautiful (she really does look like Snow White), and very talented. It seemed as though there wasn't anything she couldn't do. I envied her so. Patty could read five books at one time without getting confused, and her handwriting flowed evenly and beautifully across the page. Heck, she could even write on unlined paper using a fountain pen. She was a constant reminder that I was less than.

In junior high school, I joined the chorus because Patty was in chorus, not because I had a burning desire to sing. Patty was an alto, so I forced myself to sing low so that I could be with her. She had a beautiful and powerful voice. Mine, on the other hand, was painful to listen to. When the school decided to present *Oliver*, the musical, the tryout list was posted. There was such excitement. Patty got cast in a leading role, Nancy. She had solos to sing as well as lines to memorize. I got a part also: I was one of the peasants who sold knives in the street. On opening night, I was instructed to just mouth the words in the song, and the other knife-selling peasant girls would sing the monotone line, "Knives! Knives for sale!" My only line, and I didn't even get to say it. Well, the play went off without a hitch and Patty was great. I was so proud of her. After that evening's performance, my parents took us all out for ice cream, and I reveled in the attention. I felt very much a part of the whole thing, as if I had played the leading role. And, in a way I had. I knew all of Patty's lines and songs by heart, and when she was out there, I put my heart out there as well. I love music, but I now believe that I was meant to appreciate it through listening to it and not trying to make it. By the time I reached high school, I gave up on the chorus and just watched in amazement.

My brother, Mark, and I have an extraordinary bond. We think, feel, and behave in a similar manner. We fought as children, often putting each other's well-being at risk, but it was nothing out of the ordinary for siblings. Mark was two years behind me in school and was also labeled as LD. He did not go to the RR, but to the "Learning Community." What a lovely name! You can call it what you want, but it was the same thing. As children, we never really talked about our experiences within the walls of the school. It has only been over the past ten years that the stories have started to surface. I was talking to Mark just this past week, explaining my involvement in this book, when I realized that he, too, was never properly diagnosed while in school. He, too, does not know what is wrong. We started talking about what it was like for me to be diagnosed, and he wanted to know what it did for me. I did not really know how to describe it. "Do they give you a gold card with your name embossed saying *Certified LD?*" he asked sarcastically with a twinge of pain in his voice. No one wants to be dyslexic, but when you are, you know something is wrong. Although you cannot explain what's wrong with you, you always hope that someday something will click, and it will all go away, and you won't be stupid anymore. Deep down, you know, it's with you to stay. And if you get diagnosed, you get a definite label, and then you *know* it won't ever go away. Both Mark and I are very hard workers, and we found a great deal of satisfaction in doing a good day of hard work. We both found jobs that did not require a great deal of reading and writing but physical work and effort instead.

My sister, Marie, who is ten years younger than I am, was never a real threat to me when she was young because she liked me and I adored her. I lived through her at times the way a parent sometimes does with a child. I believed in her so. When she started to learn new things, she was encouraged by all of us. I can remember how thrilled I was the first time she crawled and how I loved her to perform for us. She had nothing to hide. She was not going to be stupid like me, and when she accomplished something I would beam with joy. I was so proud of her. She was my little sister. When I moved out of the house, she was only eight. She loves me and I her. But as time passed and we lived apart, our relationship changed and grew apart. Marie went on with her life and grew into a beautiful young woman with many of the same talents as Patty. They are almost carbon copies of each other. I am still very proud of Marie and all that she has done, although I do not think she feels the same about me. I think that she is ashamed of me and embarrassed by me. She has an intellectual facade that she carries off very well, which makes me feel all the self-loathing that I felt as a child. I love Marie, I really do, and think that maybe her persona is just part of her age and that in time she will be able to see the good in me and stop judging me for what I cannot do and start judging me for what I *can* do.

Not long ago, it became very clear to me that I would have to come face-to-face with my feelings about being stupid if I was going to find peace within myself. Four years ago, my mother encouraged me to go with her to an open house at a local community college, the same college that I had flunked out of ten years earlier. I agreed to go, but I had no intention to sign up. I went just to satisfy her, to say that I went. I started to talk to a woman about my diagnosis, and she guaranteed me that if I wanted to learn, they could and would teach me. The next thing I knew, I was agreeing to give college another try. I can still remember sitting in class the first day and thinking to myself, "How long are you going to carry on this charade?" I was certain that I would last only about a week or two. But, I kept hanging in there. I was facing the monsters of my past. I was no longer going to be held back. I had to admit what I was. I heard myself saying out loud to my professors that I had dyslexia. It's not that it all came easy to me, because it didn't. Saying it made it very real. All the promises that were made to me on that open house day didn't quite pan out. I was supposed to have my books on tape, have extra time to do assignments, and be given untimed tests. This all sounded good, but it took a lot of work and persistence to get the things that I needed. I really learned to become an advocate for myself. I no longer fell into the role of helplessness; I knew that if I did, I wouldn't make it. As the semester went on, I realized that I wanted this. Not only did I want to succeed, but I wanted to be one of the best. I had a goal.

No longer were my classrooms "special." They were real. I was with real students. At first, I did not say anything, because I was sure that they must be so much smarter than me. After all, this was college, someplace I thought I would never be.

As time passed, I realized that I wasn't the dummy in the class. The professor would ask a question, I would have an answer in my head, and most of the time someone would say what I was thinking. I wasn't so different after all. In time, I began to ask questions or respond to those asked. And I was learning, right along with the normal students. The gap that was once about the size of the Grand Canyon was beginning to close. I couldn't believe it when my fellow students asked me for help. This sounds very childish, but it was an experience that I had missed out on as a child, and it was a wonderful feeling. I was not worthless, and my opinion mattered. My success at that college was a milestone for me. Not only did I graduate with an Associate's Degree, but I did so with honors.

My success at the community college gave me the strength to believe in myself enough to continue my education. So here I am, a junior at a four-year college with a goal. Being LD has become less important to me. There are arrangements that I make due to my disability so that I am able to learn, but no one is giving me the answers. I certainly don't get a free ride. I don't have a tattoo on my forehead saying that I am dyslexic, but I don't hide it either.

In junior high school, being LD was a big part of my life. At that time, the universe revolved around me. I was my biggest concern. I was self-centered. My world consisted of very little, and so being LD was a big part of who I was. But as I became older, I grew out of the self-centered mode and into a more complex way of being. As my life evolved, being LD became a smaller piece of the whole.

Above all, I thank my parents for their unconditional love and support. I am fortunate to have had parents who emphasized my attributes rather than my shortcomings. They always saw in me what others could not, and they taught me to love myself for what I could do. It is from their encouragement that I found the strength to face my fears and become who I am. While my disability will last my lifetime, it no longer has to limit me.

I now strive to see myself as my parents see me.

3

Revolution

Aaron Piziali

Aaron is a 22-year-old, middle-class, white male who has nearly completed his bachelor's degree in anthropology. Until the age of 13, when he was first evaluated by a psychologist, Aaron was usually assumed by his teachers to be a discipline problem rather than a child with a learning disability (LD). Aaron's learning disability is difficult to classify, but it mainly affects his ability to sequence and organize thoughts and words. Accordingly, his disability has had the most severe impact on his efforts to write the kind of ordered, conventional prose that schools usually demand.

In this essay, Aaron uses a series of letters—each of them written to persons who have tried to "correct" or "heal" his disabilities—to address his own educational history and to call for a radical reconfiguration of the relationship between the "abled" and the "disabled." Aaron argues that teachers who try to erase a disability are misguided and potentially destructive, for these efforts often have the effect of causing the student to distrust and reject his entire thought-world. Instead, teachers ought to help students establish an affirmative, open, and curious stance toward their own mental processes, permitting them to think, write, and speak in the ways that are most natural to them.

Aaron does not, however, propose that persons with disabilities wait for the "temporarily able-bodied and able-minded" to make the needed changes. Instead, Aaron encourages persons with disabilities to direct their own futures, in part by banding together as a political and moral community.

Introduction

In our society, there is a class of individuals who experience life based on their displacement via their disabilities. Many of these individuals—including those with learning disabilities—have disabilities that are invisible to society, *invisible* because they can't be easily seen or explained. The spaces in which learning disabilities manifest go beyond their origin in the classroom and overlap upon all aspects of one's lifeways. Those who have to negotiate life with learning disabilities are often disenfranchised from the mainstream's ability to create real adaptive choices for the production of life's needs.

For those with invisible disabilities and those who have configurations that fall into undefined spaces of disability, there is a constant haranguing of them to get it together and figure their problems out. If they can't do this, then the response is usually to ask them to be *okay* with their difficulties and limitations. After doing a great deal of reading and conducting a general review of my own experiences, my general feeling is to say *bullshit* to every person who can't take onboard my concern.

Assessing the factors that play into learning disabilities has become so important in my life that most of my self-deconstruction revolves around it. Thought—or, better, the cognition involved in forming theories, expectations, decisions, and resolutions to personal and public tensions—has all been held suspect, my belief in its integrity has been worn thin by constant worry. *Class clown, fidgety, rude,* and *a discipline problem* were the standard accusations made against me up until mid-elementary, along with praise for being mature, smart, athletic, and creative in the arts. All of this was woven into a confusing spiral of feedback that was not yet organized under the notion that I might be learning disabled. But everyone knew there was *something*.

It is in such moments and spaces that our disabilities are contested, and we are rendered as ghosts; we have occult disabilities, and our experiences are invalidated, because those who want material substance cannot see what we experience.

As we get further out on the periphery of definable disabilities, the prescriptions we are offered comprise nothing more than a bad-spellers' dictionary, repeat visits to the doctors, and special education plans. Where is the opportunity to articulate an alternative view?

It is at this point that the so-called "disabled" learner may come forth as the genius to piece together our collective experiences and produce a reading of the nature of learning disabilities. Learning disabilities exist, but they may be nothing more than an accumulation of various culturally determined blocks and flows—*flows* being the states in which educational production is in tune/touch with the individual and *blocks* being the crisis points in which the individual is unable to produce what the educational world requires. Thus, whenever some teacher or parental frustration becomes the mirror of who you think you are, you're in danger of being blocked.

I am a prisoner, a survivor, a target, and a struggler, continuously defending, negating, and recreating myself. My disability? My disability is that I have been disabled, as well as discouraged and discounted by a temporarily able-minded, able-bodied general public. My success and failure have been based on an existing value system created by the dominant majority. Although I am now constantly disabling myself through a process of disbelief, exacerbating disabilities already in work, I know that I shouldn't be compared to anyone else. My evolution is the only standard against which to check my progress. That I now struggle as I do for self-acceptance, may, in fact, be my learning disability. Thus, my learning disability is something I must perpetually fight to define and also something I must fight to reject.

I.

Dear Dad,

I am sitting down here trying to trace out reasons that may have contributed to my learning disability. This is coming out of my belief that my learning style is something that was molded, and that due to this, it has put me at a disadvantage in almost all the educational situations that I've been in. Also I feel that any physical reasons that may contribute to my learning disability don't close the book on me. There were methods and experiences that were given to me that I believe accentuated these physical aspects. Thus I believe now that my learning disability is a holistic manifestation of life experience and physical facts at work within me.

You are a very important person in the development of my learning style and my relationship to school work. Both you and Mom have struggled with me throughout my educational life, which happens to be all of my life. It is evident to me that you sincerely did your best with the resources available as well as what you thought was best. But I want to focus on you, Dad, because this letter is about writing and the anxieties that I have about writing. This is about remembering and reclaiming a time when I was beginning to emerge as a reader and writer back in elementary school. This is about the weekends and about the book reports that I had to start doing in the fourth and fifth grade. This is mostly about your help but it is also about how you failed to help, because the failure on my part to complete papers is a fresh feeling.

Saturdays were the days that we had together. Mom was at work, and we would spend hours together going here and going there, this museum and that tavern. All day, my attention was consumed and my questions were flowing. This was the standard up until sixth grade. Saturdays were book report days. I still can't relax on weekends during the school year; I never get much done, but worry about what needs to get done. So we have worry, anxiety, and homework all bound up on the weekend.

You were the first one to read and give me feedback on those early book reports. I would usually have to finish the book and then set out to write a simple book report: title, author, year, and publisher, and then a page on what the book was about. It all should have been so easy, but even the process of picking out the book was difficult.

I remember vividly and viscerally the process of writing a book report, giving it to you to proof, and then getting it back with the corrections you pointed out. I was never satisfied in my ability to revise my book reports, and over time, I developed strategies to avoid aspects in the process. These strategies have lasted into the present, as if I were still trying to avoid the frustration, blocked to begin and blocked from meeting deadlines. I still have this sense that another person is going to judge whatever I write. I feel chased by a ghost that I can't understand. Is this feeling a cause of or a response to my learning disabilities, or both?

What you didn't realize, I feel, was that your experience as an English teacher was not helpful to you as a teacher for me. It left you with some very real difficulties in addressing ways to contribute to my learning and work styles. The forces that surround one's life experience contribute to every aspect of one's responses and abilities. So you passed on to me a set of expectations that I felt I couldn't meet. If the cognitive disabilities were there, then they were marginalized because you weren't able to see their manifestations. Therefore, the red pen gouged at my difficulties and bound them into a tight sense of failure in me. This effect followed me from classroom to classroom, year after year. My avoidance of your help also contributed to my inability to accept and reorganize myself around an idea of relearning the way that I learn, an arrested development because I was too distracted by work and its frustration to really get to a centered moment and resolve upon a plan of action to relieve the frustration.

Then there was Fred, a writing tutor appointed to me through the college learning disabled student services. The first day I met him, he asked me what I wanted him to do for me with my papers. I told him to just read my papers for the ideas. I didn't want him to proof a single misspelling or imperfect grammar. All I wanted was his response to the paper's conceptual and intellectual qualities. He didn't do what I asked. I wanted to hear feedback on the idea content, but all I got was the same proofing you gave me on my book reports. I had enough deep down and wanted the ideas responded to. Indeed, this outcry was ignored, and he told me for three weeks that my sentences were too full, too rich, and that I needed to spend more time trying to make the ideas clearer. My sentences were rich because I had just spent the year and a half before with English teachers in high school who gave me avenues of creating papers that were open to my style. I got support for my capabilities, not the mistakes which were treated as details to work out. All in all, I gave Fred the boot, my stomach all tight, and I told him that he stressed me out and was not helpful. Again I was cut off from a source that could synthesize my disabilities with my potentials. This left me to repeat my patterns of self-doubt and work production that feed a negative cycle.

Do you think you messed up? Well, to a large degree, you did, and you were a part of the wider network that holds you, as well. Why haven't I learned to write an essay? More importantly, why haven't I remembered a style in which to do it? My anxiety to do work is a handicap for me educationally. It has severed my interpersonal relationships with my teachers and it makes me spend too much time worrying and groping for strategies. It leaves me with little I can use as a tool or a road map to get out of the jams and into the self-aware flows. You used to play "Kick out the jams motherf*#@ers," a song about the "system" and the oppression it causes. It was a declaration about fighting against the "man" and was a song that seemed to symbolize an era of rebellion. That rebellion, the one that could have rendered a better understanding of my learning style, got inverted for me and the work that you did on my papers was not helpful at the time. Now it is only helpful in that it provides me with clues into my LD, but it comes too late in life. I will do more work on this in the future, but there is no way for me to reclaim the work I have done, never finished, and doubted.

Journal writing, essays, proposals, outlines, etc. Before I begin any of them, I hesitate. Writing them, I frustrate. There is an echo of an experience that is like a voice or a presence that really makes itself known. It manifests in the subtlest expectations that my writing will be scrutinized. Journal writing uses organizational skills to write out a poetic and intellectual analysis of my life. It should flow and expose. However, even the act of writing in my journal is difficult. There is an expectation as if someone is going to read my entry. It is a concern not about exposing myself but a distrust in writing itself. This is my point. The distrust in my own abilities to write has fused with my informational output style and caused a very disabling experience.

Dad, you are present in my writing and present in my anxiety. I am present in my cognitive pattern, the space of my disabilities as dictated by physical reasons. I am also present in my emotional ability to produce "school work." The presence of all of these things is disturbed, their borders overlapped and bungled up inside of me. I am the physical representation of all that I am and have sustained from my life experience. In the educational institution and in the expectations based in their logic I am disturbed, and this will persist, decreasing only as I find the forms that my disability takes. You learned strategies that I have not had the privilege to learn, and now you and I pay the price.

II.

Dear Don,

Your enthusiasm was unmatched. As my writing tutor at the University of Brighton, you were immediately suspect as an adversary; however, the sessions we had were healing moments. The process of writing that year had been very hard, if not painful.

What was so important about our session was that you took the time to look into and behind my papers to see how I constructed them both psychologically and cognitively. Your insight went beyond an analysis that just stated what it saw and then handed me the action prescription. You were more concerned about getting me to recognize the ways in which I could do the work that best matched my developed skills. This is the point that was never addressed in previous tutoring or study skill advice situations. You provided a barrage of things that you noticed, such as the way I would use detailed hand gestures while explaining my ideas or the way in which I would organize aspects of information. Overall, you not only painted a clearer picture of my work style but tried to teach me how to paint that picture myself. Skills were your answer to frustrations, something that others who have tried to help me couldn't really get to.

I would stare for hours at a blank piece of paper, pen in one hand and a pile of notes next to the other, ready to write the sentence that would open the flood gates in order to complete the paper. Days would pass. Finally, I came to you during the middle of my last research paper. My work style up until then was based on that pattern of trying to funnel all my collected knowledge into the first sentence, trying to write the entire thing along a linear path from first work to last. You broke that thought process up for me. We made trees of note cards, each note card numbered and color-coded by the aspects it covered. Each tree was mutable, shiftable, and able to incorporate a whole lot of segments that were unattached. Why I never strove to do that myself is the hurt over time of straining to comply with a dominant style of paper writing. There were skills that produced papers that I wanted to be able to write. But not recognizing that there existed a better way to write, I entered instead into a process of constriction of anxiety that cut the creative juice to my brain. Inner visions have so often been stolen or dulled for me by my education. The frustrating thing is maintaining that inner vision in the face of my historical relationship to dominant educational expectations. So what was powerful was the process of writing the papers with you and seeing my ideas come out and take on a shape that was much more manageable. The learning was a joint process rather than a passive donation of knowledge.

I still struggle to fracture the styles that I work with. There is a pattern of producing a paper that is still deeply woven into my style, but it is ever so clear that given an opportunity to actively practice new styles really draws out the power of my real creative/intellectual abilities. What is sad is that for years my style has been an angry and anxious reaction to demands for answers that I could not give under the educational duress that I am always under. Working with you was a bright moment in my educational career and one that reverberates across all spheres of my life, because it spoke to the ways in which I express, problem solve, and create. What we did gave me a chance to see a dynamic expression of the potentials, obstacles, and quality of my work style. Thank you.

III.

Dear Ms. Richards and Ms. Marcus,

In an uncompromised voice, I would like to extend my thanks for—as well as my deep concerns about—the support you provided to me and my comrades with learning disabilities in high school. I have many conflicting and mixed emotions about my experiences with you.

For four years, I attended the Learning Center daily. Over that time, I learned the most disabling skills ever. The atmosphere was depressed, attributable in part to the others in there who were also on the top-ten troubled students list. All the tricks of the LD trade that are supposed to enable us to learn were provided: mind mapping, better note taking, comprehension tricks. But there was a lack on the center's behalf to encourage the sense that we were there not to compensate for a disability, but to gain an insight into our learning styles and our relationships to them. A large part of me is angry that this was not provided.

Also, there was never any work done with us around the psychological impact of the learning disabled identity. It pains me to remember the amount of tears that I shed because I had no words to describe the feelings I had. A bubble is what I remember it feeling like, some membrane stretched around me that let me exert only so much and then that was it. The psychological trauma of the adolescent conception of self and LD is evident in all our lives. The ones who do "well" were exceptionalized and made into models for us to aspire to: Einstein, Bruce Jenner, Madonna, etc.—cultural icons with LDs that we were supposed to associate with and realize that we all had potential. But for me the block remained, and the lasting effects of it followed me across high school and into a repeat of the denial of an LD in college.

The center was only a space to mediate between perceived learning problems and the education community. Teachers, administrators, and other students were not clued into the pervasiveness of the aspects of learning disabilities. So, in turn, teachers never got a clue about how to change their teaching styles, and administrators carried out their authoritarian judgment upon us and tightened the tough love reins on our human rights. Dignity was at stake, and the skills and insights provided at the Learning Center were not adequate enough to support and enable myself and my comrades for the terrain of classroom, school work, and school halls. My life could have been a lot better than learning that "math sucked." I would have wanted to see those of you at the center arm us for the struggle and help us to fracture our mono perception of what was needed in order to "get it" in school. Math is something that can be done many ways, and there are strategies to help. But the opportunities to learn them don't come from those who are not aware enough to teach them.

There are so many points to bring to you, and they all rush to be said, so fast that the frustration and sadness they churn up is difficult to convey. Your center tries to nobly provide support for a class of students who are marginalized and demonized by powerful forces at work in the school system. The social impact of learning disabilities is self-destructive and alienating if it is not approached from a point of respect and nonpaternalism. This is part of a systemic problem. The center should not be considered a service, but should be seen as an integrated approach to all students in hopes of encouraging learning strategies that enable each person's best performance. You have got to help us dig ourselves out if you ever want to help us and get us started developing positive skills, and that is going to take trusting and believing in our perspective and going from there. You must define the process by way of our experience.

IV.

Dear Pam,

I was asked once, *If there was a super pill that would rid me of my disability, would I take it?* It was a difficult question to answer. I thought of all the possibilities that would glean up for me if there was no longer the threat of obstacles created by the learning disability. I thought of all the activities that would simplify and all the projects that could be finished. It took me a good ten minutes to think it over, but in the end I answered "no."

I have never taken chemicals or any other treatment for my learning disability. When I say chemical, I mean drugs and medication to help my brain function at a level of a functional student. Also it acknowledges an action of doing something to my body's processes as a way to combat the disabilities. To this day, until going to see you, I have never considered any such actions.

These past three months have been the most important chapter in my relationship with my disabilities. Going to see you for CranioSacral Therapy was a serious step outside myself. I had to accept and to trust that there was a possibility for physical treatment. The therapy and the process of our visits have given me more insight into the nature and function of my disability.

To begin to think of my disability as a result of bone displacement and restrictions of circulation is the most important possibility I have ever pondered. From the day I began to search for remedies, the abundance of alternatives created a panicked search. I tried everything from herbal stimulants to dietary changes, yoga, and other forms of exercise. And like the overabundance of study skills and coping tricks learned over the years, there is only so much that I can do to and for myself. Exhausted and well dosed on herbal remedies, I finally boiled it down and took the positives from the options. My diet changed for the better and has helped, my awareness of my body and its processes has developed, and a general stock of knowledge has accumulated about self-treatment and disability. However, never once did I go to someone else to administer a possible treatment for my disability in the alternative medical field. Seeing you was the result of the total acceptance of a biological foundation of my disability as well as the point that I was ready to step outside of the selfish heroism that I see destroy so many disabled people. What you helped to create for me was the decentralized need for another remedy, another hunch as to what may help me with dealing with my disability, and a chance to gain empowerment for the first time.

The action of manipulating bones in the body and finding points in the body where the circulation of cerebral fluid may be blocked has released a new chapter in my relationship to disability. I firmly believe that there is something real about the therapy, especially after reading about the results other recipients have had and comparing it to my own. This is a form of medicine that developed out of standard medical practice and should be used more widely.

For the first time in my life, it seems that something that was once fragmented is now beginning to align, to reconnect: all the bits and pieces forsaken by failure, bad grades, or a stuttering speech in front of classrooms; fragments that have taken the shape of a lumbering trauma that follows me around, always reminding me of my disability: a perpetual post-traumatic stress syndrome that brings me back to square one with each intended step forward. This is the first time I actually feel the confidence of change, the steady waking of discovery and awareness.

What has opened up for me, and what I hope someday for others, is a reclamation process. I want to think of my disability now as a flexible aspect of my person. It is real, it is there, and it is an impairment to deal with. What is important about receiving the CranioSacral Therapy has been the changes in my attention span, activity, and confidence. I seem to have stepped into a hyperactive state that would have served me well as a younger person. It is a state that seems to be the collective potential that possibly was stymied by the blockage of the cerebral fluid circulation. This new state is powerful, and its existence assures me something has been done, that just as with the taking of medication, there has been a physical effect upon my disability. What makes this experience fundamentally different from medication treatment is the direction, the source of authority describing the nature and aspect of the disability. In what I experienced with your style of therapy, there was a mutual discovery and, in turn, a mutually facilitated "recovery," again a reclamation.

I believe that this is a fundamental process that all disabled persons, especially those with developmental and cognitive/learning disabilities deserve and need. Our own participation in the process that gives relief and actually names possibilities of the origins of our disabilities is sorely lacking in the "professional" support usually offered to us. Authority cannot solely command the prescription for something not organic to itself; that is, descriptions of disability handed to us by the temporarily able-bodied/minded lack the critical components and bulk of disabled persons' analysis, as well as our hope for a "better" way to perform our functions. Through serious trial and error, we have analyzed what works and what does not. However, for the majority of the time, we are left without the tools to create the ideals we hope for. It is at this very point that I feel that our sessions have provided a crucial link to the reclamation of my identity.

Even though I'm soon graduating, a learning disability remains within me. However, with new insights into the causes for learning disability, I feel that many obstacles will melt away. Still a little confused about the future of my ever-changing disability, I thank you for being yet another person who goes beyond the limitations of popular healing and understanding of the potentials and paths with which to relate to our disabilities.

V.

Dear Aaron,

This is an open letter to myself, from myself. Overall, this is the letter that I have been trying to write all along. Each of the other letters I have written has been an effort to reclaim much of the trauma that envelops me and my entire learning endeavor. Reclamation is a chance to pull the hurts and memories from the depths of myself, pulling them up so I can turn the hurt into memory and finally begin to resolve my dilemma.

My question now is to know, *What do I do to survive emotionally, and how do I go about it?* It is also important to figure out how I can interrupt patterned behavior in order to change the patterns.

Some days it's going to be hard. Most days are hard. What is apparent to me now is that we (myself and my abled self) have so far failed to combine the knowledge needed to monitor my emotional state so as to develop a more resilient headspace.

To do this project right now is draining because it is a writing project I have been describing. To proceed in this project is to be constantly exposing the triggers that disallow my learning abilities from performing. The very action of writing this piece is not objective. It creates a vortex that trails behind it and begins to speed up and expose thoughts and problems that support and surround the very act of writing it. Its deep subjectivity becomes realized in the reactions it causes in the activities of learning.

I know that due to a process of essentializing each other's abilities, there has been a historical silencing and omission of the needs and self-representations of the disabled classes. I use the word "classes" because cultural integration and awareness will not occur until authority is given to the lives and self-definitions of the individuals who make up the disabled subgroup in society. In order to change, we must begin by placing those that are disabled in a powerful position of agency in the transformation of culture, especially the dominant socio-economic global culture.

As for the individual, I find that there is an overwhelming amount of agency that the individual can have in the transformation of others and their relationship to the dynamics of disability. My learning about others in the disabled classes and their self-defined lives is a powerful reference point to my own struggle. We have to keep struggling to find a niche in society, as well as to mend the emotional and mental fibers that have been systematically severed in the process of our lives. By looking at case histories, accounting for new and old teaching methods, comparisons of those students who have an "easy" time in their education, personal stories of those with LDs who have had access and who maintain the overall access to support, and biological data on the related research, we could come to a more holistic account of the dynamics at play in the lives of those deemed "learning disabled."

It is a revolution of reclamation that the disabled classes are contributing to daily. Their lives, my life, and our potentials are at stake and are competing against historical cultural hegemony. Awareness is the cornerstone of that reclamation process that becomes the psychological foundation from which to survive. Build on, band together, and go beyond survival!

4

Look in the Mirror and See What I See

Christie Jackson

Christie, a 20-year-old, white, upper-middle-class junior writes of how being diagnosed with a learning disability in her college years forced her to rethink her career goal—that of becoming a marine biologist.

Though there were signs from grade one onwards that she had trouble with spelling and memorization, Christie was a highly successful student, even to the extent of being seen in grade school as the "class brain." At a private high school, the symptoms of a yet-undiagnosed learning disability became more obvious as Christie struggled for academic success, looking "confident and able" on the outside, when on the inside she felt "meek and disabled." In this struggle, she was, for awhile, highly successful, winning science prizes and writing awards. At college, however, a poor performance in a Latin course and a disastrous one in a microbiology course suffused her with self-doubt and the sense that she was a fraud. A subsequent LD diagnosis and a reflective experience in a foreign study program changed her academic goals and worldview, and compelled her to assess where her real strengths lay—in writing and in helping others identify and deal with their learning disabilities.

The stage was a typical college frat basement, offering an assortment of social inter-actions (drunken conversations that wouldn't be remembered, provocative embraces, and less than ideal introductions), though most were obscured by the loud music. After trying to converse with a friend and not getting past "What did you say? Speak up!" I turned my attention to the group next to me playing a drink-ing game in which the inability to recite an increasing list of names wins you the chance to drink. I remember the conversation.

"Christie, come play with us!"

"No thanks, guys, I don't want to."

"Come on, *it will be fun!* You don't have to drink much!" another tipsy friend expounded.

"That's not the issue," I said.

"But we want *you* to play, you *only* have to drink what you want!" chimed the tipsy crew.

I could tell that this group was as receptive to my saying "no" as they were to saying "no" to another drink themselves. I hated it; I had to say it to make them understand, and I knew they still wouldn't.

"I just can't remember things like that. I have a learning disability." Sure enough, the same dumbfounded look I usually receive prevailed on their faces. "Oh" was the most they could muster as a response. They turned their attention away after that odd stage of silence that occurs when someone doesn't quite under-stand what you are talking about, but realizes it must be something serious by your expression. Better to leave it than try to understand.

My learning disability seems to creep into every facet of my life. It had even managed to creep into a frat basement, a place that few would call a safe haven, but which I thought might offer some escape from my LD's clutches. The learning dis-ability routine had become as commonplace to me as my daily schedule. But at least now I know what to call it. Growing up, I called it stupidity. As a child, I had worked so hard to cover it up, even from myself.

The effects of my learning disability first appeared when I was in grade school. I thrived while learning and my eagerness to explore was recognized by my teachers and family. Yet, there were times when I felt terribly alone and so inferior that I was ashamed. I remember Sister Maria's first grade class and being the last to get my spelling words corrected. You had to write each word you spelled wrong five times; when you were done, you could play. I always was the last one done; sitting among the empty desks, I could hear laughter from children at play on the other side of the room.

At home my mom used to quiz me even before the unit began for the week. I would try and learn words for what seemed like years to a grade-schooler, repeating, saying out loud, and writing them. "Hourse—no, horse," or "house." "Piece—i, e; e, i; what was that order?" In my mind, what was the use? My hand would be so tired from writing, that I would try and spell them out loud, which was even worse.

Through practice, I was able to learn the words, but I would master them for only a week at a time. Just enough time to barely rattle them off on a test. When the next week began, they were already a distant memory. Although I was able to get my As, I felt I was cheating in a way, as I realized how quickly my words slipped from reach. I felt as if all I had worked for crumbled right before my eyes. The wall of perfectly formed words lay like a rubble pile of disjointed letters.

At other times, I felt as though I had some magic spell over me, causing me to be different from everyone. I think I was the only child to ever be stressed-out by a music class. Everyone else just joked and learned the songs so easily. "Repeat this after me: 'High hopes, high hopes' . . . ." After about four words, I was not able to repeat any of the song, let alone an entire verse. The phrase I hated the most was "let's sing the whole verse now." I couldn't even remember the first word. My music teachers always thought I hated singing, but the problem was simply that I didn't have words to sing!

This same resentment carried over into my religion. I would sit and intensely listen to the church readings and feel as though I understood the messages. Then, an hour later, when the teacher would say, "Who was the story about and where did it happen?" my mind would be bare. I must not have been paying attention. My humiliation increased when I couldn't learn the responses. I felt like a mute, deaf invalid in church: unable to hear the messages, unable to respond on cue. How could I let God down like this?

During grade school, I was a very quiet, shy student. I had many passions inside of me and about four friends, but I was deathly afraid of interacting with a large group, turning violently crimson whenever called upon. Everyone saw me as the class brain, who was quiet and always slightly out of the cool group. I was not into the normal early teen fascinations: I would rather watch NOVA than MTV, rather hear Mozart than Madonna, and rather read classical books than *Sweet Valley High.*

Although I was happy during these years, I had a growing sense of unrest as a desire to explore and reach out to others grew. Unfortunately, my peers expected me to be the same sedentary, shy girl. I felt like a foot that had just grown too large for its shoe, and no one noticed the pain I was in. Everyone expected me to be in a dull, worn loafer when I really wanted to try on some dancing shoes and, in a whirlwind, see all that the world offered. Yet, as my graduation from eighth grade grew near, I became increasingly aware that, finally, I could decide who I was and what I represented. I soon found my niche at a female Catholic college prep school.

But my time in high school had another side. The first high school obstacle, posed by what I now know as my learning disability, was opening and closing my locker. After continual pre-fall practice, I somewhat mastered the art, though a hidden combo at the end of each notebook helped considerably. I also had a problem with the "always walk to the right" rule in the stairwell. The difference of left and right to me was as clear as the difference between eggshell white and ivory.

High school also presented a new type of pressure. Though I suddenly was free of others' stereotypes socially, no academic reputation preceded me. In grade school I could only achieve academic confidence by the praises of my teachers and the grade recorded elegantly on a paper's top. Here, in a new setting, I had nothing to base my academic achievements on. The academic pressure I placed on myself caused enormous stress headaches, though at the time, doctors' diagnoses ranged from a brain tumor to allergies. They became so bad, I would wake up in pain at 7:00 am; they would continue throughout the day rendering me helpless, and I would cry myself to sleep.

Academically, I was doing well in most of my classes. Spanish, however, was different. Spanish was a nightmare. I felt lopsided: My abilities in some courses were counterbalanced by my inability in others. I never knew when I would tumble over from the unequal strain. I was so scared of Spanish class that at night I woke up crying, scared by foreign words screaming in my mind. At the end of a class on Friday, I counted the precious hours until I would have to be in that class again.

I did my written work every night for hours, painstakingly looking up each word—words I should have mastered in the lesson or the year before. I would, for example, look up "with" in the dictionary and see the translation was "con." Not more than a few phrases after writing that word, "with" would arise again, but my memory wouldn't. Was it "como?" "com?" "son?" and back to the dictionary I would go. The next day I would not remember what I wrote, so before school I would write it out in English again to review.

I guess I carried myself well. I don't know how I always managed to get an "A," but somehow I came out all right. This success, however, made me feel so inferior—like I was displaying an outside shell that wasn't me. I looked confident and able, when inside I felt meek and disabled.

Oral communications were far worse. When a teacher asked me anything in Spanish, I could only hear the symphony of sounds, flowing and rhythmic; I couldn't hear the meaning. I tried to dissect each word, but by the time I reached the third word of the sentence, I had forgotten the first. My mind wouldn't process information quickly enough. The same bottomless feelings of inferiority were always there.

As my high school education continued, my other academic performances began to set me apart from the other students. I won a writing contest for an essay on peace, was on academic decathlon teams, won state academic awards, and was the recipient of science prizes. I took all the honors classes I could, commonly giving up my lunch for an extra class. I was afraid to admit that I could not remember my teachers' names, or that I had to look up a word in the dictionary four times in a row. I thought that by taking more classes, I could compensate for my deficiencies. In all areas of my life, I always was one to say "the glass is half full," though in academics I was more apt to say "the glass might shatter any moment now."

Though I loved all subjects (except Spanish), at the end of the year I realized I had a passion for science. I decided to do something about it and wrote to a well-known aquatics lab with a plea to do anything—even wash test tubes. I wanted to observe a real lab, with real scientists. A few weeks later, I got a call from Professor Tom Phillips, offering me a job.

My time at the aquatics lab, although unnerving at times, afforded me opportunities and contact with professors, something I had never experienced before. I felt I could prove myself by functioning well in a lab, and somehow, make up for all those scientific names I never was able to recall. I would show the world that I did know, I did understand, and that I would succeed. I remember cheerfully walking down the hallway that smelled like a combination of alcohol and pond/lake water, with shadows from the overhead industrial lights lining my path. My shoes rang proudly on the tiled floor and in the distance, Tom's Led Zeppelin music echoed from the radioactive lab. Here, I felt like I belonged, and I let my love of the water work its magic. I knew the combo to the radioactive lab, I knew the angle to push the cart so that it would go straight, and I knew to call the large 5-liter jugs "carboys" and not "cowboys." I knew my place; I had confidence.

During junior year, I also began presenting my science research, namely at a regional science fair. There were about 300 of us, all lined up, row by row. My three-way four foot wooden board (complete with hinges and pictures taken with a $100,000 microscope) towered over the more mundane white cardboard and loose-leaf displays. This was my thing. I knew I loved my research, and I was going to make the judges love it too—period. As I spoke, the assurance of my results, the completeness of my data, and the complexity of my problem were matched only by my eye-catching enthusiasm. I didn't even notice the semicircle of attentive judges. It was such a different feeling than in the classroom, where every test left me empty and guilty for not knowing the material. My confidence here felt right.

The next day at the awards ceremony, I received the most awards of any student, including a four-year scholarship to a local college, monetary awards, and awards of recognition. I continued to show my research, and at a statewide symposium, I won the chance to go to nationals. The best reward, however, was when Tom asked me to come back during my junior summer and work for him as a quasi-teacher, researcher, and assistant. I had my own bench space, which is like being given your own plot of fertile soil and staking your homestead on it. It was a sign of respect, of hard work, and I experienced the "I know what I am doing" feeling.

Through all my science presentations, the college question became more and more pressing. I was an overachiever, I admit, and the college admissions process was just another one of my extensive projects. I applied to 12 colleges, thinking I would not get in anywhere and wondering why any school would want me. I remember I cried a lot during this year. At times I cried because I felt I was faking my intelligence, somehow slipping through the cracks. I cried because I felt I would fail. I kept repeating "Let me get in somewhere, anywhere, please God." Somehow, I was admitted to a prestigious East Coast college, and I became known as the "Ivy Girl." I tried to keep the news low-key, but soon everyone assumed I was God's gift to academia. Yeah, right! Everyone saw me as valedictorian. I saw myself as a fraud.

Coming into college, I knew I wanted to be a biology major, as well as a philosophy major. Now I felt, as I had in high school, that I needed to prove myself, but to a much higher degree. I was with the smartest of the smart. I was in a different state, never mind a different region, where no one knew my history. I embraced my new life with my usual energy and enthusiasm: a love, a drive, a passion for life.

I thought the more I studied, the better I would do. That is what happened in high school and that's what I supposed should happen at college. This theory put enormous pressure on me. I would study for 12 hours at a time in a library mirroring an English nobleman's house, complete with tall facades of books, leather chairs, dark mahogany wood paneling—the place just shouted out "intellectualism!" I thought that maybe the environment would suddenly cause an epiphany, that I would be able to excel.

That year, my English papers and ecology labs came back with enthusiastic comments and my understanding of the material seemed comparable to any other student's. Yet, in other classes—Latin, chemistry, and math—I was miserable, receiving Cs and Ds. Latin would take me six hours of studying a day, only to see the words evaporate, slipping from my hand. At first I reached into the air periodically, not quite sure where to grasp. As the weeks went on, I began to clutch the air, frantically, wildly, until frustrated tears streamed down my cheeks. I spent hours in my caring Latin professor's office. My fear of languages grew far deeper than anyone realized. I began to doubt my decision to attend college—and myself. I had almost not come to this college because of the foreign language requirement. I knew I was a fraud. If I had once studied Spanish for four years, why couldn't I even say one sentence of it now? Why wouldn't Latin come at all? At the lowest point of my Latin efforts, I spent one and a half hours on two Latin sentences for translation.

In math, I also had a fear. Numbers. Formulas. I could do math in high school, but all our tests contained a sheet with the formulas. Here, I couldn't remember the formulas. During office hours, the professor asked what I didn't understand. I replied with a hurt voice quivering in frustration: "I don't even understand what I don't understand or else I would have come in and asked you to explain what I don't understand." My professor advised me to get a tutor (which I had), go to help sessions (I was the only one who went every night), and read the book (I had read it three times). I felt like an illegitimate academic child, always questioning my sense of belonging in the intellectual world.

In chemistry, I fared no better. For the first test, I confidently studied for 40 hours in one week. I sat down to the test and looked at the first page. I didn't understand. I flipped the page. I didn't understand. Flip. Flip. Flip. There is nothing more daunting, nothing more dreadful, than a test page with a two-sentence question and the remaining page blank, and knowing that anything you write will be wrong. My mind was supposed to conjure up formulae, equations, and notes to bring the page alive. I sat there without writing. Beside me, other people were scratching the paper rapidly—the sound of their confident, rapid-fire pencil strokes drained me of confidence. With every question I heard my inner voice ring: *You are a failure, a failure, a failure.* I received a 29%. I ended up dropping the class.

During this troubling time, I had begun to write poetry, and as my college career advanced, so too did my reliance on writing as an outlet to express feelings that otherwise might have remained hidden. I scratched out poems with the same pencils I used in chemistry and Latin, yet with poetry, the pencil knew where to go, and the figures it produced effortlessly covered the page. These poems mirrored my deeply embedded anger: Slanted words dug into the page, reeking of fear and urgency.

Late one night, a friend saw me crying in the hall as I was scribbling a poem. She came over, knowing of my hard times, and spoke softly. She asked me if I had ever been tested for a learning disability. My reaction was similar to the incredulity that I receive from others now. What? "A learning disability," she answered again. She said some people just learn differently.

I didn't know where else to turn, so I went to talk to Joyce in the Learning Center. She asked me if I confused right and left. Funny, I always did. Had I talked late as a child? Yes. As I spoke to her about my difficulty, she didn't have the usual responses: "Well, just work harder," or "You *must* be getting As with that amount of effort." Instead, she said I should be tested. I considered that "good" news of some sort; at least she didn't think me mad. However, the earliest available date to be tested was in two months. Waiting two months to find out whether I was just inherently dumb or whether I had some disability was too long. Emotionally, I was being pulled in too many directions. I felt like I would crack in a short time. Luckily, my parents were very supportive, and they agreed to pay to have me tested in Boston.

After the strenuous testing, the doctor spoke the words that changed my life: "Christie, you have a learning disability." Much of what he said after that I remember as droning words. I was half recovering from the blow, and half hearing the echo of those words in my head: learning disability, LD, handicap.

I thanked him, shook hands, and went downstairs to the marketplace, where I was meeting my parents. As I saw them walking toward me, I suddenly leaned up against the building. Tears welled up in my eyes, and I heard myself say it for the first time, "I have a learning disability." I began sobbing as my parents hugged me. Others around me must have thought I had just found out I had some fatal disease or had lost something.

I had no fatal ailment, but I had lost something. Never again would a day go by when I didn't think of how my LD would affect my work, how I needed to alter my actions to get around it, or how to express it to anyone else. Yet, over the next few days, a drastic change in my poetry flowed from my heart—a feeling of peace and assurance that I wasn't an oddity.

The most difficult task was telling those friends back home of my learning disability via e-mail, trying to keep the mood low-key. Their replies shocked me. I felt as if they didn't know me. One person said that it must be a mistake, that the valedictorian, who held a 4.0 GPA, couldn't have an LD. One friend thought it was an early April Fool's Day joke. Another friend paid her condolences, as if I had passed away or had some terminal disease. Their lack of understanding was matched only by my frustration in trying to get across to them what I was feeling. I normally could express myself well; why couldn't I express how painful, yet calming, this new revelation was?

It's very difficult to try to explain, in lay terms, something that is wrong inside of you. It's not as if you can say your hand hurts, or your eye is burning. An

LD isn't cut and dried. When I read the report and saw phrases like "language-based learning disability," "problem with memory," and "poor spelling skills," I could barely translate into words *how* I felt. Phrases like "significant intracognitive discrepancies on the WAIS-R" and "high WAIS-R performance IQ" and the confusion of how to tell people what that jargon means becomes a frustrated mixture of "kinda like" and "sort of as if." People are easily bored and their eyes drift away when I can't pinpoint with one breath what my LD means. What they don't understand is that my LD is something I can't turn my attentions from; it's always there. To this day, I still have difficulty explaining the concept. Some acquaintances think LD is an all-inclusive term, that handicaps can't vary. They don't know how ignorant they sound when they try to use the term *LD* as if it were something universal. It's like telling someone confined to a wheelchair that there are Braille boards at the top of each flight of stairs so they can tell what floor they are on. Sound idiotic? That's how I feel sometimes when my LD is defined by someone else.

In addition to my diagnosis, at the end of my freshman year, a number of other circumstances tested my faith in myself, in family, and in God. I had decided to take a heavier course load than normal; I was working in the science lab doing research 15 hours a week; I was a member of six student organizations; and I became confirmed in the Catholic Church. This was an insane amount of work. I felt as if I needed to redeem myself, since I had dropped out of chemistry earlier.

Then came a switch. That summer and my sophomore fall focused my attentions elsewhere—on the sea and all its beauty. During the summer I sailed in Nova Scotia as part of an oceanography program, soaking in the mysteries of the ocean. That fall I continued my love affair with the sea by going on a maritime studies program. I could study the sea, write poetry, and be a free spirit. I received all As that term, an accomplishment I had not achieved since high school. I had forgotten the elation, the complete satisfaction success brings. I thought my success was a fluke, but how wonderful it was to soar again!

With the ending of my exchange programs, my college routine continued. However, I was slowly learning to ask professors and friends for special LD considerations. I also began to realize *all* the insignificant tasks that gave me difficulty. In my step aerobics class, I never got the left-right confusion in check and had to follow everyone else from the back of the room. I had forgotten the combination to my post box, and feeling like a young 'shmen, had to ask for the sequence three times. Then there were all those meetings where I entered the building and found I had forgotten the room number.

The fall of my junior year marked the utter collapse of my academic self-esteem, as well as of my energy. I had decided to stay at my college—despite the fact I was scheduled for a break. This decision worried my parents. I remember telling them: "I'll be all right, Mom, I promise." I believed it, mostly. I knew I was burning out, but I couldn't stop. If I did, I thought it would show weakness, that my LD had won.

That fall started with excitement and energy; I went into my classes with a vigor and drive to do well. I stayed on top of the reading and seemed to have double the amount of notes of anyone else. In microbiology, our lab had one write-up for the entire term, which consisted of the identification of eight unknown bacteria strains. Because of my experience in Tom's lab, I immediately fit in and answered other students' questions. Then it started, slowly. The first test came and I got a 45%. The test had identification of bacteria strains on it, and I got every fill-in-the-blank question wrong.

I went into the professor's office, started crying, and asked what I should do. The options were either drop or stay. I heard those words again, "drop." Disappointment. Disaster. Failure. Again. I couldn't get away from it. I honestly had hope that endurance and effort would get me through it. What a false sense of hope I had; I see that now. But naively I decided to stay in the class. I had wanted to take this class too long to give up now. I loved the material; I loved the lab. I walked out the door wondering whether I had done the right thing. I thought I had. Maybe I was reading into it because my self-esteem was already so low, but during our conversation, I thought she was smugly questioning my LD. I can remember how she seemed to lower her eyes down to me as the words "learning disability" rolled off my tongue.

My term after that plummeted. Slowly. Then faster. I began studying so much microbiology that I let my sleeping slide; I became so tired I couldn't stay awake in class and felt too stupid to ask friends for notes even though they were always willing to help. My energy diminished, I started lagging in my other classes. In my introductory philosophy class, I began doing poorly. In my aquatics class, I couldn't do much better than the mean, and yet this class was based upon the same material as my college research. I felt horrible.

On my next microbiology test, I got 30 points below the mean. They hung a copy of the distribution curve on the wall to the lab. One student commented: "God, can you imagine how it would be to be at the end of the curve down there? You could kiss med school good-bye!" My eyes were locked on the lowest bar on the graph: That represented my failure. I had to stay in the class at this point. I felt as though nothing I did was right, had been right, or ever could be right. I received a D. I felt I crawled away from the term, on hands and knees, my fingernails scraping into the dirt as I cried out, without anyone hearing. I was alone.

During this term, my academic performance affected how I approached everything. I was a tour guide for the college. Admissions officers, students, and parents loved my style and enthusiasm. How could I not be enthusiastic? I loved the place, and I wanted to give back to the school that had given me so much. Yet, I began doubting that I should be a tour guide. Did I really represent the "ideal" college student? I even began thinking I wasn't qualified for my upcoming exchange program to Costa Rica. I seriously thought about telling them I was a mistake and to ask another student.

Finally, the term ended, and it was time to move ahead, if I could. I had the mental stamina of a drained battery. Still, I could fill these pages with captivating Costa Rica images. The program rejuvenated a soul that yearned to be held and embraced. I slowly regained hope and assurance that all would work out.

After I started seeing the beauty around me, I was able to temporarily separate myself from my LD to see that I did have something worthwhile. I began to write more poetry and the pockets of my khaki army field pants, mud stained and not washed in three weeks, held not only a field notebook but my journal. I wrote 300 poems while on this program, and many speak from my soul. They were not filled with the previous hate and mistrust in my abilities, but with an assurance and peaceful beauty. I was able to do what has always been my goal: to learn for the sake of learning. This goal was so often in direct conflict with my LD. Here, I could just do research. No tests, no finals, no fill-in-the-blanks. My spirit soared. The clutches of the LD had directed not only my academic performance, but my mood, my smile, my eye for detail. With it, I had become consumed with an anxiety that made my heart ache.

One day in Las Crusas, we were unexpectedly asked to memorize plants, 30 of them in two days. As the class groaned and complained with a tinge of laughter, my eyes fell to the page in front of me. I thought I would escape it this term, that I wouldn't have to utter the words that sometimes disgusted me: *learning disability.* Suddenly, I was left with the same feelings of isolation and lost hope I had suffered in the fall. I knew I would fail, even before I had begun.

That day, I did a rare thing. I wrote a journal entry, not in the form of a poem. The words speak from my heart, with the pain I can sense even now:

> February 6, 96 —Today was difficult when my LD became unbearable once more. Of being confronted with a list of memorization. Without a previous botany knowledge nor a quick mind to memorize, I felt behind, dumb, inadequate. I start to question why I am here and why I deserve to be chosen for this program. Harry told me the quiz actually counts for nil, but the inferiority remains—the reminder of my fault surfaces, yet again. Frustration sets in.

When I was outdoors trying in vain to memorize the list, I ran into our teaching assistant, Harry. He was concerned about why I had not been myself in the last few days. He grabbed a plant and supportively asked for its name. "I do not know" was my response. He repeated this gesture a few times, and always my response was the same, the same as it has always been too often in my life. Finally, I couldn't take it anymore: "Harry, I just can't do this, you don't understand; I normally would study this for weeks to learn them all."

My voice trailed off. I burst into sobs and let go of my papers, which flew all over the pathway, the ink smeared with my tears. I explained to him I had an LD, something I had hidden so well until now. Oh, why couldn't I get through one term without having to hear those letters?

I told my professor about my LD that day, and with tears welling, expressed to him that I was trying terribly, though it might not appear so with the grade I would receive. He was very understanding, but I ended up doing poorly, despite having extra time. When my fellow students quizzed me on this "special" treatment and why I was so upset, I tried for one brief instant to invite them into my world:

"Well, you see I have trouble memorizing names like this."

"So do I, man. I didn't know how I'd get them all down in two days with all the other work we had to do!"

"But you see, I have trouble with it . . . um . . . it's like a bridge between the name and the object just won't click. . . ."

"I have that, too. I always get a few wrong like that."

"No, you don't understand, I have a *learning disability.*"

"You? No, you don't! You're at an ivy school."

With that, I let the conversation drop. It wasn't worth it.

With this experience came a revelation of sorts. The day after the test, I was sitting on a stone bench with a friend of mine. I mentioned I was upset, that I didn't feel smart sometimes. She nodded her head, and I heard something in the way she spoke, a hesitation, that seemed very close to mine. So I went out on a limb.

"Well . . . I have an LD." I was afraid that I would be branded by my intimate revelation, or worse yet, that it would be totally ignored.

"What? Well . . . so do I."

Like long-lost family reunited, we understood each other. We spoke about the feeling of failure, about the pain of isolation. Nothing is more comforting than to hear someone else speak the words you are unable to express. She let me talk mostly, yet her eyes told me that she wanted to soak in all I said, as if my words were what she longed to hear another human utter. Then she thanked me, and I will remember this as the only time I have ever been happy to have an LD.

"Christie, you just put my mind so at ease. Your way with words, with expression, they speak of all that I can only try to express but can't. You have a communication skill to comfort people by saying exactly what they are unable to say, but need to hear themselves. Thank you."

I realized then that God may have given me an LD not only to make classes much more challenging but to help others identify and deal with their LDs. How long had I suffered silently? How long had my LD been able to break me down into tears? How long had it taken me to say "yes, I have a learning disability"?

I have also continued to take comfort in my poetry; through my poetry I live. I have written for the past eight years, but in the last three, my poetry has let me grow and share, what at times, I don't know how to express.

Now, in my senior year I am wiser as changes occur around and within me. I realized that my first academic love, marine biology, may not be the career path I want. I have not been able to gain the self-esteem in science that I had hoped for, that I once had. I am not sure how much of my frustration is with science and how much is with my LD. I am tired of my mind churning with the heavy burden of, "Am I going to be all right?" Working with people, I feel as though I have no disabilities, nothing to prevent me from doing my job. I never feel such joy as when I have assisted others. I was put on this earth to help people. No LD could stop me here.

Now, I am better able to talk about my LD and not let the leash around my neck strangle me with fear. That day in Boston marked the moment that I was changed forever. LD is a label and, as a label, stereotypes will always surface. But that label is also part of me. It's as much a part of me as my middle name, as my smile, as my love of lilacs.

I do not know where the future will take me. I do know that my LD has influenced my life. I know there are some people who will not understand, never understand, choose not to understand. I do know that I am intelligent and that people are drawn to confide in me and gain comfort from me. I know that I must continue to try to understand my LD, and my strengths, and grow with them. I know these things. My challenge is to learn to believe them, to be able to say them to myself without worry.

I end with a poem about my LD, one which captures my constant struggle to realize that my identity is strong and vibrant, regardless of my learning style. If my story has helped others understand what it means to have a learning disability, then this story has served its purpose. For if you can look in the mirror and see what I see, my job is complete.

> I have
> witnessed
> the beauty you
> have repressed
> out of fear
> or rejection
> or unassured belief in
> yourself
> (all without just cause).
> But I have seen that
> shimmer of delight
> and intellect
> the impressionable wonderment
> that elated you
> beyond the credit you give yourself.
> And, when you believed aloneness prevailed,
> I, in the corner, watched your beauty
> unhindered
> glow
> as you lived life
> as you thought life
> and no self-doubt surfaced
> for you were (are) above that
> deep cavern of lost esteem.
> Without the weight of measuring to other's standards
> I see you soar
> above the dreams you create
> and witness the beautiful nature
> of your spirit
> And with my eyes I watched
> And with my soul I felt the joy
> And with my heart
> I beg you to let
> the actions seen only in the shadows
> carry beyond
> into the light
> you create by beauty.

5

Trusting My
Strengths

Michael Sanders

Michael, a 21-year-old middle-class, African American senior, grew up in a home in Texas dedicated to education and religious practice. A positive experience on the debate team in high school had a profound impact on Michael's self-confidence and sense of identity. Having discovered the "winner within [him]self," he was able to shrug off his classmates' taunts about his academic striving and what they perceived as his "difference." Michael's confidence in his powers of oral communication, however, were undermined by consistent difficulties in his Spanish class—difficulties attributed initially by his parents to insufficient effort. It is not until a disastrous experience in a college Spanish class makes it abundantly clear to Michael that he has a learning disability that he seeks help and accommodations for his problems. Recognizing that this learning disability has had a powerful impact on many areas of his life, and that he has been the victim of discrimination as both a racial minority and as learning disabled, Michael is unbowed and unapologetic. He knows that the challenges he has undergone have helped, in his own words, "shape who I am."

Sighing impatiently with a cross look upon his face, my Spanish professor entered his office as I followed closely behind. After he had taken a glance at his e-mail, he said disinterestedly, "OK, now, let us speak about your work. It seems that you have been having trouble in this course. Your exams reflect this, as do your written assignments. How do you explain this? Are you doing the work for the course—going to drill, completing the workbook assignments, reviewing the class material?"

Feeling frustrated by his casual manner of addressing problems that were very troubling to me, I seriously questioned his commitment to helping me succeed in the course. I said, "I spoke to you about my problems in language courses at the beginning of the term. I am doing the work for the course. It's not that I'm not putting forth effort. I mean, in comparison to most of the other students that I know in the course, I do more work. Most of them do their class assignments in drill. I always have mine finished."

Turning again to his e-mail, he blurted out, "Well, then what's the problem? If you're doing the work, you should be performing well in the course."

I thought to myself "Well, if I knew, I wouldn't be here, would I?" Though offended by what I felt was his half-attention to my concerns, I said only, "I don't know what my problem is. All I know is that I'm working hard and getting no results."

As if to wash his hands of the matter, he replied, "Well, I'm not very experienced in these matters. Go to the Academic Skills Center." I wondered if the same lack of care that he displayed for me would have hurt him if he had been on the receiving end. Put off by his abrupt attempt to rid himself of my problems, I told him that I had already been there numerous times and was still not doing well. His manner was confusing to me, as virtually all my previous interactions with professors had been pleasant and some were very helpful. Yet here was one who wouldn't work with me, even though I was obviously putting forth a lot of effort.

But the worst was yet to come. He caught me completely off guard as he jumped up and began to yell at me, stunning me with his choice of words, "God, man! What am I supposed to do with you? Huh? What is wrong with you! I don't know what your problem is—and I don't have the time to try and figure it out. I heard about you. I heard about you from other people. I told you the course would be demanding, and I was reluctant to let you enroll in the first place. Now I know that I made a bad decision because you've been nothing but trouble. All of the other students are getting along just fine, and you're the only problem."

Momentarily, "Wow," was the only reaction I had. But, as he finished his tirade, lots of thoughts began running through my mind all at once. Why was he screaming at me? Was I really such a bother? Why wouldn't he at least try to listen to me, to work with me? Other professors had worked to develop other techniques that would make it easier for me to learn. Why wouldn't he do so? Was it too much work for him? Or did he just not care about a black man's problems in learning Spanish? I also wondered from whom had he heard about me. What had he heard? Who was discussing me with their colleagues?

Becoming increasingly angry, I couldn't believe he was treating me this way. Wasn't it his first responsibility as a professor to work with people in order to help them learn? I was also steaming about apparently being discussed throughout the

Spanish Department. I resolved that if I ever discovered who had spoken against me, I would give them a hefty piece of my mind, and I also would inform my Class Dean.

Trying to compose myself, I said testily, "It's not because I haven't been doing the work. I've been over to Academic Skills and I'm doing all that I can do!" He yelled back, "Well, what do you want me to do! What am I supposed to do? I am a teacher, not a psychologist. What is wrong with you! I don't have time for this. I don't know what to tell you. Pull yourself together and go back to the Academic Skills Center. I can't help you any further." I was sure that other professors in close proximity could hear us, and by this time I was not only angry, I was also very hurt. After all, I had not done anything wrong! When I finally broke down and cried, my professor made a feeble attempt at kindness by telling me to pull myself together. Outraged and disappointed, I walked out of his office in worse shape than when I entered.

Although this incident took place almost two years ago, I still remember it in detail. However, unlike then, I am now aware of certain, special abilities that allow me to learn in ways different from most people.

The motivation to write this essay stems from my experiences in attempting to learn foreign languages. The problems that I've overcome have had such an impact on me that I want to share my feelings with others. In this essay I explore the particular nature of my abilities, the limitations and difficulties associated with my language learning, as well as my strengths and accomplishments. I hope my experience will not only increase the understanding of those who have no experience with learning disabilities, but also help those who do have learning disabilities to succeed.

My experience with learning foreign languages at college has been disturbing and disheartening, at best. During my sophomore and junior years, I was working to complete the college's foreign language requirement. When I was unable to complete several courses, I was evaluated by Dr. Pam Koval in order to determine whether I had certain processing weaknesses associated with language learning. Dr. Koval found that I have great difficulty processing novel language forms and associated weaknesses in computation. I have very real problems in hearing individual syllables and the pronunciation of words in other languages, which makes it difficult for me to distinguish some words from others, and thus to participate actively in class.

It is important to note that these problems were exacerbated by the college's use of the Rassias method for teaching languages, which is a fast-paced alternative to more traditional forms of teaching. It is comprised of several components, including drill sessions, textbook and workbook exercises, and class dialogue. During drill, instructors dictate phrases and sentences that students must repeat or modify using clues from the instructor. This is meant to help students become more familiar with hearing and pronouncing words in another language. Drill fails for many students, some of whom may need to understand the meaning of sentences and phrases before they can respond satisfactorily. This was the case for me because, whereas drill's sole purpose is simply to pronounce and hear words, I needed to understand the meaning. Because drill sessions often consisted of speaking in incomplete thoughts or segments, it benefited me little.

In addition to drill, the Rassias method incorporates a class segment during which teachers and students speak only the foreign language. I had trouble maintaining the fast pace, and when professors asked questions, I required significantly more time than others to hear the question and respond. Because they relied solely upon an oral approach to learning languages, both drill and class sessions exacerbated my learning problems.

As a result of Dr. Koval's diagnosis of my disability, I was granted a waiver of the language requirement. My time in college has been molded by my ordeal in recognizing, facing, and overcoming this disability, all the while maintaining my academic interests. Although I feel that my learning disability does not pervade all areas of my life, it has significantly affected me in many ways, including my academic performance, interests, and personal relations. My learning problems have hurt my grades and discouraged my study of China, my main academic interest; but despite these considerable stumbling blocks, I continually face my weaknesses and rely upon my strengths to obtain the best education possible.

It is important to note the effect that the language experience has had upon my self-image. As a former debater, one of my greatest assets has been my ability to communicate. I was a debater throughout high school and was recognized as one of the top debaters in the nation. Because of my hard work and success, I was recruited to debate at a New England college, which is the main reason I am here. Debate has been the mainstay of my self-confidence; I derive much of my self-esteem and confidence from my ability to manipulate language and ideas, something on which I have always depended. In short, oral ability has been my strongest skill. Yet, I couldn't even complete a language course! I continually asked myself, "Why can't I pass any of these language courses?" Because I derive much of my confidence from my oral skills, in using language to influence other people's perspectives and thoughts, failing foreign language undermines that confidence, and in fact strikes at the very heart of my academic mainstay.

It is important to look at people's general perception of disabilities, because I held some of these perceptions before I was forced to deal with my own problems. I would guess that most people are not very knowledgeable about learning disabilities. In my experience, mostly involving students and administrators, people tend to react two ways when informed that someone has a learning disability. Some react with sympathy, while others react by taking measures to help deal with it. I do not resent people who express sympathy when hearing that I have a learning disability, but I don't want anyone to have sympathy for me because I have problems with foreign languages. Rather, I appreciate individuals who try to understand my problems and help me find a way to deal with them. I don't see myself as being mentally or intellectually deficient, though some people may view it that way. Instead, I recognize that I think in a manner that is different from the mainstream. This is not to say that I shun my identity as having a learning disability, but I do think that it should be looked at simply as a matter of people learning in different ways—ways other than the norm.

Some people may say that being learning disabled is comparable to being physically handicapped, or belonging to a racial minority group, or like missing a part of yourself, but it's not! I am not physically disabled, so I can't comment on that experience. But I am a racial minority, and I think comparing this to a disability is highly problematic. I happen to belong to both groups and thus have a unique perspective.

Though people with learning disabilities and racial minorities both encounter discrimination, the similarity ends there. First, while having a learning disability isn't visually identifiable, racial identity is, which means that racial minorities bear the greater brunt of discrimination. Those with learning disabilities don't have to tell anyone if they don't want to, which gives them a certain amount of control over their own fate that a racial minority does not have. Second, the learning disabled are not subject to the overt brutal racism and discrimination that racial minorities suffer. I've never heard of anyone with dyslexia or quantitative problems being lynched, burned, or beaten. Racial differences have historically been a motivation for violence, while differences in learning have not. Thus, I don't think that placing learning disabilities in the same category as racial minorities is fair to either group of people.

Nevertheless, it is important to note that I have experienced discrimination as both a racial minority and as learning disabled. In order to fully understand how both experiences have shaped my character, it is necessary to know something about my family and background.

Both my parents were brought up in poor, hardworking, devoutly religious families. Despite many difficulties, my mother and father both excelled in high school. My father was a track, basketball, and football star and also maintained high grades. My mother was also an excellent student. Though both were quite frequently held out of school to help the family, they graduated from high school and went on to attend a university. After two years, financial strain forced my mother to drop out of school to work, while my dad went on to earn a degree in Biology. He then went to work for a chemical company. Soon after, I was born.

My education began when I was yet unborn. During her pregnancy, my mother would sit and read to me in hopes that her efforts might put me on the learning track early. She continued reading to me after I was born. The book that I most vividly remember from my childhood is the Bible. She would read each story to me over and over again, hoping to instill in me vivid images of the events of ancient times—which she did! I can still recite in great detail stories of love, hate, murder, and sin from the books of Genesis and Exodus, the books of the law, and the history of the kingdoms of Judah and Israel. Due to my mother's efforts, I began reading at age three, and writing at four.

My formal education began at age four, when my mother enrolled me in a local preschool. After first grade, my intelligence was tested, and I was placed into an accelerated learning program. I stayed in the accelerated learning program through elementary school. During that time, my teachers noted my creativity, my interest in reading, and the ease with which I achieved high scores in all of my subjects. Though I won many awards during this time, one in particular stands out for me. Mrs. Burnett, my third grade teacher, took a special interest in me, noticing among other things my great love for books. She sometimes lent me short classroom books to read at home. During the awards ceremony at the end of the year, she announced to the school, "And finally, I have a very special award. It is one which I give very enthusiastically to a special student who shows a profound interest in reading. That student is Michael Sanders." As I walked to the stage and she handed me a newly purchased science book, I was proud and happy, but most of all surprised. No teacher had ever recognized my interests in this way. It felt like she was telling me, "Use your talents and let your interests take you to be all that you can be!"

My parents' guidance, so critical to my early development, continued when I entered high school. In their efforts to point me in the right direction, I was enrolled in the standard Honors courses—algebra, English, chemistry. Against my wishes, my mother enrolled me in debate. I wanted to enroll in football—it was the most popular sport at West Orange-Stark and I wanted to play so badly! However, my mother insisted, so I stayed in the class. As the year progressed, however, I didn't learn that much about debate. The first in-class debate that I had was an absolute disaster! But later that year, my partner and I did well in a tournament, and our coach approached us about going to debate camp during the summer. It was the best move I could have ever made!

At debate camp, I discovered a winner within myself, and I knew I would be one of the best in debate. My partner and I were placed in a championship lab composed of some of the best debaters in Texas. It was fast-paced and intensive, and though my partner and I were way over matched, we learned so much that we would not have in the beginning lab! At the end of the debate camp, a tournament was held and we lost all of our rounds. We were the worst team in the entire debate camp! But our lab leader gave us some advice that still echoes in my ears: "You guys are a year younger than everyone else here, and you have a lot of time. If you work hard for the rest of your high school years, you can be really, really good." I let those words drive me from then on. I knew I could be good.

By my sophomore year, I was already one of the best debaters in Texas. During that sophomore year, I became known around the state by coaches and judges, and debaters alike. I continued to work hard. I was smart and knew my evidence. The following summer I decided to go to one of the best debate camps in the nation—The National High School Debate Institute Coon-Hardy Program for Seniors at Northwestern University. Once again I felt over-matched, but I benefited greatly because I learned so much from the more experienced debaters and so made another big jump in my level of debating. Despite the limitations that I had during this period, I was able to work hard, make good connections, and succeed in championship debate.

During my first two years in high school, I was very active in other activities besides debate. I played the saxophone in the marching and concert bands, and I taught private lessons to younger saxophone players. I was also a member of my school's academic team, an active member of the math club, the science team, student government, and Junior Achievement.

Because of my success, many of my classmates regularly ridiculed me, calling me "nerd," " teacher's pet," "sell-out," and "prep." Many of the people who made fun of me did so because I was different from everyone else. While most of my classmates were into drinking, partying, and basically having a good time, I was concentrating on debate and other school-related things. I was not daunted by their taunts and ridicule. I maintained the view that none of them contributed anything to my being, and that little of what they said or did had any effect on me. I knew that my talents could take me somewhere, that later in life I would be thankful that I had maintained my purpose. I believed that the same people who had once degraded me for being different would one day look up to me.

While I excelled in classes and activities, my main foundation stemmed from my experience and teaching about God. I have a very strong religious life. Both branches of my family have always been religious. From my earliest times up to the present, my parents have indoctrinated me with the Gospel, and I really enjoyed learning about God's word. My parents helped to shape my character by the Gospel, deriving the principles that guided our lives from the Bible. During my sophomore year of high school, I became the song leader of our congregation, a role I continued throughout high school. I also led songs at other congregations and became a leader in the church.

All of the activities I was involved in at that time helped shape my character. I was able to balance many things at once, while maintaining a standard of excellence in each area. Although I had many things going my way, I was not lifted up with pride. Rather, I knew that I had been blessed with such advantages, and I took time to appreciate them.

Though I was engaged in so many activities, debate was my first love. Much of what made me love debate more than other activities was implicit within it. In order to be the best and remain ready to debate any particular issue, I had to stay abreast of all that was going on in the world. This fed my insatiable appetite for knowledge and provided a medium through which I could profit intellectually and competitively.

I considered debate a sport—a sport of the mind. I was exhilarated by it! I had always wanted to play organized sports, and here was my chance! To me it was a test of my wit, my ability to maneuver, my ability to access resources, and my persuasiveness. Beating other debaters gave me a special feeling because I was competing against others on the highest level. I considered debate to be the ultimate sport because it prepares you for all walks of life, academic or non-academic, thus fulfilling one of my strongest desires. As I continued to get better over time, I derived a certain sense of achievement, which fed my self-confidence. The most important factor in my love of debate was that I was doing the best that I could do. You see, my parents took great pains to teach me about the rewards of hard work and putting forth your best effort. Thus, I always put my best effort into debate. The pleasure that I derived from this was simply the fact that I worked hard and it paid off. And once I found a relative degree of success with debate, I worked, worked, and worked to become the best I could be. Knowing that I was putting my best foot forward and succeeding kept me going; it was what I needed to continue through the years. And as I pursued my goals and succeeded in my endeavors, respect grew for me among my peers. Many factors were involved in my success, but my chief motivation came from the work ethic instilled in me by my parents, from knowing I was giving my all.

Knowing something of my background is significant in understanding my experiences with foreign languages. My first difficulties with foreign languages occurred in high school, where I took Spanish during my junior and senior years. My grades in Spanish 1 were always low A's and high B's. My teacher, Mrs. Farrell, was a very good instructor who constantly monitored her students' progress. I considered my progress in Spanish to be normal, though looking back on it, I can see some things that pointed to my having trouble with languages. But at that time, I did not know what a language disability was.

First, although I did all of the work for the class—including vocabulary, homework, and in-class exercises—I found that I had difficulty grasping the vocabulary. I did not know then that my trouble represented certain weaknesses. I often had trouble on vocabulary sections of the exams and in oral exercises in class. For instance, although I studied, during exams I would routinely forget the definitions of Spanish words, and often had so much trouble understanding the words in the questions that I couldn't adequately answer the questions. Or during oral classroom exercises, when the instructor called on me to answer questions, read, or lead the class in a workbook exercise, I would have trouble translating questions asked or simply hearing the question. This was frustrating to me as I didn't know why I had trouble in Spanish or how I could improve my performance. I did not want my teacher to call on me for fear I would not be able to answer her questions.

Second, I always had trouble on the exams. I never seemed to do as well on exams as other students, though I knew I was at least as intelligent as all of them. I usually had trouble finishing exams or simply could not answer the questions, despite having studied. Thus, though I did all of the work for the class, I was still deficient.

Though I had these problems with languages in high school, I was unaware that they could be attributed to a learning disability. It was not until I went to college that my learning disability was identified. Because students at my university are required to complete the language requirement by the end of their sophomore year, I had been forced to take language courses term after term. When I saw a pattern of problems developing over time in my language courses, I told my parents first. Their initial reaction was to tell me I should work harder and not give up. They instructed me to get a tutor, go to my professor's office hours, and check with the Academic Skills Center to see what I could do to improve my study habits, memory, and performance on exams. What they did not know was that I had long since done all of these things. Being unaware of what a language disability was and some of the problems associated with it, my parents were somewhat insensitive. They, like teachers, told me that I didn't do well because I didn't work hard enough. The fact that they blamed my difficulties on my supposed lack of hard work troubled me, but I knew my parents were caring people and wanted the best for me. I knew that they were trying just as hard as I was to sort this out and that my lack of effort was the only reasonable explanation for them. I don't think they meant to be insensitive or to burden me—I just think their lack of knowledge made them less likely to respond as I needed.

However, as I took more language courses and continued to have problems, I began to explain to my parents that I thought I had a learning disability. I told them what it was, describing my problems to them in terms of known problems associated with learning disabilities, and I asked for their advice. At this point, they began to respond in a different manner. When they learned that my lack of progress in languages was likely due to difficulties and weaknesses that to a certain extent I could not control, together we began to seek help in identifying and dealing with my problems.

My relations with my friends have not been at all adversely affected by my learning disability. I have told a few of my friends about my problems with languages. Some of them have also had problems in this area, so they understood the difficulties that I was going through and tried to be supportive. They offered me tutoring and assistance with assignments, and even others who knew nothing about learning disabilities were generally very understanding and helpful.

My girlfriend, who is bilingual, was also very supportive and tried to offer her assistance. Being of Spanish descent, Manuela speaks both English and Spanish fluently, and is also proficient in French. It took her a while to realize that I was having big problems with languages, but by the time I was into Spanish 1 the second time, she began to understand. She wanted me to learn Spanish for many reasons, but most of all because we could then grow closer. Her culture—including music, literature, and food—is very much influenced by the language. She especially loves music, and when she sings to me in Spanish she often stops, saying, "Oh, I wish you could understand this." She often speaks in Spanish with her friends, frequently excluding me from the conversation. Perhaps this situation is most difficult when she calls home. She always wants me to speak to her mom, but her mother speaks only Spanish. I, understandably, find it hard to communicate. So, besides hurting me academically, my difficulty in learning the language was excluding me from certain parts of my girlfriend's life. When I came to her with my problems, she offered all of the assistance that she could, including tutoring, special help with essays, and vocabulary exercises. But this didn't help much either—I continued to get low grades on my essays and to fail my exams.

I feel that my friends and family have all been there to support me and to help me in exploring and learning how to deal with my learning disability. And as I continue to learn about how I think and the language problems I have, we continue to discover new things and new ways to deal with those problems. The fact that I have been blessed with people around me who are understanding and caring enough to try to help me provides a big emotional lift for me, because I know I always have family and friends to lean on.

I have a wide variety of friends and try to be an amiable person so that I can make friends easily. I do not feel that I have problems socially. Additionally, I am also in a fraternity. Our mission and founding concepts are community service, scholarship, and brotherly love. We try to set an example as upstanding men in our community who are here to serve others. When my learning disability was identified, I had already made many friends across racial, religious, and gender boundaries. My friends accepted me for the person that they already knew, and did not change their view of me or the way they treated me. I do not tell everyone that I have a learning disability explicitly, but many of them know at least that I have had problems with languages. I don't think it does or will make a difference in our relations, which is important to me because it lets me know that my friends choose to be my friends because of the way we interact. The fact that my friendships rest on firm foundations reassures me emotionally and helps me deal with what is perceived as a disadvantage in a positive way. I can rest assured with the knowledge that my friends will be my friends for who I am, and that will not change.

One of the main benefits of my support network is that I have been freed from worry about issues of acceptance. This freedom allows me to think about what my disability means to me and the ways it has helped me to progress. This is important because it helps me to maintain a sense of my strengths and weaknesses, while further developing an understanding of myself.

There are three main areas in which my language experience at college has adversely affected me: self-esteem, finances, and academic work.

As you may sense by now, the use of language in debate and other arenas is an area from which I derive confidence. My difficulty learning languages struck at the very heart of that confidence, causing me to struggle with my sense of self-esteem. At this point, I have attained a sense of balance in knowing that I can learn languages using other methods beyond the Rassias method. I also work continually to refine my ability to speak effectively and convincingly. I know that I have certain skills that contribute greatly to my success, but equally important is my understanding that everyone has weaknesses. I must understand and cope with mine, maintaining a sense of balance between my strengths and limitations.

My experience with languages in college has also affected me financially. Because I have been forced to keep taking language classes term after term, I have been wasting courses and, subsequently, money. Each language course that I took and dropped could have been a completed major course, and up to now, I have wasted a complete term's worth of courses.

Finally, my problems with languages have affected me academically, depressing my grades and discouraging my study of China. Second, because of the extra strain and pressure of the language classes, my grades in other disciplines fell. I put so much time and effort into my language courses that it detracted from the time that I had for my other courses.

My interest in China originated during high school. I was assigned to research a debate case involving the Chinese coal industry and became interested in knowing more about China. I've since maintained this interest, most recently undertaking a significant research project in preparation for a senior fellowship proposal. The fellowship allows students to substitute a year-long project in place of the final year of courses. Although I was not granted a fellowship, I did acquire greater knowledge of Chinese philosophy, religion, and culture while successfully developing a research topic that deals with the dynamics of local and central government interaction in China during the Great Leap Forward. So, although economics is my major, Chinese studies is my main academic interest, although virtually no courses exist in this area at my university.

When I matriculated, I had no idea what lay in store for me. I was unaware of the difficulties I would encounter due to my learning disability. However, as I've progressed both academically and personally, I know I have experienced difficulties and problems that would have precluded my success if I had been of weaker character. These experiences have been critical factors in shaping who I am.

In short, by writing about my problems with languages and language-related courses, I am exposing myself, allowing others to examine my person and look into my fears, doubts, and weaknesses. However, I find confidence in knowing that I have great strengths, which I continually use in facing and overcoming my weaknesses. I know I am unique and that if you choose to delve deeply into my character, you will get a glimpse of an individual full of unique interests, talents, mettle, and potential.

6

Bad

Gretchen O'Connor

In this essay, Gretchen, a 21-year-old white woman, tells the story of her eventual recovery from the psychological injury done to her by others' misunderstandings of her ADHD. Within her family, Gretchen was early on labeled a problem child: poorly organized, prone to school failure, and apt to become distracted. Perhaps as a result of her parents' marital difficulties—which destabilized the family generally—Gretchen was afforded little room for error, and as her problems persisted, she was subjected to escalating emotional and physical abuse by her mother. Finally, during her senior year of high school, Gretchen dropped out and ran away to live in the city with her boyfriend. After months in a drug rehabilitation center and a stint in an outdoor therapy program, she chose to return to high school.

Writing as a college sophomore, Gretchen challenges the conventional belief that ADHD is nothing but a problem, a syndrome to be cured, a disease to be eradicated. Instead, based on her own experience, Gretchen believes that ADHD can be a source of joy and life-energy, a part of a person's cherished uniqueness. Accordingly, Gretchen advises her readers to adopt a more curious and open stance toward ADHD, warning that failure to do so can result in the misjudgment and abuse of persons like herself.

I woke to the sound of my mother's footsteps hammering down the stairs to the kitchen. Through sleepy eyes, I looked out at the glorious fall foliage, the bright sunshine warming my face as I sat up and stretched my small body, thinking, "It's finally Saturday!" I loved Saturdays in the fall; it was soccer season, and Saturday was the one day of the week I spent with my dad. As part of our Saturday ritual, Dad would always bring doughnuts for me and my sister, one chocolate and one honey-dipped. The smells of coffee, doughnuts, and the newspaper surrounded him when he came to pick us up for my soccer game. I loved the way Dad looked on weekends, his hair messy, his face unshaven and salty from his early morning jog. Handing me the doughnut bag, Dad asked if I had my gear ready, and I realized I didn't know where my uniform, cleats, or shin guards were, though I did know where to look.

I darted upstairs to examine the heap of things on my bedroom floor. I first looked under the bed, where I found one shin guard and one cleat behind my Scrabble box. Beginning to feel frustrated, I scurried around my room, finding only two dirty soccer socks in my doll clothes drawer and a pair of soccer shorts from last year's uniform. Wanting to appear organized, I threw on the mismatched pieces of my uniform, just in time to hear my father's call up the stairs, "Ready, Gretchen?" As I ran down the stairs, I was something to behold wearing my wrinkled shirt, still dirty from my last game, a pair of shorts that were too small, and my dirty soccer socks, carrying one cleat, and one shin guard that had a doll hat stuck to the Velcro strap. I squirmed as my father examined me, his thick, dark eyebrows raised, his eyes squinting skeptically. I spotted my sister's gear stacked neatly in the corner; dropping mine, I scooped hers up and followed Dad out the front door, feeling somewhat relieved by the cool morning air. My very organized father followed with a shopping bag full of cookies and punch for the team; it was his turn to bring the post-game refreshments, and I thanked God for letting me remind him of that yesterday, and not on the way to the field.

We sat in silence as we drove to the field, but I was happy just to be with Dad. I loved watching his strong hands shift the car, which smelled just like his office: a mix of leather, paper, coffee, and new carpet. I liked to feel part of my father's world, and this for me, this time alone was a bonding experience. I would often pretend I was one of his clients and that we were on our way to a meeting. I'd also pretend that the air of seriousness that surrounded my father was comfortable.

Before the game, I huddled with my team, shivering because I had forgotten my sweatshirt. When my coach shouted, "Get out there girls, let's hustle," I stared blankly, wondering why she hadn't put me in the lineup. Then I heard my dad yelling from the sidelines, "Weren't you listening? GO! Get out there, you're playing defense, pay attention! GO!" I ran onto the field, with my too-small shorts riding up my behind. My mind drifted as I watched my teammates dominate the game at the other end of the field, and I started mentally going over the moves I had learned in gymnastics that week. I started to do a cartwheel, and as my legs kicked over, I saw the ball heading straight toward me. My coach screamed from the sideline, "Gretchen, for Christ's sake, this isn't GYMNASTICS, it's SOCCER! Why are you doing flips in the middle of the game? PAY ATTENTION!" I glanced at the laughing parents standing on the sidelines, saw my father's embarrassed look of disgust. My coach took me out at halftime, and I sat with my back to my father for the rest of the game, hating myself for being so stupid, wondering why I could never be as organized as everyone else. The car ride home was silent. I was filled with shame and devastated that my day with Dad had been ruined. I was not, after all, his client, but merely his unreliable child whom he couldn't understand.

"I would hear my name being screamed from the front of the class."

When I think back on my years as a young student, I can laugh at some of my behaviors in class. I was constantly told to sit down, to stop talking; if the teacher gave instructions, I was always one step behind everyone; if we were supposed to hang up our coats, I would be easily distracted by something else. I was constantly yelled at for being disruptive, and I remember feeling very guilty, but, also confused: I did not mean to disrupt my class, and I often didn't even realize I was doing anything wrong. I realize now that I was not a child with a discipline problem, but a child with ADHD.

But, at that time, nobody knew what my real problem was, and at school embarrassing things would happen to me daily. I was constantly in trouble for taking too long when I went to the bathroom or to sharpen my pencil. I would look out the window and totally forget I was in class. Then I would hear my name being screamed from the front of the room. The thing was, I could not control my behavior. I felt I was not in control of my own mind and body. My frustrated teachers and my parents always wanted to know why I was not paying attention or why I was acting up in class, but I would only tell them, "I don't know, I just did." Often I couldn't even remember what I was in trouble for! But no one ever believed me, and soon I was pegged a liar—a label that followed me for a long time. Every teacher at my school knew me because I was always in trouble. I was regularly kicked out of class, which bruised me emotionally because I could not explain my behavior. I felt like a really bad kid.

"There are days when I can actually feel my ADHD taking over my mind and body."

ADHD is not merely a part of me or an influence in my life. It *is* me. It is the main force that controls me mentally, physically, and socially. I cannot separate it from myself or keep it under control. It is hard for me to explain what it feels like to be driven by an inner force that is so powerful and primordial. There are days when I can actually feel ADHD taking over my mind and body. It's kind of like being on a ride at the fair that goes 'round and 'round in circles as it jolts up and down and side to side, and everything is a huge blur of lights, smells, and noises, and you try really hard to single out your friends down on the ground watching you, but you can't focus because it's spinning so fast. That is how hard ADHD can hit. Imagine that happening when you are in class trying to listen, or when you are trying to do your homework. In class, I often have the feeling that I am sitting in the middle of a drain, and I sit there at my desk, spinning furiously, trying to stop the motion. When the force erupts, my anxiety starts to take over, and I have to fight the urge to scream with frustration. My body reacts to this rush, and I have to move. There is nothing that can bring me back to the moment, and the only thing that helps me to relax is space and open air. An escape! This is an extremely complicated psychological state to have to describe when someone asks, "What's the matter?" or "Why can't you just sit still?" I feel that someone would think I was psychotic if I tried to describe the feeling.

The strangest thing about this state is that, though I know what I am supposed to be doing, I have absolutely no control. I can have a huge list of things I know I have to do, or else pay severe consequences, but I still will not do them. There is a force stronger than my own will controlling me. For example, if I have an important assignment to complete for school the next day, I'll go for a run or clean my room, all the time thinking, "I'm not doing my assignments." Then I might read the paper or go out with my friends, still conscious that I have this assignment, but still not doing it. I want to, but I really can't stop *not* doing it, can't stop doing something else. This also happens in class: I get the urge to do something else, like go for a hike, and I go. It does not matter what else I should be doing—I have to go. I'm driven.

"How come no one ever saw the fear in me?"

As a child, the hardest part of the day was the bus ride home. I always had a bag full of notes from my teachers, and I knew the school had already called my mother to tell her I had them. I would get off the bus scared to death and very sad. I would contemplate running away, or wonder whether things would be better if I were dead. I would close the front door very quietly, knowing what I would get when my mom knew I was home. I always felt like I had worms in my stomach, and would sometimes vomit from the anxiety. I'd develop a migraine, which my mother would say I was faking because I knew I was in trouble. I often felt like I was spinning out of control, and my parents would make me spin even harder, until finally I would just shut down and cry myself to sleep, feeling worthless and scared. I always felt very misunderstood.

My mother had a mean and violent temper when I was a kid. I know now that she was unhappily married and felt neglected by my father, and she would take out her anger on me and my sister. But as a child I just thought that this was how my mother was. I always got it worse than my sister—I added more stress because of school. When my mother got mad, she screamed so violently that I did not recognize her. She also hit. Instead of sitting and discussing why I was having trouble in school, she would usually beat me. This made me fearful; I started to lie to my teachers and hide my bad reports from my mother because it was my only defense from the abuse.

The first time I was caught forging my parents' names to a progress report was in the third grade, when I was eight years old. The consequences of lying were always worse than the bad report, but I could not stop. I had to protect myself somehow; nobody else understood what it was like for me. I felt that the only way for me to avoid punishment was to lie, and though I was often caught and punished, for some reason it didn't stop me. It became a habit, and I found myself lying even in situations where I did not have to. I never got in trouble at school for problems like fighting, but I was very dishonest, which gave me a bad reputation. My parents and my teachers overlooked my learning problems and focused on my behavior.

How come nobody ever saw the fear in me? Why did I have to be so deceitful so young? This overwhelming fear started very young, and stayed with me until recently, like a terrible weight I carried inside. I was a nervous child, and the stress caused migraine headaches and a nervous stomach. Stress can do many things to people, especially children, which I feel is one of the largest factors behind my failure in school.

As I got older, things only got worse. I was evaluated several times at my school, which showed only that I had deficiencies in copying from the board, work completion, math, and spelling. I was always off the charts on my vocabulary and comprehension abilities. They always told me that my testing scores were way above average and that I was capable of the work, but that I was careless and lazy.

I was often told that I didn't have my priorities in order, which was why I was doing so poorly in school. When I was in seventh grade, my parents decided to put me in private school, hoping that it would solve my problems. This may have been a good idea, but, in fact, it only brought on a new wave of problems. The private school had parent advisory slips—commonly known as PA slips—that would be sent home if you were disruptive in class, did not do homework, or if you were basically not doing well in a class. I probably hold the record at Cabot Academy for the most PA slips! As I explained, bringing home PA slips was not an option for me because I was so scared of my mother. So, once again I forged and lied daily. I would hand the forged slips to my teachers, but they usually found out my mother had not seen them and would then tell me I was caught. For the rest of the day, I would conjure up possible escapes, imagining myself living on the streets or in the woods, lonely and afraid. But I always went home. I would get home, where I would be verbally tormented by my mother. I would try to explain that I didn't know why these things were happening and that I was as confused as she was, but all she could say was, "You're lying," or "You're a lazy, stupid, selfish, child." I was called an "insensitive brat," a "lazy, fat ass," and I often heard my mother say, "I could fucking kill you!" As she screamed at me, she would twist my arm or smack me or push me, then send me to my room, saying, "I don't want to see your face for the rest of the night." I would wish that she could understand that acting that way was only hurting me and killing my self-esteem. I wanted her to realize that I was not doing these things because I was a bad person. I wanted her to realize that my problems in school were caused by something that I didn't understand. Instead, my mother only added to my problems.

Several incidents will never be erased from my memory. I hope that sharing one will help explain why I stayed in this pattern of lying, why I was just too scared to stop. I was in bed one night when I heard the phone ring. I thought it could be one of my teachers telling my parents that I had failed a math test. I heard my mother say, "Thank you very much for calling and letting me know." I knew I was right. I heard my mother scream from her bedroom and come flying down the hall-way to my bedroom. The door burst open, and standing in the light of the hallway was my mother. She stormed into the room with a belt in her hand and started to whip me where I was lying in my bed. She was screaming cruel things at me and whacking whacking whacking me with the belt. Finally, my sister ran into my room and pulled my mother off me. It was total chaos. My sister and I were scream-ing and crying, and my mother was totally flipping out. I was confused and embar-rassed that my sister had seen this. I know she felt bad for me, but I also know that she was angry at me for causing this. I put a chair in front of my door and huddled under my blanket, crying and getting sick to my stomach until, finally, I fell asleep. All this because I failed a math test. By the time my father got home from work, the house was silent and we were sleeping.

"I don't ever remember my parents getting along well."

It is amazing to me how much my family influenced how I see myself and shaped who I am. I will start with my parents. I believe that my parents' marriage was doomed to fail from the beginning. They were married at 25, and within two years they had my sister Meredith and me. My father started a job at an account-ing firm in Boston, where he has worked for the last 21 years. My mother stayed at home for the first few years to take care of me and my sister. The main reason my parents are no longer together is that my father is married to his job; it's the reason they started fighting. My father worked 12 to 14 hours every day of the week. My mother thought it was unfair that she was left home all day with two babies to take care of and that she was totally alone all the time. When my father did come home, my sister and I were usually asleep; we never spent time with him. I believe that my mother felt neglected, and that she felt bad that my sister and I never saw my dad either. My mother could not handle my father's work schedule, and she became very depressed and angry, and my parents fought regularly over the fact that my father was never home. I think my mother was so angry that she couldn't tell my father that the problem was that she really missed him and wanted to have a better marriage, so she would yell and scream and push him away even further. Eventually, their arguments became violent, and my mother would hit my father. The first time I witnessed this was horrific. It is hard to see your parents acting so irrationally. I was scared my parents would end up killing each other.

Looking back, I understand my mother's frustrations. I know she needed much more affection and communication than she was getting from my father. I know she tried to make their marriage work in many ways. She became an excellent cook and homemaker. She kept herself looking great, always beautifully dressed, and in great physical shape. She was envied by her friends for being so domestic and desirable. Only my father never recognized her efforts, never complimented her or gave her more time. That is why my mother became a very angry person.

My mother's temper became the thing that scared me the most. She would hit me and my sister when she became angry, often enraged over little things like spills or messes around the house. My mother treated every situation with violence. My father never really knew what was happening, and there was no one to help us. My mother's erratic behavior was confusing: After she hit me, she would give me a big hug and a kiss and tell me she loved me, but it never made me feel better. I wanted her to feel bad for what she had done, not kiss and make up. I often felt I was living in the middle of total chaos, but was too small and powerless to stop it.

"The doctor told them I had ADHD."

When I was in eighth grade, my parents decided to take me to see a specialist. I had been evaluated many times throughout the years, but I was still not improving. My parents were desperate to get some help for my problems. I remember the ride to the hospital: It was no big deal for me, since I had become accustomed to being taken to psychologists and doctors. As I went through yet another series of testing—the ink blots, the puzzles, the building blocks—I wondered how these simple games would tell these people anything about me. At the end of the testing, my parents and I met with a doctor, who told them that I had ADHD. He said the drug Ritalin was the latest treatment and told my parents how it was used. I had never heard of ADHD, and at the time it did not mean much to me. I just figured, "Well, that's one more thing we can add to the list, so can we go home now?" That was the extent of my diagnosis; we never got any information about ADHD, and we never talked about it again. My parents never thought to seek any advice about my condition, and, for me, it was just another name of another syndrome that was not going to change who I was. It didn't really bother me that we never talked about it because the doctor didn't seem to think it was a big deal. By the end of that school year, I was kicked out of private school and back in public school, still without any mention of my ADHD.

I now regret so much the way my parents and I let my diagnosis be pushed under the carpet. If I had had some help, I could have accomplished so much more and been spared the humiliation I felt when I was expelled from school. The guilt was even worse; I was so tired of disappointing my parents. I knew I was doing poorly in school, but I never expected to be kicked out. I think this was a turning point for me in many ways. I think this is when my parents finally gave up on me, and when I gave up on myself. I was tired of not being understood and of being hurt so much that eventually I stopped caring about myself. I became so afraid of failure and admonishment that I was unable to take a risk or try really hard for things. I became scared of conflict or even the possibility of conflict. I couldn't trust anything I believed, and I became a sponge for other people's opinions. I never told anyone my feelings because I was so embarrassed about myself all the time.

Yet all of this did lead to something positive: I became a listener! The one area of my life that gained something from my bad experiences was my ability to be a good friend. I have had the same friends for many years, some since the first grade. I always put a lot into my friendships. All my friends would come to me with their problems because I was a good listener. I wanted to make sure these people felt that their problems were significant and that they were being understood. I never wanted anyone to have their feelings misunderstood, as I did. I would change plans for my friends, even if it meant missing the biggest events; I would never desert a friend. I never let myself be in a clique and made it a point to try never to hurt anyone's feelings. I stuck up for kids who were being picked on and felt good about helping people. I was so well liked that I never had to worry about being picked on like I was at home or by my teachers. I was never a victim. Many teenagers have a hard time socially because kids can be really mean, but I never experienced that. This was great for me, but it also became a problem. I became so involved with everyone else's lives that I totally ignored how I was really feeling. Helping other people did make me feel better, but it was not enough.

During my sophomore year in high school, I became involved with Rob, a boy I had known throughout my school years. Rob gravitated to me because he had a lot of emotional difficulties. In elementary school, he had cancer for seven years, but cancer was the least of his problems. When Rob was diagnosed with bladder cancer, his father took off, and Rob never heard from him again. After later bouts with lung cancer and a tumor on his spine, Rob went into full remission when he was twelve. A week later, his mother announced that she had cervical cancer and that it was too far gone to help. She had never told anyone because she wanted Rob to be taken care of first. She died when Rob was a freshman in high school, and he blamed himself. This kid had major problems, and he became my new project.

I went out with Rob for five years, devoting myself mainly to his problems. I believe he'd be dead by now if not for me, but it sure didn't get me anywhere. He was a drug user, and I got into heavy drugs with him—acid, pills, coke. For two years straight, that was all we did. It was great: I was "helping" Rob, and I was too fucked up to feel my own pain. Rob hated school as much as I did, so we stopped going after a while, and if I did go, I was high. My parents separated the year I met Rob, so they were dealing with their own problems. My mother was such a wreck throughout her divorce that it was easy for me to get away with things.

But midway through my senior year when my mother had an emotional breakdown, I totally lost it. She wanted me to affirm her and comfort her, but I was so angry at her for what she had put me through that she made me sick. I could not even feel bad for her, and I let her suffer. My dad and sister were gone, so I was left alone with my irrational mother. And I just lost it. I quit school and ran away from home. I got an apartment with Rob and two of his friends in a part of the city surrounded by crack houses. This was the worst possible environment, but I did not care. I felt like I was losing my mind and just had to get out of my house. I have never been so depressed in my life; I totally hit rock bottom. I was still seeing my therapist through all this, and one day I showed up for a therapy appointment to find my dad waiting there with two guys in white coats. My father forced me to take a drug test, after which I was locked up in rehab for a few months.

"Those three months in Minnesota were a period of rebirth."

When I got out of rehab, I had a hard time motivating myself to do anything. The whole world felt dead to me. My relationship with my parents was not great, and my self-esteem was at the lowest place it had ever been. I couldn't pretend I was happy; I couldn't even smile. I was able to put a lot of effort into figuring out what I needed to do to be happy again, and the one thing I was sure of was that I needed to get away from my family, my friends, and my hometown. I needed to see myself in another setting, to cut myself off from the rest of my world and totally concentrate on myself. My father suggested that I try an Outward Bound course for the summer, and I instantly agreed with him. I knew a little about the philosophy behind Outward Bound, but I didn't know what to expect from my trip. I think the main reason I agreed to do the trip was because the distance and seclusion sounded so right.

I spent three months in the woods of northern Minnesota backpacking, kayaking, and canoeing. There is something so amazing about living without a clock or a schedule hanging over your head. Getting away from the noise, hustle, and stress of life, I was able to reflect and think. I found a calming silence in nature that soothed my mind and gave it the time to expand without unnecessary chatter and noise.

My Outward Bound course was the most significant experience I have had, the best choice I have made in my life. The changes I experienced during my trip were so strong and unbinding that I could feel them as they were occurring. I had moments of great clarity that allowed me to separate myself from the cloud I had been living in for years and to free myself from insignificant worries and fears that I had been holding on to my whole life. I think this was the first time I recognized myself as an individual person, rather than as a mere part in the lives of all the people I knew and all that I experienced. Before, I had absolutely no sense of who I was; I viewed myself according to what other people told me I was. Outward Bound gave me the personal freedom to explore inwardly and form an identity for myself. This freedom was the crucial aspect of my experience. I was in a group of seven strangers who did not have a clue about my past, and this was the first time that I could be the person I knew I was. I did not fear that these people would analyze my behaviors like my family did. I had lost the faith of all the people who were close to me and was used to getting few words of encouragement.

Those three months in Minnesota were a period of rebirth. I shed about 19 years of unwanted skin that was trapping my spirit. With every step I took, I sweated out the toxins in my body and mind. Every day, I struggled and cried, and I released and released all the pain inside me. For the first time my nerves settled, and the sick feeling I had in my body left. My stomach felt empty and happy without the butterflies that had lived in there for years. I smiled and I laughed out loud, and I was happy!

Equally important to my rebirth was that I gained a lot of insight into my family. I had had so much anger at them for so long that I could not distinguish the good in them. I know that I had an inner demon eating away at my spirit, and my family was that demon. In time, I was able to conquer the burdens my family had placed on me and to recognize my own faults and the ways I had contributed to the deterioration of our family. I had put so much emphasis on defending myself that I couldn't see my role in the problem. I went home from my trip feeling settled and open to my family. The trip also gave me time to decide what I wanted in the future, and I decided to go back to high school to get my diploma.

There is a part of me that would never want to change the fact that I have ADHD. I believe that this condition can be positive in many ways for the person who has it. The main setback for most people with ADHD, especially children, is that they are misunderstood. If I had been taught to believe that ADHD was a learning difference rather than a learning disability, I feel I would have had a more positive view of myself while growing up. ADHD has caused me problems as far as learning goes, but not because I cannot learn. I just do not learn the same way other people do. But then, everyone learns differently, not only people with ADHD. ADHD becomes a learning disability when teachers try to put many different kids together in one room and expect them all to learn the same way. I feel that a lot of the problem for children with ADHD lies within the education system. Most schools have a set curriculum and routine method of teaching, but it is ridiculous to believe that all children will be stimulated by the same things. The problem is that not all classroom settings incorporate a multimodal form of teaching. There are simple strategies that can be incorporated into the classroom that can greatly help all students learn more effectively according to methods that work best for them.

Many specialists believe that medication is the most effective treatment for ADHD students. This is something that I am very afraid of. I have experimented with a few of the drugs that are prescribed, like Ritalin and Dexedrine. When under the influence of these medications, I am a completely different person. I lose all my energy and emotions. It is like the driving force behind who I am is sucked out of my body, leaving me feeling like a hollow shell. My ADHD is the source of my energy, and it is vital for me to have that. I feel that my personality would not be what it is if I did not have ADHD. There are so many positive aspects of ADHD. For example, I can do many things at one time successfully. My mind is always in motion and always looking for something to do. My main goal is to be able to control my ADHD in certain settings, and to use my ADHD as an advantage, rather than taking drugs to suppress all my creative energy.

Although most people look at ADHD as a negative condition, I disagree. I believe that if you were to ask anyone that has a friend with ADHD, they would say that all of these crazy symptoms are what they love about that person. ADHD makes a person an individual unlike anyone else. I know that at times my erratic behavior and spontaneity aggravate my friends and family, but those are the qualities that make them laugh and appreciate me. The problem is that most of the literature about ADHD is written by people who do not have ADHD. They generalize ADHD and say that the symptoms are concrete. This is extremely offensive to me. I understand my symptoms, and I know how my ADHD affects me, but it's all personal. My situation can be totally different from another person with ADHD.

I am happy that I have the opportunity to write about my experiences. They are me, and they are real. I hope this essay will help some people see the importance of dealing with learning disabilities so that they or their child will get the help they need. I also hope people can learn from my story so that they will deal with this issue differently from the way my family did. I want people to understand that ADHD should not be labeled a disability, that it only becomes a disability when it is not understood and when people fail to see the benefits and the positive aspects of it. I believe that my ADHD caused people to look down on me and tell me that there was something wrong with me. I had hundreds of tests for that reason alone; everyone wanted to know what was wrong with me rather than just seeing the energy and passion that I had for so many things. My teachers and parents overlooked all the areas in my life where I was succeeding and instead concentrated on my faults. If I had learned earlier how to turn my ADHD to advantage, I would have had a better outlook on life and I would have had more respect for myself as a person. It has taken me a long time to be able to see the good in me. Because of all the people telling me there was something wrong with me, I was unable to recognize any part of myself as positive and "normal." All I wanted was for people to listen to me and to really see me, not what the doctors were seeing.

7

ADHD

Window, Weapon, or Support

Joshua Green

This story, written by an upper-middle-class, white, 21-year-old college senior, explores vividly the impact of late diagnosis of ADHD and a learning disability on a highly intelligent young man.

Joshua's school years are marked by chronic disorganization—by missed appointments and forgotten test dates. He finds he cannot live up to his parents' expectations for him of high academic achievement and personal responsibility. To cope with his frustration and his fear of disappointing them, he embarks on a period of lying and deceit, all the while sensing his parents do not know the real Joshua. What had been perceived earlier by his parents as his moral failure and lack of intellectual commitment are diagnosed at college as ADHD and a learning disability in the area of auditory processing—diagnoses that illuminate for Joshua patterns in his personal behavior, social relationships, and academic record. Accepting that his learning differences are an integral part of him, "burdensome, [though] no longer intrusive," and even embracing these disabilities, Joshua looks forward to the future and a career as a physician.

For as long as I can remember, I have had problems keeping track of everything I had to do. Despite my best efforts to keep a daily planner and a "things to do" list, I constantly forget school assignments, payment and registration deadlines, and practices or meetings. When I was younger, teachers and coaches often accused me of being lazy because of missed or uncompleted responsibilities. This criticism hurt because I knew it was not true, but it seemed that the harder I tried, the more things slipped by me unnoticed.

The first really negative consequence of my chronic disorganization occurred in seventh grade. All of the students in my class were given a permission slip for our parents to sign so we could go on a field trip to a museum. We received the form two weeks before the trip. I put the form in my notebook and didn't think about it for a week. When I finally remembered it, I found I had lost it. I managed to get a new permission slip from my teacher, but then the unexplainable happened. For some reason, I never asked my parents to sign it. Even now, looking back, I cannot explain why this happened. It was as if a cloud descended upon my brain and blocked out the existence of the slip. Two days before the trip, I remembered that I needed to get the form signed immediately, but this paralyzed me, even as I watched my chances of going on the field trip diminish.

This is the first time I remember being afraid of my parents' reaction. My parents are kind and loving people, but they have always demanded a high level of achievement and responsibility from me. I couldn't bear to tell them I wasn't going on the field trip, so I lied and said that I was going. Later I described the trip in detail. Three weeks passed before my lie and the entire story were discovered. Throughout the ensuing discussions, I was unable to explain why I had not had the form signed. Although my teacher's and parents' disappointment hurt me, this did not cause my tears the day we met at school. And my being grounded for a month and having a week of detention did not cause my tears either. I cried tears of frustration, not knowing what had gone wrong and not being able to make anyone believe that I had actually tried.

Although I was perceived as very intelligent by most of my teachers and schoolmates alike, I constantly underachieved in high school. My parents criticized me for being lazy and unwilling to apply myself in classes. After many frustrating efforts to explain why I hadn't turned in certain assignments or had forgotten about certain tests, I was unwilling to make excuses to my parents any longer. Instead, I started to distance myself from their concerns, not because I didn't care about my parents or my schoolwork, but as a defense mechanism against their expectations and disappointment. It also was a way to protect myself from the pressure of my own high expectations.

In school, I started to take the attitude that students who did all their work and really cared about their grades were brownnosers and to disdain students who emphasized improving their chances of getting into a competitive college. Accordingly, I refused to participate in any activities to improve my transcripts, such as clubs or community service projects, and I said that those who engaged in these activities were superficial. I told my friends that grades were simply not important to me.

So, while my friends described me as a genius, they understood why I wouldn't achieve at the highest level. They presumed that I lived under a different standard than other people, and they admired and even envied me. I would help other people with homework problems that I hadn't done myself, and I understood difficult concepts on tests I had never studied for. When I got above-average grades, everyone hailed me as a wonder who didn't have to pay attention or study to do well. Outwardly, I was successful, and even my parents could not argue when I refused to study for the PSATs and then became a Merit semifinalist based on my scores. But this was not the whole picture. What nobody knew was that my supposedly different standard for living was only an excuse to myself for my poor performance. Inwardly, I maintained a quite different standard for myself.

I have always been proud and competitive intellectually, although I would deny this to anyone who asked. I was regularly dismayed when students whom I perceived as less intelligent than I achieved at a higher level. I portrayed myself as an intellectual snob, someone who cared strictly about the pursuit of knowledge and who could not be contained in a banal school system based on uniformity. I would bring books by philosophers and poets, and read them in class.

Behind my behavior, however, I was frustrated and afraid. I was frustrated at not being able to master a school system that I thought should have been easy. I feared that even if I tried my hardest, even if I allowed myself to care, I still wouldn't have been the best. I might have been smart enough or even dedicated enough, but something else was there. Something that would never let me be the best. This scared me.

If I hadn't been able to work and read very quickly, I might never have graduated from high school. By eleventh grade, I was regularly forgetting assignments and test dates. To compensate, I often studied during breaks or devoted lunch periods to finishing homework that I had just realized was due in the next class. I was able to finish most of my assignments and achieve reasonably well, but not without cost.

I will always remember that sick feeling I got in the pit of my stomach when I knew I had more work to do than could possibly be done in the time I had left. It was the slow-growing panic of being trapped. Longer-term projects such as research papers presented a more acute problem. While many people would break such a project into simple steps, the prospect of such a big paper overwhelmed me and prevented me from starting at all. I only became motivated when the panic of a due date set in. In eleventh grade, I had a major history paper due on the same day that I had a trigonometry test. I started the paper only five days before the due date, although it had been assigned for a month. Because I worked on the paper the entire night before it was due, I hadn't studied for my test that was only two periods away. As that familiar sick feeling started to set in, I thought I had found a way out. The period before my math class I had gym, which you could miss if you were sick and had a note from home. I forged a note so that I could miss gym, and I used the time to study for my test.

Although I got a very good grade on the test, I was caught when the school compared the signature on the note with my mother's signature, kept on file in the school office. When told that I was going to be suspended for two days, my mother turned to me and said, "I hope you're satisfied. You'll never get into a good college now." I never felt more distant from her than in that moment, but her words didn't affect me nearly as much as my father's, who said, "Well, now I hope you have learned why you have to start projects on time."

It was as if he didn't know me at all. I already knew too well why projects had to be started on time and worked through steadily, but I couldn't do it. My father acted like this had been an isolated act of procrastination, but what neither of my parents realized was that this was not an isolated incident. I lived daily on the brink of academic failure, and I could not tell them.

Through a combination of luck and friendly assistance, I managed to slip through high school with decent grades. College, however, was a different story, because for the first time I had to be self-reliant.

When I first entered college, I was optimistic. I believed that college would be more conducive to my style of learning. I had heard that college students had only a few tests or papers per term. I figured that I wouldn't forget about only one or two major tests, and that I would finally get organized. But from the first day and for the next two years, I was constantly in academic trouble.

The first problems occurred during freshmen orientation week. I failed to show up for placement tests for two classes I had enrolled in. As a result, I was not allowed into the two classes and started out my first term with only one class. Because one class is below the limit, I had to enroll in two classes that had space left but which I had no interest in.

The only subjects I perform well in are those in which I take an acute interest, and I hoped in college to take only interesting classes. Yet in my first term, because of my inability to deal with college bureaucracy, I found myself in two classes I found especially boring. I was scared because I knew my grades would not be good and would not be acceptable to my parents. They had made it clear that if I did not work harder than I had in high school and receive satisfactory grades, they would refuse to pay my tuition.

Because of this threat, I found myself in a difficult moral position. Fall grades were sent home during the Christmas break while my parents were away visiting my grandparents. I found the envelope with my grades, and when I saw I had only a 2.7 average, I panicked and hid the envelope.

I knew that hiding my grades wasn't right, but I felt I had no other choice. I couldn't explain to my parents why I had taken those two courses. When my parents returned home and asked me if my grades had come, I said, "No." This bothered me to no end, but I felt trapped in the situation that my poor organization and performance had caused. I desperately wanted to stay at school, and I feared that I would have to leave if my grades were discovered.

On New Year's Eve, while I was at my friend's house, the phone rang. My father was on the phone, and he asked me to return home as soon as possible. Fearing the worst, I slowly drove home. My father had opened my desk drawer to get my scissors, and he found the letter containing my grades. When I returned home, my parents were waiting for me at the kitchen table.

The ensuing conversation involved yelling, swearing, threats, and tears on both sides. I don't remember exactly what was said, as the moment I saw the letter on the kitchen table I went numb. The only thing I recall is sitting alone at the kitchen table, with my head in my hands, hearing the countdown to the ball drop at Times Square from the family room. And quietly below it, the sounds of my mother crying about what she had done wrong in raising me.

I wish I could say that this awful New Year's Eve was a turning point in my life. I wish I could say that it caused me to get organized and start following through on my responsibilities. I wish I could say that it brought my parents and me closer together. I wish I could say that all my problems were finally solved. But this is not true. My poor performance in school continued for at least another year. My parents had reluctantly agreed to let me return to college, but they were more distant from me than ever. Perhaps most disappointing was that within two weeks, I didn't care about what had happened on New Year's Eve. My apathy about anything besides myself was almost complete.

Though the next year of my life was socially very fulfilling, I continued to suffer academically. I no longer seemed to care how I performed. Perhaps this attitude was a defense mechanism, but the ramifications carried into every aspect of my life. I did get better grades, though I was not learning anything or living up to my potential. Ironically, by reducing the pressure on myself, I improved my performance.

Spring term of my freshmen year I received a 3.7 GPA while taking hard classes, despite not going to any class for seven weeks and playing lacrosse full time. On one occasion, I had to be woken from a friend's bed after a long night of drinking, an hour before a chemistry test. With my grades improved, my parents resumed their normally supportive position. Although one foreign language professor, when I dropped her course, said I might want to be tested for a learning disability, the comment did not phase me. Heading into the winter of my sophomore year, my academic and social life had never seemed more positive.

It was at this point that my problems started to interfere with my life on a more daily basis. This eventually led to my diagnosis and made me the person that I am today.

One of the college's graduation requirements is the ability to speak a foreign language fluently. I had taken a few foreign languages previously and had always done much worse in language than in my other classes. Tenses, male and female endings, plural and singular—all were lost in a jumbled tangle somewhere in my brain. In college, I enrolled in Spanish 1 because everyone said that's the easiest language to learn. Spanish was easily the hardest class I have ever taken in college.

Midway through the term, my professor suggested that I drop the class because, in her words, "I do not see any hope of you ever passing my class." Feeling rage and humiliation, my first impulse was to yell at the professor. My second impulse was to heroically refuse to leave the class, to prove to the professor that I could pass, but my pride and stubbornness were quickly defeated this time. Though staying in Spanish would have been stupid, I still had to pass out of my language requirement. My professor suggested that I be tested at the Academic Skills Center, because a diagnosis of an auditory learning disability was grounds for an exemption. Soon, I found myself striding confidently up the stairs to the Academic Skills Center, ready to prove that I had an auditory learning disability. I imagined myself as more intelligent then the testers, ready to fool them and their tests to serve my purposes. Within five minutes of walking in the door and talking to Elizabeth, the learning specialist, all of these ideas were gone.

After listening to a list of my symptoms, Elizabeth encouraged me to go through a series of tests with a psychologist, Dr. Frank. After we had talked for about 20 minutes, Elizabeth said, "I can't believe that you haven't walked in here sooner." I remember the knowing way she looked at me, as if she recognized things after our brief discussion that I had never noticed in my whole life. With a vague feeling of apprehension mixed with interest, I called Dr. Frank to make an appointment.

Dr. Frank was a nice, receptive, middle-aged woman. For five days, she gave me a barrage of intelligence, personality, and perception tests and conducted some interviews. On the first day, upon hearing my academic history, Dr. Frank said I had the hallmark signs of a learning disability. She added, "I can't believe that neither your teachers nor your parents noticed this sooner." This theme—late diagnosis of an obvious problem—was to be repeated again and again.

On the day I walked to Dr. Frank's office to get my diagnosis, I felt a degree of uncertainty about myself for the first time in a long time. I had become so used to living with certain facets of my personality that I viewed any redefinition of them with much trepidation. I was so used to hiding all my problems and trying to deal with them alone that I was scared of what this lady, who had finally seen the true me, would say.

Dr. Frank reported that I had Attention–Deficit/Hyperactivity Disorder (ADHD), as well as an auditory learning disability. ADHD is a type of learning disability where people have a hard time focusing on tasks and difficulty with organization and concentration. It is a challenge for a person with ADHD to concentrate on one task, as lack of stimulation in the brain causes the mind to wander or think about many other things to further stimulate itself.

When Dr. Frank reported her findings, my first impulse was to fight the diagnosis. The idea that my eccentric personality, the way I accomplished and thought about things, and the majority of my problems could be defined as a disorder, an illness, was difficult to accept. I certainly did not feel sick, and I did not want to admit to being imperfect in any way. I suddenly felt less like an individual and more like an organization of chemical macromolecules. Learning that I had an auditory learning disability didn't disturb me, but the ADHD diagnosis was hard to swallow. I disassociated myself from the diagnosis and went out with a group of friends that night.

The next day my parents came to meet with me and Dr. Frank. Dr. Frank explained that this disorder probably had affected my entire development. She said my frequent underachieving could be explained as a learning disability, not a flaw in moral character, and that my high intelligence had enabled me to develop several coping strategies. At some point during that meeting, I began to believe in my diagnosis. I grew happier and more inquisitive. If I did have ADHD and it could be ameliorated to help me academically, perhaps there were good points to my diagnosis.

My parents, conversely, grew increasingly quiet as the meeting continued. My mother, who had entered the meeting brimming with her usual self-confidence, was soon quite withdrawn. My father looked almost sick. When Dr. Frank finished, my mother turned to me and apologized. "I always thought you didn't want to work hard," she said. "I always blamed you for not getting the grades you could have. "

After leaving Dr. Frank's office, my parents' guilt quickly escalated. Their complete change was almost incomprehensible, but I did understand it. It was hard for them to hear that they had overlooked my learning disability until my sophomore year of college. I was not ready to let their apology break the ice in our relationship.

Though my parents always seemed to care about me, it seemed a close second to their concerns about what was going on in their respective offices. They also seemed more concerned about what was going on in school than in what was affecting me as a person. As long as my grades were good, it didn't seem to matter to them if my life was not. My parents are both overachievers and fully expected the same from me. When I struggled in school or did not show the proper amount of career motivation, I knew that I was disappointing them. The pressure to excel was always great. Their insistence on academic excellence made it impossible for me to confess my problems to them. I preferred to struggle alone and make them think I did well rather than admit I needed help. In my family, help always came with a lecture on trying harder, wanting it more, using your intelligence.

My parents put a picture of the Swiss Alps in my crib when I was younger to make me, they said, want to achieve lofty heights, as high as mountains. Alone, confused, and struggling in high school, these mountains never seemed further away, and neither did my parents. A rift was formed that will never be filled with parental-filial love. Though this rift is slowly filling with friendship and respect, we keep the conversation away from the one unapproachable topic: my life.

When my parents traveled, they often left me home alone, and I enjoyed spending time just with myself. I enjoy being completely alone, with my own thoughts, taking time to look inward, probe, and reflect. Reaching inside yourself, finding only yourself for company is how you fill any void that is there and elevate yourself to higher heights. To this day, these moments alone are some of the most cherished of my childhood.

I think my childhood made me more serious and introspective than most people. I have never really enjoyed drunken revelries like many of my friends. I prefer serious conversations and often find myself giving advice to friends or trying to work out situations between people. Knowing that something was different about me, even if I did not know what it was, has made me more sensitive to others' feelings and to social interactions. This has drawn me closer to people, especially those who are depressed, troubled, suffering. Maybe in the face of my own imperfection, I can only be happy with people who are also imperfect. Maybe I just like to feel needed, as people with their own problems draw me to them like a moth to a light. Hearing that people are scarred makes me think better of them.

I used to think that my attraction to life's dark side was a result of my dissatisfaction with my life. I vowed to myself that college would be different, that I would be re-created by getting away from my parents and out of high school, where the same things happened every week. I thought that a change in the outward aspects of my life could change my attitude, allow me to reinvent myself. What I did not know then was that the dissatisfaction was inside of me, as much a part of me as my name or my body. This dissatisfaction with life is something I must work to overcome every day. It would be easy to blame this attitude on the ADHD as a disorder that has created a void between other people and myself, that keeps me from being satisfied. But I refuse to see ADHD as a handicap; it simply is part of me. My social aloofness, my brooding introspection are part of who I am and I wouldn't change that.

It is at college that I achieved this understanding, for my attempts to re-create myself were an overwhelming failure. College did not change me; it merely offered new arenas for my traits to emerge. At first, college was an exciting new environment for me. I was surrounded by people I did not know, and I attempted to be everything that I was not—gregarious, outgoing, enthusiastic. I embraced a new lifestyle, drinking five nights a week, telling jokes and teasing people, mock fighting, all of the things that I had only watched in high school. I had a multitude of friends, and I reveled in the attention. All of my troubles seemed to melt away, and I thought I should be satisfied. But, deep down, I knew that I was not being true to myself. This knowledge gnawed at me, threatening to erode my new self-confidence. Moreover, my trouble concentrating on conversations was growing worse. I started feeling a pressure to perform, which started to take a toll on me. I came to hate the way I was behaving, to feel I had betrayed myself, my true nature. I had hidden my disabilities, sneered in the face of my handicaps, refused to embrace my shortcomings. My confidence and grades slipped, my girlfriend broke up with me. With nowhere to turn, I turned to myself; never has introspection been so vengeful.

This was not a happy time for me. Self-doubt and self-criticism proved the weapons the real me used to rid myself of everything that I had recently tried to create. I knew that I had lost a part of myself, and I retreated into my memories as a way in which to retrieve it. I felt paralyzed; in three weeks I rarely went out.

Finally, I turned to sports to break me out of my lethargy. Sports have always given me an outlet for my energy and frustration and are among the few arenas where I never feel unequal to other people. I spent the whole spring term concentrating on lacrosse; it gave me an outlet, somewhere I could dedicate myself and my energy. When lacrosse ended, I was left with a vague sense of uneasiness, especially because I knew that I would have to return to college for a summer term.

Before the summer term, I told my parents that I wanted to drop out of college for a year or two. I felt I needed to go out and see some of life, to travel, go somewhere to work a menial job and live among normal people—basically just to live and be happy with myself. After a series of fights, we made a deal: If I got through the summer term and still wanted to leave, I could take off two terms, but no more. This seemed fair, so I returned for the summer term. The first two weeks of the term were very different. I was no longer drinking, and I soon made some new friends, people more like myself.

Now, as I write this, I am set to graduate from college with a modified major of psychology and chemistry. I do not have the highest GPA in the school, but I have improved steadily, especially since my junior year. I plan to apply to medical school this summer. I have a group of good friends with whom I am comfortable being myself and enjoy being around. My life has reached a comfortable medium. Some days I am in the deepest slump, some days life sails along, carrying me on its coattails. For the first time, I can accept this. I feel that I know myself and have at least some control over my life.

I am ready now to take on whatever the future may offer. The imminent end of college both excites me and scares me. Though it will be good to leave, I know the challenges that await me will be of a more severe nature than any I have yet faced and that fewer people will be there to catch me should I falter. It is hard to fight the fear and depression that constantly threaten me, but at this important moment in my life, I have quietly begun to believe in myself.

If I had been diagnosed with ADHD or a learning disability earlier, my life might have been easier. My trouble at school would have been explained, and I probably would have gotten treatment. Certainly, my relationship with my parents would have been closer if they had known that it was a disability that hindered my schoolwork. A closer relationship with my parents might have made me more accepting, perhaps happier and less withdrawn. Perhaps I would not be so scared of the future, so full of the fear of failing.

But there is no future for me in such might-have-beens. Surely the ADHD and my parents' shortcomings have had a tremendous impact on me, but my life is my own creation, driven by waves of discontent, by a need for something more, always something more. There is no simple explanation for why I seem to be constantly unfulfilled, and I refuse to make excuses, refuse to blame. I have spent 21 years living with my particular burdens, and they are simply an integral part of me.

Nevertheless, my learning disability and ADHD are a pervading factor in my life. Though burdensome, they are no longer intrusive. Rather, these traits provoke bursts of creativity and mental activity that I could not accomplish otherwise. They make me sensitive to the world and to the people who are important to me. Most importantly, ADHD and my learning disability make me more sensitive to myself.

Because of my ADHD, I have had to spend a lot of time thinking about myself and why I am different, which has had positive results. I know now that a learning disability does not have to be a handicap, that it can be a window, a weapon, or a support. In sum, I do not think it has hindered me more than it has helped.

When all the people I am close to are far away, I know that I can take comfort in my solitude and emerge renewed and ready for another day. I would not have such inner resources without the ADHD. This is what having a learning disability means to me.

8

Lovelvet

Velvet Cunningham

This essay was written by a 26-year-old white woman with severe dyslexia who has recently completed an associate's degree at a college exclusively for students with learning disabilities. The essay's title, "Lovelvet"—a conflation of "Love" and "Velvet"—serves as an emblem for the idiographic spelling that has characterized her writing throughout her life. In this essay, Velvet writes of her efforts to cope with her learning difficulties while maintaining her own identity, both privately and socially. Although eager to find a positive learning environment, Velvet has little success, and so is drawn increasingly into the adolescent counterculture, where, true to her title, she establishes herself as a person of both rebelliousness and goodwill. Leaving high school at the age of 16 to tour with the Grateful Dead, Velvet continues to search for an environment that "fits," a search that leads her to various jobs and almost into an abusive marriage. A turning point in her life comes when her dyslexic spelling *suddenly becomes cause for humor rather than despair. Finding that she can, finally, laugh at herself—a major step toward self-acceptance—Velvet decides to again pursue her education.*

I have asked the help of my family in writing my autobiography, because not only did my dyslexia have a large impact on my life, it also had a profound impact on my family's life, and I wanted to have more than just my perspective. Throughout the autobiography, there will be inserts from my family which are direct quotes from them. You will see quotes from four different people: my mom, who stood by me even when I was pushing her away; my dad, who taught me how to climb my mountain; my sister, who is two years older and was an idol, then a punching bag, and now a cherished sister and friend; and Sky, my dad's partner of 20 years, who has always supported and encouraged my spiritual growth. There are also poems and journal entries throughout my autobiography. All the poems are mine. In writing this autobiography, I have truly come to own my learning disability and I am wanting to share it with you.

> *Velvet was born quickly and without preamble during the hot summer of 1971. When the nurse brought her to me, it was immediately evident that my daughter was in perfect health; she was the loudest crier of any of her birth mates, without a doubt! (Mom)*

> *When she was a newborn, holding her was like holding a cat that did not want to be held. From the beginning, she would arch her back and push with her hands and feet against me. And she would cry an impatient cry. It was a slight trick to cuddle with her. (Dad)*

From what I have been told by my mother and father, I spent the first summer and into the early fall of my life living in a tent out in the country of Michigan, while my father was building our house (a geodesic dome). When I was about four, my parents separated, which eventually led to a divorce. They said that it got pretty bad. About one of the only things they agreed on was that they were going to co-parent, meaning that my sister and I would spend the weekdays at Mom's house in town and the weekends at Dad's house out in the country. The best of both worlds!

The first school I went to was Country Roads School. Their philosophy was that when a child was ready to learn, the child will learn. (It took me 23 years, but I'm learning.) I liked that school. English was studied by doing plays and writing poetry. Everything was pretty much hands-on stuff; building things was math class, vocabulary was knowing the names of wildflowers, and it was all done at the child's own pace. I guess my pace was a little slow.

To be honest, I hardly noticed that Velvet couldn't read. What I vividly remember about her early years is sitting around the breakfast table listening to her recount, in great detail, her colorful dreams and astral travels of the previous night. Generally speaking, children under the age of seven feel a great sense of oneness with the world. Velvet's close affinity to the natural world lasted well into her teens, perhaps because she couldn't read. Her vision of the world was not contracted down to the printed page. (Sky)

When I was in fourth or fifth grade, I was diagnosed with dyslexia. I don't know why my mother decided to have me tested. It may have been when I gave her a new name. It was Valentine's Day, and my class was making those cutout hearts from construction paper. Mine was the prettiest because I was the one that used up all the glitter and sequins. I think it took the rest of the day to dry because there was so much glue on it. I was so proud of it and even prouder to give it to my mom. At the end of the day, I carefully picked up my card and took it home to my mom. When I gave it to her, she said, "This is so beautiful! Thank-you, honey." Then she started to laugh.

I thought she was laughing at me. I was so upset that I started to cry. I thought that she did not like it. When I found out what she was laughing at, I felt even worse. She was not laughing at the card, just at how I had spelled MOM. Instead of "Dear Mom, I love you," it said, "Dear Wow, I love you."

I think that was the turning point for me and my self-esteem. Even to this day, my mom signs her name "love, Mom/Wow." I like it now and can laugh at it, but little things like that can completely change a person.

Before testing, she was outgoing and lighthearted—she just couldn't read. After she was diagnosed, she turned into a troubled upset child. (Mom)

After being diagnosed at around age eight with dyslexia, I thought that was it, that was as far as my learning was going to go. I was never going to learn anything again. I felt that I was stupid, dumb, and incompetent. The funny thing is that I did not even know what dyslexia was. I think that after that I just shut down, stopped even caring. So, obviously, it all went downhill from there.

I was allowed to finish up the year at Country Roads School. Then my parents decided to send me to public school, which was a total disaster. I was being judged for what I could not do and not for what I could do. I felt like a total idiot—someone with a severe problem—and everyone knew it.

(F-U-N. God, I don't know how to spell "phenomena." How the hell do you spell it? I don't want to ask Ms. Cartwright. She always snaps at me, but I want to know. I can ask Chris, but she will laugh at me. Ho, Jesus!)

Student: "Ms. Cartwright, how do you spell "phenomena?"

Teacher: "Look it up in the dictionary."

Student: "How am I supposed to look it up if I don't know how to spell it?"

Teacher: "Sound it out."

Student: "F-U-N . . . "

Teacher: "No!"

Student: "What?"

Teacher: "That is not how you spell phenomena."

Student: "Well, that's why I asked *you* how to spell it."

Teacher: "Do you know how to spell 'phone'?"

Student: "Yea, F-O-N-E."

Teacher: "No! That's not how you spell 'phone.' 'Phone' is spelled with a PH, that is what makes the F sound."

Student: "Why?"

Teacher: "Because that is how the English language works."

Student: "Why?"

Teacher: "Just because. So how do you spell 'phenomena'?"

Student: "I don't know."

Teacher: "It starts with a PH. Now look it up!"

Student: "OK . . . But."

Teacher: "Just try to look it up."

Student: "Ph . . . Ph . . . Ph . . . Pha . . . Phe . . . Phi . . . Pho . . . Phu . . . They all look the same to me."

(Tears came to my eyes.)

Student: "Ms. Cartwright!"

Teacher: "Yes."

Student: "I tried, but I can't find it."

(The bell rings.)

Teacher: "OK, kids. That's all for today. Bring your homework in tomorrow."

Student: "But Ms. Cartwright, how do you spell 'phenomena'?"

Teacher: "We will deal with that tomorrow. Run along now, I have lots of work to do."

(That night I pondered over the spelling of "phenomena":—"Ph . . . Phi . . . Phu . . . ")

I was not only dumb, I was the tallest, oldest, and biggest-boobed blond in fifth grade. I did not think that my life could get any worse than that, until I went to junior high.

Next came one of the most absurd meetings I have ever had. I had arranged to meet with Velvet's special education teachers and her special education counselor to talk

about strategies for teaching her to read. It was their professional opinion that pho-
netics was pointless. Context was the key. "Velvet has no context to begin with!" I
heard myself saying in disbelief. "A kid who can't read doesn't have a context! Get
it?" No, they didn't. (Dad)

I went to Portland Junior High in eastern Michigan. Things seemed to be OK
for the first year. I was a cute little preppie, and rather popular. By this time, all the
other kids in my grade had caught up to me in the physical aspect, which was a big
help. Then the summer before eighth grade, my mom/wow got remarried to a
man in a wheelchair, and my father and I had a falling out. My father and I were
very close. We would take hikes and horse rides all the time, discovering new
countryside. But then my friends became more important and parents were not as
cool anymore, as is the case in most adolescents' lives. My father and I parted ways
for about four years. Since he was the closest to me, he went first. Just recently my
dad and I have started to take walks again. This time in my life was a turning point
for me, even though I went in the wrong direction.

I hated the thought of my mom marrying a cripple. My sister and I had her
to ourselves for so long, and now we had to share her with somebody that would
take all her time because he couldn't walk. The fights that came out were dreadful.
Steve, my mom's new husband, and I were at each other's throats all the time. I
hated him. My mom was pulled into every fight. Then one day, after about four
years of fighting, I heard my mom tell Steve that if it comes down to him or the
kids, he was out of there. After I heard that, my fear of losing her just kinda
stopped, and so did the fights. Now Steve and I get along pretty well, and I even
think that he is a pretty cool person. I even look up to him and ask him for guidance. But at the beginning of the relationship, hellfires were conjured.

Velvet is a survivor, as are all children with learning differences, and she began to
develop what she considered strengths to deal with the suffering she was experienc-
ing. Slowly over the months, the open, forthright, adventuresome little girl changed
into a protected, overly sensitive, angry, tough, and bitter youngster. Only reflecting
now, 15 years later, can I see this shift. When I was caught up in it, I felt as if I had
been hit by an unforecasted hurricane, and I was completely adrift. (Mom)

After that summer, I came back to school with two different colors in my hair:
black and white. My friends just flipped out. Just because my hair was a different
color did not mean that my heart was too, but they did not see it that way. They
thought that I had gotten wrapped up in some pretty hard drugs or something.
This really hurt, so now I was mad, and now my heart was changing, too. I hated
my friends, my family, and myself. So you can imagine what happened from there.
I just got more hardcore. Anger hovered over me like a storm cloud visible for
miles, and it rained on everything I came close to. My sister and I started fighting
at frequent intervals, and my school work went downhill. I think I skipped more
days of school than I went.

I sat in class trying to orally read a paragraph out of a history text. When I came to a word that I could not read, anxiety hit me like an ocean wave. The room started to swirl, and I started to break into a shaky sweat. Just as the undertow pulled me under and began dragging me out to sea forever, I heard my mother's voice, "Velvet wake up." I rolled over and looked up into my mother's concerned eyes. The lines around her eyes looked deeper this morning, I thought. As I was about to roll over and go back to sleep, my mother grabbed my shoulder and said, "You either get up and go to school, or get up and get out of the house!" I wrenched my shoulder away from her grip and slowly crawled out of bed. I turned around and faced my mother, sending her hate through my eyes. I told her to get the hell out of my room.

My room was my world. The bed, a mattress on the floor, was covered with red and black satin pillows. The wall opposite of the bed was spotted with silverware, mostly knives protruding from the cracked plaster and chipped paint. Between the knives rested memories of past visitors written on the wall, like "F.T.W." signed John, and "Love is Vain" signed no one. I never wrote on the wall because I was afraid that I would spell something wrong, and my handwriting was embarrassing (every once in a while this fear still rears its ugly head). The rest of my room was eclectic; I guess you could call it punk paraphernalia. There was the bottom half of a mannequin that I had made into a table: It was embraced with barbed wire with a birth control sign pasted on its privates. Also, a gross collection of crumpled up papers (homework) lay in a corner. This safe haven I created protected me from the realities of the evil world.

After my mom sheepishly left my world, I started to prepare myself to fight the elements of reality. This was not an easy task. I felt like I could truly say that I know the hell the medieval knights went through preparing for a battle. Armor is not an easy thing to put on, especially by yourself. First, the clothes. *Tattered jeans? No. Stretched pants? Oh, what's this? An old black plastic bag. I can just cut it here and put it on like this and tie it off here, a mini skirt. Great, now what shirt? This one looks good* (faded black and ripped across the back). *And my faithful flannel, where is that thing?* Digging through a pile of clothes, I retrieved it from the bottom. Tying it around my waist, I headed into the bathroom where my altar of hair spray and makeup awaited me.

No need for a shower. My mohawk is still in pretty good shape. Just a few teases and a splash of Mop an' Glow. Perfect! It will stay up all day. Now the face plate. This part was easy. I just held the black eyeliner up to my eye and drew a straight line from the bridge of my nose to the middle of my temple. That was it for the left eye. The right eye was a little trickier: four straight lines that connected my eyelids to my eyebrows, giving the effect that the eye was behind prison bars. A couple of brushes of black blush and a kiss of red, and I was done.

As I headed out of my bedroom door, I put on my most prized possession of armor, my leather jacket, smashed on my combat boots, grabbed my smokes, and I was on my way. As I was stomping down the stairs, my mom yelled from the kitchen, "Where are you going?"

"Why do you care?" I snapped, and then stormed out the door.

Lost
I was told that I lost my way when I was young.
My way was the hard way.
Don't go over to the left, they would say.
It's much easier to the right.
But what they did not know is that I did not know
My left from my right.

I had to cut through two neighborhoods and part of a golf course to get to school, which took just the right amount of time for me to get my attitude "bad" enough to be able to face all the other kids at school. I could time it perfectly so that I was always five minutes late, so the other (smart) kids would not see me going into the SPED class.

The whole angry world I created around me was to protect me. The clothes and make up were a disguise: I hoped that people would see me as a freak, instead of stupid. I would rather have everyone think that I had done too many drugs and that was why I was slow, instead of them knowing the truth. My "bad" attitude was a way to keep people away from me. Not that I didn't like people! I really liked people, but I thought that they would not like me if they really knew me.

The simple truth was that I had dyslexia, and I could not bear the thought of it. Everyone always told me that I was special, but I thought they were just trying to make me feel better. I truly thought that if you were not born being able to do something, if it did not come naturally to you, then you were never going to be able to do it. I did not like myself, so how in the world could anybody else like me? I thought that I was the only kid in the world that was going through this struggle, and my life was always going to be like this. There was no light at the end of the tunnel.

It would have killed me if I tried to do something and failed, so I didn't even try. If I had put all the energy and effort I spent on trying to divert attention from my learning difference into my education, I probably could have had a Ph.D. by now. The evil "realities" were mostly my own, but I was in the stage where I knew everything, so there was no telling me anything different.

> *I don't think that she meant to hurt us, but V was so caught up in trying to be accepted into something and for everyone around her to forget that she couldn't read, and that was how she did it. Everyone was too busy dealing with what a bitch (family), how cool (friends), or how tough (enemies) she was. (Sister)*

I sit back now and can see other kids going through the struggles I did. Maybe they aren't acting-out as radically as I did, but they are still suffering, and my heart is wrenched by this. One thing I can say to them is, "You are not the only one."

After *the year of the freak* at Portland Junior High, I was transferred in ninth grade into a private school for kids with LD.

Class
I think my mind is going to pop
    With the tick tock of the clock.
And the hum of the light
    Will probably start a fight.
The scratching of pens and the thoughts that pass
    Are definitely becoming a pain in my ass.

The "specialized SPED" school just made me feel like all the horrible feelings I had about myself were true: dumb, stupid, incompetent, ignorant, lazy, useless–as–a–human–being, ugly, mental, etc. I remember sitting there saying my vowels out loud and just wanting to hide under a rock. Here I was in the ninth grade, and I was practicing my alphabet. I only had one friend there, because most of the kids there were on major meds for hyperactivity, depression, or some kind of mental disorder.

One day I just could not take it anymore. I got to class early, and the teacher was not there yet, but this one kid was. I think he was there for some reasons other than an LD. He came over to me and grabbed my shoulders, pinned me on the table and said, "Take off your clothes, bitch." I was not scared at this point. I was just pissed off. As he was trying to climb on top of me, I kneed him in the balls as hard as I could and threw him off of me. I only got scared when he started destroying the lockers with his face. That was it. I walked out of the room, went to my locker, got my shit, and walked out of the school for good. *This is a mental ward and I am not mental. I just can't read,* I remember saying to myself. I still think that place helped deplete my self-esteem account even more than it had been depleted already.

After quitting halfway through ninth grade, I started to hang out in the park with the "dealing Deadheads." The Portland municipal park was a place for all the dogs to take their yuppie owners for walks. It was a rather large park with a brook running through it to a duck pond and a playground for the little tots. This place became my new home from 11:00 A.M., when I woke up, to 8:00 P.M., when the park closed. Most of the time I would go home to my mom's to sleep, but more than a few times I would stay out all night. The people I hung out with in the park did not care that I could not read or write (not that I told them) or what I looked like. They just liked hanging out and shooting the shit. I guess you could say that I went from mosh pits at punk shows to drum circles at Grateful Dead shows. It really wasn't difficult to change like that. I just had a different type of armor to wear. I tried to cut all ties with my family. They did not understand what I was going through, and I tried to think that they did not care.

Velvet, I think that you are going to hate to hear this, but from this side, I think that the reason things were so fucked up was not because you are dyslexic. I think that you had a very bad attitude. The attitude may have been because you had dyslexia, but from the outside of your mind, you were such a bitch that no one could get close enough to figure out that you were hurting. (Sister)

When I was 16, a couple of months after quitting ninth grade, I started to tour with the Dead. I would be gone for weeks at a time. I was known as "the Nurse." I had this really bright/ugly banner that I would hang from the car that would tell people where I was. I never did a single drug on tour. I did not need to. Things were so out of hand already. I would like to think that I saved some people's lives or at least their sanity. When people were having a bad trip (did way too many drugs at once) and the cops were going to take them away, I would beg and plead with the cops to give me 20 minutes with the freaked out party, and if they did not calm down by then, the cops could take them away.

I never lost anyone to the cops. I would try to get them to lie down and close their eyes, all the while telling them to breathe deep and relax. It sounds simple, but more than once I was slugged, bitten, or kicked. But my efforts came through, and eventually they would calm down and relax. When people are having a bad trip, you have to just let them know that they're safe and loved. You have to make them feel the love by holding them with your soul and let them see that (it's amazing what they can see when they're "tripping"). I don't remember any of their names, but I remember their souls.

So here I was almost 16, saving lives, selling peace bracelets, and panhandling for a living. Sounds great, huh? It would have been, if I wasn't running away from myself and taking care of others. The tour finally took its toll on me. I was drained, and I was so busy taking care of everyone else that I forgot about myself. I was tired and hungry, so I went home once again.

Facsimile of a Page of Velvet's First Draft

When I was sixteen a cuppel munths after quitting ninth gread I started to tuer with the Dead, and would be gon for weakes at a time. I was knowen as the nirce , I head this really brite / ugley banner that I would hang from the car that would tell people where I was. I hever did a cingel drug on tuer I did not nead to, things were so out of hand arledey. I would like to think that I saved some peoples lives or at least there sanitey. When people were haveing a bad trip (did way to meny druges at once) and the copes were going to take them away, so I would beg and plead with the cops to give me twntey minites with the freaked out partey and if they did not calm down by then that the cops could take them away.

I never lost anyone to the cops. I would try to get them to lay down and close there eyes all the whiel telling them to breath deap and realx. It soundes simpel but more then once I was sluged bitten and kicked. but my effertes came threw and evenuchley they would calm down and realiz. When people are haveing a bad tripo you have to just let them know that there safe and loved. you have to make them feal the love by holding them with your soal and let them see that (its amising what they can see when there "tripping".) I dont rember any of there names but I rember there soles.

So hear I was almoste sisteen saveing lives, selling peace braclets and panhandeling for a liveling. Soundes great hu? it wo. Wuld have ben if I asent running away from my self and takeing care of others.

Now I was almost 17 and feeling really bad about myself and my family. My mom found a school in Vermont that she was sending me to. I did not have anything else to do, and I did not want to get a job, so I agreed to go. It was a rather lax school, which eased my fear a bit about learning.

It was the first day of classes at my new boarding school, and I was scared. I woke up really early to arm myself for the day. I wanted to look, feel, and act perfect so everyone would accept me. It was the only way I knew how to go about it. I planned to go to class and impress teachers and the other students so they would all like me and maybe not rag on me for not being a well-rounded student (not being able to read or write).

Well, that all changed as soon as I walked out of my room. My room was right off the common area where the students would gather after meals to hang out and socialize. This particular morning, there were more students than usual and all but one of them were sitting on the floor. The one student that was standing yelled out to me, "We're protesting because they did not serve cereal for breakfast! We have decided to watch *A Clockwork Orange* and *Easy Rider* instead! Sit down and hang out! None of us are going to class!" I wanted to fit in, so I sat down.

What happened here? I was all gung-ho to go to class, and since there was no cereal, I protested? I don't even like cereal! My need for acceptance took over, but the cool thing was from that day on, I was able to be me because I realized that no one gave a shit about academics, not just me.

That school, I have to say, was one of the greatest and worst experiences I have ever had. I don't even recall learning any academic stuff, but I sure as shit learned a lot of other stuff. The school was small, about 50 to 60 students, more like a mob of misfits. It was a college prep boarding school, and boy, did it prep me for college: I could smoke, drink, and drop with the best of them. I even learned a little horticulture by growing pot and shrooms in a crawl space next to my room.

Since academics was not an issue, I was able to excel in other areas. People came to me for just about everything. Some would even just come cry in a safe environment. They would come to me for drugs when campus was dry. When someone got hurt, I would be there to stitch them up or dress their leg. Once I even had this guy want me to have his virginity, which I politely declined. I was trusted and respected. I was important and had a place there. People knew me for what I could do, not what I couldn't do.

Throughout my three semesters at this school, I amused myself by hitching around the state and checking out east coast Dead shows. The school never seemed to be too concerned when I would be missing for a couple of days. And if they did piss a fit, friends would cover for me, but that rarely happened. All the kids there were lacking a solid family, so we created our own. I don't know how to explain it, but the bonds that were created there between all the students have probably saved some of our lives by teaching us how to take care of others and not just our selfish selves. After three semesters of this hell I loved, it was taken away.

The state of Vermont ended up shutting the school down for sexual misconduct (a student and staff member had a relationship, and the student got pregnant), drug abuse (no argument), unclean living facilities (the buildings that we were living in were built in the 60s as a Peace Corps training camp and were supposed to last only two years; I was going there in 1987), not up to par academics (no argument), and pornography (a student broke into a staff member's apartment and stole pictures of the staff member engaging in sexual activities with another staff member). I understand why they shut the school down, but that was our home, and we all had a place there. It was like a joint family. We fought a lot, but what family doesn't?

My three semesters at the Vermont school seemed like a lifetime. When they shut it down, they didn't only break up our family; they also took away the credits we had acquired there.

> *Life*
> *I have climbed . . . and climbed . . .*
> *and climbed . . .*
> *To get where I have fallen . . .*

I guess it does not matter now, since I ended up dropping out of school anyway, but at the time it made me feel like a failure and believe the system had failed me, too. Could I have done something to keep this from not happening? I don't think so. I was a year away from graduating and now I'm two and a half years away. All I can remember thinking was *Go figure . . .*

My mom decided that I should try school again. She found a school in California. They said I would have to go there two years, and then I would graduate. Well, after a year, they told me that I had two more years, so I bolted out of there.

That was one of the reasons I left. The other was that I was doing way too much LSD. I was tripping about four to five times a week. I loved it. It was the only time I laughed. I loved the feeling of my cheek muscles cramping from a perma-grin. It was the only world I enjoyed at the time. I knew that it would eventually kill me or that I would just wish I was dead because my mind would be so fucked up. I wanted to stop, but I knew that I would not be able to if I stayed there. So, I left and have never done acid since.

> *I ask myself after all these years, why was I in such a fog about Velvet's problems? Did I think by ignoring them they would go away? By passing off responsibility for Velvet's education to the schools, did that free me of the responsibility of parenting her? I can't answer those questions yet, but I can say I felt guilty and responsible. Twenty years ago, learning problems were considered more a problem of poor parenting than a genetic link (at least that's what I heard from the educators), and certainly I felt I had been a poor parent. (Mom)*

After quitting school for the third and final time, I went home. For five years, from age 18 to 23, I just kinda hung out doing what my mother thought would be good for me, all the while I was trying to find "something": myself. Eventually, I thought that I found it.

I was a week and a half away from the most exciting day of my life. All my dreams were coming true. I was going to be married to the greatest guy in the world and live happily ever after. He was so gorgeous: tall with dark hair (when it was not shaved), tattoos, and the cutest little nose. He never really showed emotions, though he had his angry side, his happy side, and (when we were alone) his goofy side. We had so much fun together. We could have a nice time just taking walks, and we could have fun going to a rumble. I was never scared of other people when he was with me. I knew he would risk his life to protect me. I was so happy. I was his queen, and he my king. Then the plans we had for our life together shattered. The night of July 21, 1993, we got into a fight. I was sick and tired of him leaving his shoes in the middle of the living room floor. I thought that it was just as easy to take them off at the door as in the living room, but he did not think so. Well, this is what started the end. The fight escalated and ended on the note of money problems. I needed to take a walk and cool down. He did not want me to leave. The more I tried to leave, the madder he got. He finally got really mad and punched a hole in the wall next to my head. Then he threw me across the living room.

After that, I snapped into the happy little passive housewife, not knowing what else to do and not wanting to anger him further. I was scared because this man's favorite pastime was fighting. He broke his knuckles so many times that they fused together and made a kinda permanent brass knuckle on the top of his fist. He was known as being one of the best fighters around. Not too many people would fuck with him, and if they did, they would usually get their asses kicked. He did not care if he won or lost. He just loved fighting. Guys would even have to ask his permission to talk to me, or else they would get pounced. I was a queen— I was his queen. Even when the band he played in was on stage, he would be watching to make sure no one was bothering me. I loved it. He made me feel so important and cherished.

To this day, I don't know if he would have really hurt me, but I did not stick around to find out. After the fight, I said all sweetly that I was tired, and I think we should go to bed. The next morning, I got up, made him breakfast, and packed his lunch like usual, and kissed him off to work. As soon as he was in his car, I ran upstairs and started packing. I just packed the necessities, threw it all in my car, wrote a quick note, "The wedding is off. Velvet," and took off to my mom's house.

> **Broke**
> *My heart is broken, but hardening with hate.*
> *You took it all away from me.*
>
> *The dreams of a little girl.*
>
> *Now broken.*
>
> *Broken like a crystal vase.*
>
> *The bond we had is not strong enough to repair it.*
>
> *It wasn't enough that you broke it.*
> *   You had to also lose some of the pieces.*
>
> *Never allowing it to hold love again.*

I had to send back all the wedding and shower presents. My mom sent out cards to let the people that were coming to the wedding know that it was called off.

But the worst of it was how I was feeling about the whole thing. Was it my fault? Did I make the right decision? I wanted him back. I hated him. What was I going to do? All my dreams of a happy life were gone. The one chance in life to be happy, and I fucked it up. I wanted to pretend that the fight never happened. I loved him so much. People were telling me that I was so strong and brave for doing what I did, but I felt like a worm. I felt like a conniving, sneaking, little crawling thing that not only had to ruin my life, but his, too. It was easier for me to put the blame on myself, and I did for a long time. We tried to get back together a couple times, but there was just too much pain and guilt between us. I don't know how he felt about the whole thing. He was never one to share feelings.

I thank God, the Spirits, or whatever they may be practically daily, because the best thing that ever happened to me came out of all this. My whole world was turned upside down, and I could put it back together any way I wanted. I had so many options, but the only thing I could think of was going back to school. I had not gone to school for five years, because basically school and I have never really gotten along. But I wanted something for myself that would help me get back on track, and school was it. This was not an easy decision because between the ages of 8, when I was diagnosed with an LD, and 23, I took myself so seriously and could not laugh at myself under any situation, especially when it came to my LD.

> I have fallen . . . and fallen . . .
>   and fallen . . .
> To get where I have to climb.

Then one day when I was about 23, my life changed again: For the first time, I laughed at myself. I was working at a pizza joint, and my job was to make salads and run the cash register. Not too bad. At least I did not have to write anything down. But on this particular day, one of the order girls was sick, and I had to fill in for her. I thought that the world was coming to an end. Well, I hoped it would have. It was a really busy day, and I was completely freaked out about having to write orders down.

I took an order from a man and sent it back to the kitchen. A few minutes later, the cook came up front and asked me if what I wrote down was right. I looked at the slip and said, "Yeah, a meat ball hoagie." The cook just started laughing and said that I wrote down *beat ball hoagie.* I started to laugh too, not out of nervousness, but because it was funny. I think I laughed at myself because I was caught with my guard down. It was so busy that day that I did not have time to put my guard up.

That was the first time I ever laughed at myself, and it changed my whole life. I instantly felt the walls that I spent so much time building to keep people out and protect my scared little self crumble like they were made out of pastry dough. I never realized how restrained I was, and I had no one to blame except myself. For the first time, I tasted freedom.

I went home that night in a great mood and realized that I could do more with my life than just running a cash register. I was so excited and scared. Options were coming to me in every direction now that there was no wall to keep it all silent. Something clicked, and all I wanted to do was go back to school and make it work for myself, not anybody else. I knew for the first time that I could do it.

As parents, we have this feeling of omnipotence, that we can control the world our children see and experience. But this is only a fantasy. Velvet is at the wonderful spot she is today, not because of me, but because of her. For years I battled with her to follow a road that was of my choosing and she grudgingly did. But if I have learned anything, it is that our children choose their own roads to walk; and that we as parents should act as the support and follow-up team rather than the boss-student as well as teachers. (Mom)

It took me three months and an outrageous phone bill trying to find a college that was for adults with learning differences. I knew that there had to be something for me out there. Once I found the college, I did not waste time applying.

When I started college, I was 22, without a high school diploma or G.E.D., and I was at a third grade reading level and a second grade spelling level. Let's not talk about my self-esteem: I don't think that I even showed up on the chart. I think the hardest thing was owning my difference and incorporating it into who I was, instead of trying to hide it.

Well, after nine straight semesters, including summers, I finally graduated with a 3.5. I think that the most valuable thing I got there was self-esteem. I know now that I don't have to be a housewife, if I don't want to.

Sometimes, I think what it would be like if I didn't have a learning difference. What would I be like? I know one thing for sure: I would not be as understanding of differences. I probably would have been one of those kids that teased everyone who was different from me and tried to make them feel as bad as possible about themselves, only to make myself feel better. Now, I might be regretting the horrible things I had done to those kids, and I would be lacking self-esteem. It's more like the opposite. I lacked self-esteem then, but now, I feel pretty good about myself and who I am. I never purposely tried to hurt anyone—well, except my mom—when I was a kid, but I can assume that the kids that were running around tearing the shit out of other kids feel pretty crummy about it now, and if they don't, they are really fucked up. Having an LD has given me the option of knowing how to cope with things outside the traditional way. If I'm hurt, I don't hurt others. If I'm scared, I don't scare others. I problem-solve within myself and find a way to work it out. And I bet that I can speak for other people with LDs when I say that, if nothing else, having an LD has made the world of opportunities much larger. To see this now and to know how my family feels makes a world of support that I never wanted to know was there. These are some last thoughts from my wonderful, loving family:

I have always known Velvet is special and that the road she walks is unique, however difficult. Sometimes it has not been easy for me to participate in her life. But as I have watched her grow and mature over these years into a remarkable human being, it is easy for me to feel immense pride and to be grateful that I am her mother. (Mom)

I think that I never used to admit you had a learning disability, but you know what I do know? I brag that you are graduating college. I am so proud of you, Kiddo. So, things heal with time. I'm still working on growing in the hair patch you ripped out in our last fight, but the heart doesn't hurt so bad anymore. Actually, its bursting with pride and love. (Sister)

When I was doing my Waldorf teacher training, one of those teachers ventured the opinion that it is not always a bad thing to come to reading late, as most of the reading material for post-picture book age was trash. I think Velvet's "slow shuffle" towards reading allowed her to develop in areas she might otherwise have missed. (Sky)

As she was sitting down in the car, she picked the flier up. She looked at it for a moment. She seemed to study it slightly, for just a moment. And then almost formally, she began to read it. I was stunned! It was not simple writing. It was somewhat erudite and formal. I heard her read on with interpretation and understanding. She only hesitated on the word "neighbor," although much of the rest of the vocabulary was not common speech. Then she finished and placed it in her lap. That was one of the most amazing things she has ever done. It was something I had begun to resign myself to perhaps never seeing. (Dad)

Through writing this autobiography, I have come to know myself and I am proud of myself. I don't regret any of my experiences or actions, because I was taking care of myself the best way I knew how. I would not be who I am today without all of the joys and trials of my life. To realize this is a great accomplishment in itself. Although I now have many different suits of armor in my closet, creating a wardrobe that I can arm myself with when and where it is appropriate, the fear of having people really know me has faded away through taking chances with friends and family. I now know that I am a good person and I can be loved and accepted for who I am and not hated for who I am not.

9

Finally Saying What I Mean

Garett Day

Currently a graduate student in his university's special education program, Garett already holds both a bachelor's and master's degree in history from the same institution. Some of Garett's learning and social difficulties are related to early medical problems, including occluded auditory canals and Stevens–Johnson Syndrome, a condition sometimes caused by toxic levels of antibiotics. Professional attention to these medical problems led to early identification of his neurologically based learning disabilities, an event that Garett suggests was at least somewhat advantageous for him. Partially because of his early diagnosis, Garett developed unusual insight into the ways that his disabilities—which include auditory and linguistic processing deficits, as well as verbal memory and reading comprehension difficulties—affected both his ability to learn and his social relationships. Although Garett's self-awareness of his disabilities resonates throughout his essay, it is not until he reaches college that he learns how to transform this self-awareness into self-advocacy.

In this essay, Garett focuses on how his teachers and peers influenced his academic development and social relationships. He continually reminds the reader *of his need for specific accommodations essential to successful learning—such as a noise-free environment and the additional time needed to complete assignments.*

During my first few years, I was a very active baby; the type who learned to climb stairs before learning to walk. Yet my mother could tell that something was wrong because I did not respond to any sounds. This provides the first lesson on *ablism* in our culture, for none of the doctors believed her. It was not until I was three that my mother finally got a professional to acknowledge her observations. That one visit started a year-long avalanche of medical discoveries and problems. They found that two things had formed incorrectly in my ears. First, my eustachian tubes that allow the fluid to drain out did not form and, second, in my right ear, the ear drum lodged itself against the bone. Artificial eustachian tubes were used to restore part of my hearing through a course of nine operations.

Compounded onto this medical history was the discovery at age three that I had Stevens–Johnson Syndrome (SJS), the more severe form of erythema multiforme, which is similar to an allergic reaction to phenylphalein drugs. When you have SJS, rashes quickly develop over your entire body. What makes the condition special is the speed that the rashes attack the body. They start at the head and quickly affect everything inside and out: the eyes, the lungs, the stomach, everything.

I was placed in a bubble for three weeks because the reaction was overloading my immune system, and I was vulnerable to any airborne disease. In the end, the only way the doctors could battle SJS was to pump in steroids to boost my immune system. It was the doctors' belief that without the steroids, my eyesight would have been affected. After three weeks in the bubble, my mother had to spend another three months wrapping my body with bandages filled with medicine. And I had to spend extended time away from the sun because my skin had become as sensitive as a newborn baby's.

After my hearing was restored, attention shifted to my verbal skills. As the educators worked with me, they found that I was not responding as I should to the tutoring. When they explored why, they discovered that I had a complex learning disability (LD), which I'll try to describe as I go along. Do I feel that this hard beginning has deterred me from reaching my full potential? No, or at least not anymore. I feel that this background has provided me with a mixture of advantages and disadvantages. The early diagnosis, for example, created some advantages. I, for one, never had to suffer through any schooling without a proper diagnosis of my learning difficulties (a very minor advantage at best). Fact is, most learning disabilities are not diagnosed until second or third grade, after the student has already gone through two or three years of failure. Most of my educational difficulties, on the other hand, came from the school's failure to meet the accommodations recommended for my diagnoses.

Among other advantages was a better understanding at a young age of my limitations and weaknesses. Though this might not sound like much of an advantage, one must remember that every person has their own weaknesses and limitations. I was able to realize, for example, that to get through math, I should draw out the problems. This system let me visualize what I was trying to do.

A natural disadvantage is that I felt different from the rest of the students, and at times was reminded that I was different.

These beginnings have had a significant role in shaping who I am if only because I have had to accept the way I learn and perceive and react to my environment. My learning disability will always be part of my background and the core that makes me who I am.

Before I continue, I should provide some family background. I grew up in a suburban town with my mother and older brother. Dad was around at first, but only periodically. By the time I was six, he was out of the house permanently. For those who believe divorce is ruining society, I am stating this divorce was a good thing. Dad would drink and sometimes take it out on Mom. I do not have many memories from before six, but this is good, for what did last are horrifying sounds of my mother being abused. Thus, luckily, by the time I was six, Dad was gone (though I will add in fairness that he has since taken steps to clean up his life and thus is back in the picture). But, Mom still went through many years of raising two children alone. With the help of extended family, she managed to do quite an excellent job.

The elementary school I attended was built in the 1960s when the "open classroom" was the controlling theory of the day. However, this school went beyond open classroom, as it was an open building. If one was to stand in the middle of the library, you could peer into all six grades. This design meant that a student in fifth grade could spend his or her time watching what the people in grades 1, 3, 4, and 6 were doing, as well as the people in the library.

This school was the worst design I can think of for a person with a hearing deficit or a learning disability. The last thing either kind of student needs is any extra background noise. The more background noise there is, the harder it is to concentrate and hear the person talking. In addition, for some students, an LD can manifest itself by making it difficult to maintain a normal attention span. Having to live with both disabilities, school was torture at times. Thinking back on it, I am surprised I learned anything.

Unfortunately, this problem is only a sign of how I would be treated by the special education department throughout my schooling at Rockford Elementary School. If they had been doing their jobs, they would have at least made sure I was positioned in the least distracting section of the classroom. If they were really doing their jobs, they would have made sure I attended a different school.

I also experienced social problems in school. Because of the steroids for SJS, I was larger and clumsier than the rest of the class. Because of my hearing, I was still talking with a slight stutter in first and second grade. Lastly, because of my LD, I was not a fast thinker. All this contributed to making me a target of ridicule from other children. Hence, school was not a happy place. Yes, I had friends, but they were mostly kids who were not part of the community. In the end, I believe that my inability to orally defend myself was the biggest problem for me with the other children.

Academically, what sticks out in my mind the most is third grade. My teachers were enthralled by the concept of letting the children learn at their own pace. Though this idea might be wonderful in theory, it was lousy in practice. The way the school implemented this theory was to provide individual study packets. The teacher would provide some instruction, but the children were basically left to progress as fast or slowly as their capabilities would allow. The children could not collaborate in trying to learn the new material. When a worksheet was finished, it would be handed to the teacher for correction. If you passed, you moved to the next level and continued to work on your own; if you did not pass, you were sent back to figure out your mistakes on your own. This system became a double-edged sword for me. First, it called for me to learn in a way that is not helpful for my LD: It called for learning on my own. With very little support or encouragement, I failed to push forward. Second, the teachers did not implement the plan as it was intended. The instruction time was short, and very little individual assistance was provided. Instead of guiding the students through the learning process, the teacher would let the students succeed or fail on their own.

I suffered the aggravation of constant failure with reading. Because of my LD, learning the rules of writing and grammar on my own was an impossible task. On most worksheets, I would end up failing a few times. It became a routine for me. For a while, I would keep trying, but I knew that each attempt would lead to naught. However, because of the system, the teacher would not provide any in-depth help. I was left to flounder. Many times, the teacher would simply tell me to skip the rest of the worksheet after I had, in repeated attempts, failed to figure out my mistakes. Naturally, this helped create a big dislike toward grammar and reading. A little direct instruction to guide me might have gone a long way toward creating a happier reading experience. Considering that these early experiences formed my attitude toward reading for years, the negative treatment had lasting effects.

I also had problems socially. Often, my mother was called in for teacher conferences because of my behavior. Lucky for me, her reaction was to blame the teachers for mistreating me by letting the other children tease me. As the teachers tried to blame me for the way I was treated, Mom would ask them what they had done to try to stop the others from singling me out. Their reaction was that I needed to learn to take the abuse at some point, even in first grade. Mom would tell my teachers off and walk out. Though she was right to treat the teachers in this fashion for their attitude, I was probably a bit socially immature. It reached the point that even if a child was not looking to hurt me, I would still react at times. But, I mostly kept to myself, choosing not to react at all.

The next major events in my life came while I was in "Three Years of Hell," trying to survive the trenches of school and social warfare in junior high school. This is the period of life when everything changes. The hormones kick in, and self-doubt balloons as the ego erodes. You are positive that the only purpose of those around you is to make your life miserable. School structure changes and becomes increasingly formal. As the work gets harder you are left to fend for yourself both academically and socially. All you want to do is fit in, be part of the crowd.

In junior high, I started to take more advanced math classes and Latin. In both cases, I believed that I could have learned the information taught. However, I was not prepared to provide the effort. As the classes became challenging, I came very close to failing.

I would find out later that my difficulties in Latin, and later in Spanish, went beyond bad study habits. In learning a foreign language, a student needs good auditory skills for learning new words and good reading comprehension. My hearing deficit interfered in the oral aspect of learning Latin, and my LD was a road block against the cognitive reading comprehension process. Unfortunately, I did not learn this until I was in college.

Latin class represented the beginning of the end of other aspects of my academic innocence. Specifically, the class started my trend toward abandoning any hope of getting more than five to six hours of sleep a night (let alone eight). When I started the class, my initial reaction toward the workload was the same as always: Ignore it as much as possible. This system had always worked for me before, but then school seemed simple until now. As I started failing tests, I woke up to the reality of the situation. I started to study quite a lot. I would spend more time on Latin than all other classes put together. Yet, despite the extra work, I still entered the final exam with a failing grade. I had to get at least a B on the final just to get a D for the year, a disheartening predicament. My reaction was to pull my first all-nighter of my academic career at the age of 13. As I sat in class on the last day of school, I was fixated on the results of the test. Expecting the worst, I was afraid to see my grade. Though I had developed a new level of concentration for the test, I knew there were items that I had not been able to answer.

Latin class represented a great pivotal change for me. More than the actual Latin, which I have completely forgotten, the one enlightening lesson which I gained was that I was driven by a fear of failure. What I have realized is that throughout grade school, I ran into situations in which failure seemed like a possibility if I did not provide some extra work. My reaction was simply to withdraw. If the activity was not going to come easily to me, I was not going to try it at all since a window for failure was not an option. Unfortunately, I could not quit school, although I do not know exactly why. It was almost part of my nature. Also, education has been a part of my life since I was three. As soon as my hearing was restored, my family did all they could to help me adjust and catch up in my language development.

One reason I did not feel my grades were very good was that my results only equaled my friends. I had less personal time, having put more hours into working than my friends. I knew that they were spending more time playing while I worked. Yet, I could do no better than them. Furthermore, I was not finishing my work. Books were going partially read, tests were prepared for at the last minute, and papers were written the day before they were due. If I had more hours in the day, I could give each test the study time needed, but there was not enough time. This feeling of getting smaller results from harder work was very discouraging at times.

Not all of junior high represents bad memories of classes. One of the more exciting changes was experiencing my first joy from reading. The first book I enjoyed reading was *Where the Red Fern Grows.* I do not know what caused the change. All I knew was that I could not read the book fast enough. It made me feel empowered. I now knew that the possibility of reading without feeling tortured existed. This did not cause an overnight change in my reading habits. I still read really slowly and had problems understanding what I was reading. Further, I would still encounter books that gave me extra trouble. However, I now knew that reading could bring joy.

Academically, there was one other major step that I went through in junior high: My position as a person receiving special services changed. When I started junior high school, I was still spending time in the resource closet. Although I had been receiving special help since preschool, the only period that I remember going to the resource room is during junior high school. Why I do not remember getting help before seventh grade is beyond me, but there are some good reasons why I remember the work I put in during the subsequent years.

I believe that I remember these days because I have positive memories about working in the resource room. I had problems in all aspects of life throughout junior high school. I did not get along with most of my peers, and certain classes were starting to become difficult for me, especially without an understanding of what it meant to have an LD.

However, I did not have these difficulties in the resource room. In this room, I reigned academically. I worked with two other students from both ends of the social spectrum. While working with these students, I knew that neither could match my abilities. In this setting, I became a helper for my fellow students, since with the one-to-one help that I was receiving there I could excel. In this smaller, more intimate setting, I developed confidence that was lacking in every other part of my life (school, friends, and family). This confidence enabled me to converse with my fellow students as equals. This is a feat I could not accomplish in any other setting outside of the resource room.

Unfortunately, by the end of ninth grade they had pulled me out of the resource room, claiming that they were going to monitor me. I never heard from the special education department again, and as far as I can tell, neither did any of my subsequent teachers.

I was not immune to the hormones that started to kick in during junior high. I became interested in dating Brianna, who was in one of my classes. I would try to talk with Brianna or her friends in an attempt to get a date. The best I was able to do was skate with her during a school roller skating party. Beyond my difficulties starting conversations, my LD also interfered in one other major way. I could never remember her name. I was told it dozens of times. Yet, whenever I talked with her or talked about her with others, I could not recall it. I wanted to say her name, but the word retrieval problems that I have because of my LD meant that I suffered a constant mental block. Needless to say, no one is impressed when you cannot remember her name. If I had known that it was my LD interfering with remembering her name, I might have been able to do something, but the school system never felt compelled to educate me on how having an LD would impact my life.

Entering high school is usually a disheartening experience for any student. The school doubles in size, and the amount of work expected of you increases, with less support from the teacher. Most importantly, relations with your peers become vital to a pleasant experience during these three years as parents assume a more subdued role in your everyday life. All of these links lead to a greater sense of either security or insecurity. For me, this experience was heightened by the disappearance of two of my closest friends and the loss of the academic support from the special education department.

When I started high school, I wanted to distance myself from my past, not only with my friends, but also with past educational experiences. Consequently, I never realized the kind of problems I could have because of my hearing. When the special education department placed me on the "monitoring" system at the end of junior high school, not only did my mother and I never hear from them again, it seems none of my teachers were contacted by them either. This lack of contact violated the laws protecting me as a student with special needs. The school was obligated to inform my teachers of the needs I might have in their classrooms. Further, parents are to be kept informed about progress. These legal requirements were supposed to ensure that I was not placed in a situation where my disability became detrimental to my classroom performance. Though I found a new support system in high school to offset some of the damage, problems did arise that could have been prevented if the school had complied with the state's special education law.

One of the unforeseen problems with losing the academic support for the special education department centered on my hearing. Because of my hearing loss, the best place for me to sit was in the front of the class so that I could hear all that the teacher was saying. I naturally never volunteered to sit in the front. I was in high school, and it was important to sit with someone I knew. Consequently, I would often sit in back since my friends and teachers did not know that I needed to sit closer. I did not take the initiative to sit in front because I did not realize how important it was.

Math and science—subjects which had been strong for me—became difficult because my school let me take another shot at the advanced college prep classes. The pace was faster, the material was more conceptual, and the teachers had higher expectations. However, this time I did not buckle under the pressure. Part of my success was due to the teachers. My high school subscribed to the age-old practice of placing the best teachers with the high-achieving students. With these teachers, I felt I could ask anything if I ever had difficulty with the material. I knew they cared about how I was doing, and this caring made me feel comfortable. However, teachers were not the only reason I succeeded in these subjects. My peers were just as critical to my success. Outside of the resource room, education had always been an individual act for me. The teachers whom I had never created a situation where cooperative learning among the students might flourish. Within school time, everyone worked alone. This situation changed with high school math and science. What I found was a group of kids who were helping each other learn and teachers who were providing the freedom to allow this cooperative learning to flourish. I learned more about who I was as a learner from this group of peers than I had in my previous ten years of school.

I learned how helpful it was to talk about what I was learning. This forced me to more thoroughly process the information imparted. Quite often, one of us would be confused by a new concept. However, we would help each other by reiterating these new ideas student to student. My peers would often do a better job explaining a mathematical concept than the teacher, and I discovered that I had something to contribute as well. Since we were helping each other, I would often find myself being the one to explain the concept to one of my peers. As I helped explain the idea, I also gained a stronger understanding. Bringing everything out into the verbal arena was like opening my eyes to a bright day. Concepts just became easier to understand as I talked about them. As I look back through the Individual Education Plans (IEPs) that were created for me in elementary school, it seems that the teacher knew this as well. They noted my problems with remembering written material that had not been discussed. Though it is not clear why they did not act on their findings, I have found that teachers are often reluctant to change or are ill-equipped to make certain modifications, and thus revert to routine.

One year, the math class I was taking went through about five substitutes within a three-month period before a long-term substitute could be found. None of the substitutes could teach like our original teacher, so we stopped looking to the teacher for guidance. The class became a collaborative setting, where learning was based on conversation, discussion sections, and practices. I was finally in a math class that catered to my abilities. I might be limited in the ways that I can learn because of processing deficits, but when the class is aimed at my strengths, I can flourish. Unfortunately for my classmates, the way they knew how to learn became useless. Now they had learning difficulties from being in a class that put them a step behind. I aced the class.

High school was also a time for major social growth. I did not become Mr. Popularity or fully break out of the shell I had built up, but I did find a partially comfortable niche for myself. The way I found some social acceptance was to not be a part of any one large clique. Though I did build up another core group to hang out with in high school, I found myself building this group from all the cliques.

High school marked the start of a period where I would not go more than three months without being in a dating relationship. This period lasted until the fall of 1992, almost seven years. Although the length of each relationship would vary from a few months to a few years, they all had one thing in common: I defined a major part of who I was directly through the relationship. Part of how I defined myself was by becoming the emotional support for those surrounding me. Not being able to support everyone close to me, I would concentrate on helping the person I was dating. The mixture of needing to support others, being afraid of who I was, and having to share this with another person caused me to involve myself with girls who carried a lot of emotional baggage.

I started dating a girl named Lydia, and we developed a relationship where I took the lead. I spent a year and a half dating Lydia. One of the most important things I gained was the sense of assertiveness. Her family was very controlling and protective. Her response to suffocating parents was to become a quiet, indecisive person. This made me the more decisive person (something very ironic considering that I was quiet and indecisive myself). Taking on a role of the decision maker, I was forced to step out of my comfortable position of following others, and I learned to enjoy having someone follow my lead.

However, there was something equally telling about my growth during high school in the way I treated Lydia. She was the person I would do the most self-reflecting about and with. Yet, she never knew that I had an LD or a hearing deficit. No matter how intimate I would get with Lydia, I did not let her know that I was a person with disabilities. Since I did not come out to the person I loved, I naturally did not tell the people I met in school. Having hidden disabilities, the decision was mine to make. Much like in the gay community, it is not easy deciding whether or not to come out. Among the factors running through your head is how comfortable you are as a person with a disability. There are many stages of acceptance and denial that a person can go through, and until she or he has reached at least partial acceptance of the disability, it can be difficult to tell others.

Even if you have reached a level of acceptance such that the disability is a part of who you are, there is still the social stigma to consider. It would take a lot of faith and trust in one's peers to come out about one's disabilities. I was in no position to make my disabilities public. I had never had this choice before when I was going to resource rooms: This situation advertised that I had a disability. But now, I was on my own to make this decision. I had no clue about how accepting my friends would be about my disabilities. But, that did not matter because I was not sure how comfortable I was with my disability. No one had really talked to me about what it meant to have a disability, so I tried not to think about it. The result was that my own limited understanding of my disabilities and the self-perceived stigmas about them stifled my freedom to enlighten others about this aspect of my life. Consequently, even those people to whom I felt closest could not understand the problems I had interacting in a social setting.

When it came time for applying to colleges, my options were limited. Since the school did not teach me the self-advocacy skills I would need to get accommodations in high school, I went through my classes being hindered. I received no untimed tests, no preferential seating for hearing, and no compensation for being a poor visual learner. Consequently, though my grades were good, they did not meet the standards of my first-choice university.

I had thought that I might be able to make up the difference with my extracurricular activities and the SATs. However, like with every other academic area, the accommodations I needed were not met. A few years earlier I had taken the PSATs untimed. This might seem unfair to the average student, but the average student is not affected by the time limits. As a person with a learning disability, I am affected. It has been found that the average student will receive the same score whether the SAT is timed or not. However, for the student with a learning disability, the difference between a timed and untimed test can be 200 points—whether it is because of a reading comprehension problem, a processing difficulty, or any other manifestation.

But, I did not take the PSATs under perfect conditions. Although the other students could take the test in school, I had to go to a special center an hour and a half away. If my mother did not have the time off from work, and a car, I would not have been able to take the test. Knowing these problems with the PSATs, I decided to take the SATs timed at school.

As a consequence, I did not do well. The pressure of completing the test within a time constraint that I could not meet added extreme stress. I could not process the information in the fashion and speed that was required. Thus, my first-choice college went out of my reach.

Of course, it also did not help that I did not identify myself as a person with a learning disability on my college applications. A self-disclosure on the subject, with a mention of how I had learned to succeed with the disability, might have made me a more favorable candidate. Without good advising, I did not know that disclosing my disability would be helpful. So my options came down to three schools that I really did not put much thought into when applying. I chose a large university in the northeast because my friend James was going there. As is true with much in life, I unwittingly made one of the best choices of my life. What I gained from this university I know I could not have received at the other two schools.

I reaped the benefits of my decision to attend this large northeastern university right from the beginning. At the new student orientation, I was bombarded with tests used to exempt students from certain requirements and make recommendations for classes. The foreign language requirement scared me the most. I was being told that I needed to take a foreign language, despite having taken five years of foreign languages in high school. I barely squeezed by Spanish III in high school. I knew there was no way I could pass a foreign language course at the college level. My reaction was to seek out any services that could help me. I was directed toward the Learning Disabled Student Services (LDSS). When I went over to see the director of the LDSS, I found her to be very helpful and soothing. She described my options and the actions I needed to take. This connection and support made a huge difference in my college career.

I do not know why I sought out LDSS. Having a learning disability had become a secondary thought to me while in high school, and in college it might have been the same. But this little voice inside of me said, "Check it out." This is actually contrary to what most students with an LD do when they come to college. Often, the student sees the freedom and anonymity that comes with college and uses it to become just another student instead of a student with a learning disability. However, I had my freedom in high school, and I knew it was not all it was cracked up to be.

My first challenge in college came with calculus. The problem I had did not come from the material; it came from the professor. After the first day of class, I met with my LDSS case manager, Lucas. I told him that my professor spent most of his time writing equations and facing the board as he lectured. I also informed him that the class was placed in a small, noisy room and that my professor relied on essay tests. Lucas recommended that I always sit in the front and that my tests should be untimed. In addition, my professor must turn and face his students when he is lecturing (an accommodation that would benefit all students). I did not fully understand why I had a right to ask for these accommodations, but I was grateful. Before the next class, I approached the professor and very politely asked for these accommodations. He refused. I did not know why; I did not dare question him. He was the professor, and I did not fully believe in my right to the accommodations.

Fortunately, LDSS did not take kindly to the professor's refusals. Lucas contacted the professor to see if a simple conversation could resolve the issue. What he got was a professor who was hostile toward those with disabilities. The professor claimed that he could not turn away from the board because it would deter his teaching style and that untimed tests for me would be unfair for the rest of the class. In his view, if I could not take the class without these accommodations, then I should not be in the class at all.

As I heard this, and saw the battle for accommodations drag on, I was ready to give in; LDSS was not. Lucas quickly reached his limits and turned the fight over to the director of LDSS. She played hardball with the professor, threatening to bring legal action. All I saw was that very quickly, the professor was starting to turn toward the class and, finally, I could hear everything he was saying.

Getting the accommodations for untimed tests went a little differently. Not believing that LDSS was telling the truth, the professor devised a reading test for me. The rule was simple, if I read the test at the same speed as his assistant, then I would not be eligible for the accommodation. This was a very odd and uncomfortable situation. I had to prove my right to an equal education through a reading race. Since I was being tested against a graduate student, I naturally read the test slower—as if the outcome was ever in question.

After a few weeks of arguments, threats, and this race, I received the accommodations I needed. Unfortunately, they came a few weeks after the class started, so there was some information that I missed. The end result was that I got a C in the course. But I did not care—I had survived the "professor from hell" and learned a very valuable lesson: No matter what, LDSS was always going to be there to help me through a crisis. It was a very comforting feeling.

That feeling of support is vital. As I stated, I did not understand why I had the right to ask for the accommodations. I had never asked for accommodations before, and yet I had made it through high school. I felt that I was asking for special treatment, treatment I did not really deserve. It seemed unfair to me, like I was cheating the system. No one else was asking for accommodations (as far as I could see), and they got by just fine. Why should I be different? What I did not understand at the time was that not everyone had the processing deficits that I had. So, I went through college feeling guilty about asking for a fair chance at an equal education (a feeling that has not completely gone away today).

By my sophomore year, approaching professors for accommodations had become slightly easier. Though I still did not know why I needed the accommodations, I now understood that I deserved them. I knew it was my right as an individual to an equal education, and the accommodations were the key to receiving this education. This new understanding would give me greater confidence when approaching the professors, though I must offer that any confidence is greater than what I had before. For most of my professors, it did not matter. Either as an automatic response, or as a sign of real understanding, I received the accommodations.

First semester sophomore year was the last semester I would work with Lucas. Amalia, who replaced Lucas, became one of the biggest influences on my life. While Lucas was very helpful in providing support, Amalia gave me meaning. She was the first person to stop worrying about what classes I took, and simply concentrated on me as an individual. I entered her office expecting the same routine I had developed with Lucas. I had all my syllabi ready and knew what I needed for every class. Amalia acknowledged these needs and took note of them. However, she spent most of the time discussing how my life was going and who I was as a person who happened to have a disability.

This situation forced me to change my perspective of LDSS. No longer was it a place I simply turned to for assistance in getting my needs met; now it was a place to relax and talk with a friend. Very quickly, I started to look forward to my meetings with Amalia. I would sit in her office and share what was happening with my life, both academically and socially. Never having developed a sharing relationship with my family or friends, this outlet was amazing. Amalia listened and shared in my excitement, eventually sharing parts of her life as well. She also started to teach me strategies for working with a disability. Though others had tried, she was the person who convinced me to keep an organizer. She reminded me to work in little steps and to view big social events as rewards for getting my work done. Put simply, she gave me the tools I needed to succeed as a person with a disability. Through her, I became a strong self-advocate.

The rewards came immediately. The self-awareness I gained showed in how I dealt with the professors. Though I did not fully understand how I was affected by my LD, I now had a sense of how to describe my needs, instead of just stating them. I had no problem with any of my classes.

There was one other person that would play a major role in my personal development, Catherine. She was the one serious love interest I had as an undergraduate. Fact is, she was more than a love interest: She became my partner in life for three years. She also had something no friend ever had, an understanding of what it meant for me to have a learning disability. She did not complain when I spoke in broken (hesitant) sentences or seemed to share incomplete thoughts. She understood that these were symptoms of having a learning disability. She was patient as I consistently lost my train of thought and reorganized what I was trying to say. She also helped me clearly explain what I was thinking. Not being able to easily translate my thoughts into words, I often provide people with only half of the idea in my head, thinking that what I said makes as much sense as what I was thinking. Seeing the difficulty, Catherine would help me complete my thoughts verbally by asking questions. This was a nice change from the odd looks or dismissals I usually received. Having learned how I think and believe, Catherine was also able to help me in public settings by being my translator in a rough way.

Thus, Catherine was more than my partner; she became the first person to start teaching me how to accommodate for my LD in a social setting. The more time I spent with Catherine, the more comfortable I got with meeting others. She gave me confidence and an understanding of how to adjust my approach to talking with people so that my learning disability was not as much of a social hindrance. I knew she was responsible for my more relaxed approach to talking with others, and I grew even more in love with her for it. Now that I was with her, I was not afraid to shout and make stupid jokes on a crowded street. I did not care that there were other people around, I did not notice them. All I could see was Catherine and me, thus I let myself express the fun I was having. I thought I could never be this way. I had always had problems retrieving thoughts and expressing them because of my learning disability, so I would say nothing. But now it was different. Even in a group, if I concentrated my conversation and thoughts on Catherine, the difficulties I had seemed to decrease. Words and thoughts came more easily, which led to a decrease in fear, and thus to a greater ability to express words and thoughts. For all the years I had been in a cycle of failure because of my LD, it felt good to be in a cycle of success. It seemed that I had finally found the social accommodation that I needed: Focus my conversation on one individual with whom I found it easy to talk. Through that person, I could talk with the general group.

I am going to end this essay with a movie. Movies do not usually change people's lives. However, one did for me, *F.A.T. City* by Richard Laviou. This video helps educators, parents, and friends experience what life is like with an LD through the people's natural perception of life. An awakening happened for me. As I watched the video and saw how these people acted, I saw myself. *F.A.T. City* gave me the chance to see, as an outside observer, how I viewed the world and how this view is affected by my disability. I saw how the group was quick to become accusatory, had difficulty retrieving words, and had speech that was slow and broken. I also saw how people had problems understanding the written words because of retrieval problems. Throughout the video I kept saying to myself, "This is how life is for me." Many of my life experiences became a lot clearer. I now had a personal understanding of how my disability affected me and shaped my view of the world. I was 21.

Having this door to self-awareness opened was a great relief. However, it was still hard to watch this video. I spent much of the time watching it shocked, sad, and upset. Seeing myself in many of the ways the group acted, I wondered how my life might have been different if someone had given me this understanding at an earlier age. Not only had I learned how my view of the world was distorted, but also I started to understand just how many mistakes some of my former teachers had made with me. These mistakes had negatively impacted my life, and I could not change them. It took me a while to calm down from the anger I started to feel. If only I had understood about my disability at a much earlier age, I was sure things could have been better. However, I now had the last piece of the puzzle. I felt like I finally understood who I was as a person with a learning disability. I had clinical, legal, and personal insights into my disability. I graduated from college as a complete person.

10

I Will Not Succumb to Obstacles

Kevin Marshall, Jr.

Kevin is a 21-year-old African American man who was raised in modest circumstances in a large urban center by his single mother. Strongly encouraged and lovingly disciplined by his mother, he showed early promise of academic and athletic talent, as well as a keen, competitive spirit. This spirit was nurtured at Wallings, the predominantly white magnet school he attended in his elementary school years and through engagement in community athletics in his neighborhood. Believing that exposure to his father's influence would aid him in becoming a man, he moved to Delaware to live with his father, but the visit ended disastrously after two years when his father, in fits of paranoia, regularly abused him. It was not until college that Kevin was diagnosed with dyslexia. While, in some ways, this diagnosis proved a relief and explained his poor performance in his Spanish class, he is adamant that the key to his self-identity lies not in his having a learning disability but rather in his academic and sporting successes, particularly in basketball. He will not let anything hold him back from what he wants in life. Kevin wrote this essay in his senior year.

When I began my freshman year at college, I anticipated a rigorous academic program that would challenge all my abilities. As I prepared to go off to college, I was told by many people—high school administrators, adults, and friends—how tough it would be to earn my Ivy League degree. Many people had the gall to tell me they would pray for my success! When I told my summer league basketball coach where I had decided to go to college, he was disappointed. He first told me that the Ivy League was a step down for me athletically—not as big as other schools that had recruited me, such as Temple, Stanford, Loyola, and Delaware. I think he dreamt of me playing in the NBA, but I don't think that he respected the importance that I placed on academics and the opportunity that an Ivy League education provides.

When people asked me where I decided to attend school, I was generally greeted by a look of astonishment and what I took as a warning about the difficulty of the school. When I spoke with one of my uncle's friends and told him my school of choice, he was typically surprised. He began to grill me about how much research I had done about school and whether I thought that I, as a young Black man, would be able to handle the rigor of such an education. These questions, coming from a Black man, implied that race played a role in my education; this was something that I looked to combat in college. This man went so far as to ask whether I would be able to graduate in four years. For some reason, he thought that at such a tough school, I would not be able to handle the normal course load of an average student due to the added pressures of basketball. This concern was actually legitimate at other schools where many athletes graduated a year late, if at all; but I took his concern as an insult because he knew how much I valued my education. From all of the negative feedback I received prior to going to college, I was prepared and excited to prove everyone wrong and be successful in every aspect of college life. In fact, that focus put me on a very solid academic path. Nothing would stop me from attaining my goals.

Mom

To fully understand me, you have to understand my life circumstances. I was raised in a large midwestern city by my mother and brother, Joseph. Five years my elder, Joseph had many things to teach me. Unfortunately, his lessons were mostly from what my mother calls the "school of hard knocks." From his trials and tribulations of growing up, I picked up many of the things that were acceptable and unacceptable in society at large, and within our household. My mom taught me all things valuable: right and wrong, good and bad, smart and stupid. I would not be anywhere near where I am right now without her love, support, encouragement, and friendship. Now, as an adult, my relationship with my mother has blossomed into a friendship that is deeper and more meaningful than any friendship I have with my peers. I admire her for the many things that she has accomplished, the way she has lived her life, and most importantly, the way she raised Joseph and me.

My mom showed her support by encouraging me to be serious about basketball and stay on top of my academics. She did this while maintaining a strict "iron fist" style of raising her two sons. What I mean by "iron fist" is that she demanded respect and fear from her two sons. What makes Mom amazing is that she raised my brother and me, worked, and went to school to earn a degree in criminal justice (she is now a parole officer), while staying very active in the community—she volunteers for the National Association of Black Social Workers and Toastmasters, for example. While I was in school, Mom rarely missed a parent-teacher conference, and she always helped me with my homework and taught me the value of success. Initially, it was through incentives for good work in school (she gave me a dollar for an "A") that I achieved, but eventually the pure desire to dominate in school and sports pushed me to do well.

Mom made sure that church played a large role in my life, as well. My mother and I went to church twice a week: once on Friday for choir rehearsal, and then on Sunday for Sunday school and service. We would also attend Bible studies in the middle of the week. My mother encouraged me to read the Bible every night before I went to sleep; often we would sit and read the Bible together, and she would interpret the meanings of the stories. My mother and I were always able to communicate well. She would tell me that I was wiser than my years, and she treated me as such. There were many times when she and I would get into deep conversations about her childhood. Instead of speaking to me like I was a child, she spoke to me as an adult (or as close as she could without confusing me) and I appreciated that so much that I often longed for our serious talks. My mother was different from other mothers in town in that when we talked about my father, she never spoke poorly of him, even though he wasn't there. She carefully let me know that he was a very good man who cared for me but had his own personal troubles. These discussions about my father would often end with her holding me in her arms while I sat on her lap, my head on her shoulder, crying. The crying came from my utter confusion about not having a father. As difficult as these situations were, my mother taught me to fend for myself and learn from my father's mistakes, and strive to be a good father myself someday. These sad discussions became fewer as I grew older, and I soon became independent, largely because of this hardship.

Joseph

My brother and I are very close, even to this day. Sometimes it amazes me how different we are. We are around the same height but his skin is lighter. He is also much heavier than I. Our personalities are very different, too. My brother is more pensive and emotional than me. But with his emotionality sometimes comes rage, and from this, he has shown some tendency to be violent and out of control. Joseph has always had a much more acute love of women than I. Ever since his early teens, he was deeply involved in romance and physical relationships. Through his aware-ness of sexuality and his experiences, I learned much about the opposite sex. Some-times he would have girls over at our house and would make love to them in our bedroom or my mother's bedroom. Interestingly enough, he encouraged me to watch him and learn from his sexual experiences. I don't know how the girls felt about this practice, or even if they ever saw me.

There were other important stages in each of our own personal developments that we lived out together. Joseph was very mischievous (we do have some things in common) and was in and out of trouble with Mom throughout most of his ado-lescent life. It seemed like every other day he was on "punishment," losing privi-leges such as the chance to watch television or go outside. We developed a support system for each other in these circumstances. There were times when Joseph or I was on punishment, and the other would keep lookout for our mother so that the other could still enjoy himself. It was a bit lopsided, though, because Joseph was five years older and had many more things to get into when he was on punishment.

A part of my relationship with Joseph that I do not look back upon fondly is our confrontations. Since my brother was in trouble so often during his teenage years, he was hostile, and it seemed that he thought the whole world was out to get him. Rage built up in him, and he often took it out on me. Joseph would hit me, push me, or body-slam me on a whim. There were times when I would be scared once my mother left for work, because if he and I had a disagreement, it would usually end in punches. Even with the treatment from him that I now characterize as abuse, Joseph and I have remained close. He was very supportive of me and was proud to have me as his brother. He took delight in knowing that he introduced me to basketball and that I was excelling. Instead of being envious of my accomplishments as an athlete and student, he was always one of my biggest supporters. He was not an avid ath-lete, for he was more interested in women, but he helped me to develop my love for basketball by letting me play with him and the older guys when I was small and not very good. As I got older, Joseph supported me by coming to my games. He saw my ability as a source of pride and he would challenge kids in our neighborhood to play me, showing his support for me through his confidence in my ability to beat anyone my age. Considering that my brother never excelled in school or athletics, his sup-port and pride in my accomplishments are commendable qualities.

Wallings and the Glen

Ever since I can remember, people have told me that I was smart. My mother's friends and my teachers constantly told me that I was a really "bright" or "gifted" child. After hearing that for so long, I think anyone would begin taking it as the truth. It was around fourth grade that I really began to believe it. Beginning school at Wallings was one of the most important stages in my educational development. Wallings was not just an ordinary elementary school; it was a magnet school for gifted children. Kids who were exceptionally skilled in math, science, or English would come from their respective schools part-time, once or twice a week, so they could receive some of the special advantages that Wallings had to offer. But unlike most "smart" children who lived in my city, I went to Wallings full time, because I had abilities in all of these areas. Attending Wallings was important not just because it offered accelerated programs, but, more importantly, because it was filled with a majority of White students. The racial make-up was a vital issue, mainly because of where I was raised and my own family's economic situation.

When I began attending Wallings, my family was living in the Exeter Glen townhouses, one of the rougher developments on the south side of town. We referred to our neighborhood as either "the Glen," or "Beirut." My mother was adamant that living in the Glen was merely temporary. She was not content to raise me and my brother in such a dangerous environment. The Glen was so dangerous that one day the ice cream man got robbed in broad daylight, and nobody reported anything. After he was robbed and beaten up, he abandoned his ice cream cart, and everyone in the neighborhood, including myself, went and robbed him of all his "push-pops" and ice cream sandwiches. In our demented delight, we did not think twice about the battered ice cream man, whom we all knew because he lived in the Glen. We were just happy to have some free ice cream for the next few days.

I experienced a few difficulties while living in the Glen and attending Wallings, the worst of which came from within my own community. Children my age considered me a "nerd" because I went to Wallings. Most of the kids in my neighborhood attended Barker, a neighborhood public school that was nearly 100 percent Black. This created a problem for me, because my everyday school experiences were different from those of all of my neighborhood peers. I had a very difficult time trying to integrate myself into their lives. The children in my neighborhood also had a severe problem with my mode of speech. My mother took pride in the fact that I read a lot and was blessed with the ability to speak relatively "good" English. Unfortunately, my "good" English translated to "proper" English among my neighborhood friends—which was only spoken by Whites. Because of this natural ability to speak well, my own manhood (even at a young age) was challenged often. The problem that my friends had with my English was that they felt that I was speaking "down" to them, which they took to be condescending. Later, athletics became a great equalizer and an unspoken language that earned me acceptance among my neighborhood peers.

At Wallings, I faced a different challenge—dealing with other Black children. It seemed that the few other Black children attending Wallings came from middle-class or upper-class families. These children had nice clothes, supplies, and food, and they would make fun of the clothes I wore and the fact that I received a subsidized free lunch instead of getting one packed from my mother. Their different economic situation made these kids as far removed from me socially as the White children were. Wallings's Black children made me feel uncomfortable because of my background: These children only heard bad stories about my neighborhood, stories about gun shoot-outs and gangs. The thought of driving through my part of town invoked fear in both the White children and the middle-class Black children at Wallings.

At Wallings, I found myself increasingly motivated by competition with other children. I refused to let either the White children or the privileged Black children do better than me. I was in a precarious situation because I competed very hard to be the first done with assignments and the person with the highest average. I just wanted to be the best at everything. Along with this quest to be the best student in class, I was also consumed with the desire to be liked. These divergent thoughts led me to be quite a problem for teachers: the best student, the first one done, and the class clown. I received very good grades, but would also get bad comments from teachers about how I disturbed the class and needed to take my education more seriously.

After living in the Glen for nearly three years, we were able to move out and into a house. I learned a lot from the Glen. That was the poorest that we had ever been in our lives, and it has never been that bad for me again. As a child, you seldom realize your situation until someone points it out for you. I didn't know I talked proper until people told me. I didn't know that it was a problem not to have your father at home until my peers at school told me about their family lives. I didn't notice that it was not cool to wear your brother's old clothes until people made me see that. I left my naiveté in the Glen and was well battle-tested. The Glen did a good job of helping me prepare for the world. Forget New York! If you can make it in Beirut, you can make it anywhere.

Moving to our new house was a monumental moment in my life. It was a nice white house with brown trim and a huge backyard where I could play football, kickball, or other games. One reason why moving into our house was so important to my life was that it gave me the chance to get involved in community athletics. After we moved in, many children in the community invited me to the local gym at the Bickford School, where I made some friends who took me in and let me become a part of their circle. I was introduced to the director of the gym, Mr. Ostler, the one man who single-handedly sparked my great love for basketball. Mr. Ostler was a middle-aged Black man, short, heavy set, and very authoritative. He took me in very quickly and got me involved with athletic teams and all that Bickford School had to offer. He placed me on his youth basketball team even though I was almost two years too young to play. He allowed me to come to that gym and play and work with him even though I didn't attend the school.

Eventually, thanks to Mr. Ostler, I was welcomed into the community by all the children and local adults. Mr. Ostler gave me a nickname, Lefty, which people in town still call me to this day. I was the only left-handed kid in the neighborhood. I didn't know the advantages that followed from being left-handed, but later I found out it paid dividends. Once I began playing basketball for Mr. Ostler, he started letting me come to the gym to work out even on days when the gym was closed, or when most other students were not allowed to play. He helped me begin to love the game and realize all of the enjoyment that can come from playing. He also did a great job of motivating kids. He would curse, grab your arm, or yell if he thought it would help. He always had me shooting, and let me know that I had a nice shot, which I should continue to use in games against my friends. He helped me to develop confidence at an early age. Mr. Ostler also used strict discipline; through his style of coaching and teaching, I developed a real toughness, which, accompanied by my confidence, helped me develop into an exceptional grade school athlete. Soon, I became a well-respected youth basketball player. My name began to appear in the newspaper, and my abilities began to be noticed by junior high school and high school coaches. When I was in fifth grade, I was selected to play on the few youth all-star teams, which toured the state, playing in tournaments. My advancement in basketball and subsequent respect and recognition came quickly. Within a year and a half, my abilities had firmly planted me into the basketball world for good.

This change in location to the South Side did not change my schooling. I was still attending Wallings. I was doing much better in school by the time we moved to the South Side. My mother had been fed up by my classroom antics and vowed not to let me be disruptive in school. At this point I was becoming a much better student. I was developing great interest in music and mathematics. As far as music went, my mother made sure that I used my voice, which she loved enormously. I was now singing the lead in the church choir. I had a personal love for mathematics that was uncommon among my peers. Mathematics became a real interest for me, and I began loving the statistics of professional basketball and football. I took to reading the newspapers and finding out many various, random statistics. My favorite kind of statistics included how many points per game Isiah Thomas scored, along with how many assists he recorded in each game. I began calculating his points, rebounds, and assists just for fun. I knew everything there was to know about Isiah Thomas's statistics because he was my favorite player. Soon I began learning the statistics of all of the Detroit Pistons and Lions. I would read the newspaper every day to learn more about my favorite teams and my favorite players.

Around this same time, I started to experience trouble reading. My problem was not with comprehension, but speed. My grammar was very good, and I didn't really experience difficulties with the English courses in school. My problem was that everyone in the class could read faster than me, even the children I considered myself to be much smarter than. When I was younger, my mother had made sure that I did plenty of reading. But this trend reversed itself as I became frustrated with my slow reading level. Our class would usually go to recess once we finished our readings. Therefore, students would often race to see who could finish reading first so that he or she could be the first person out to recess. My competitive nature mixed with my slow reading ability soon led me to begin cheating on the reading and thereby cheating myself. This cheating hurt me in various ways: The most important way was that I was no longer taking my time and learning from the readings. I was rushing through my work and beginning to be satisfied with only comprehending bits and pieces instead of learning the whole thing. My frustration continued to mount. I was not at the top of my class in reading anymore, which made me frustrated and ashamed, considering that I was at the head of the class in all other subjects. I wasn't sure where this deficiency was coming from, but I soon learned that it was something over which I had no control.

Delaware and Dad

I had just finished my final year of elementary school when it was time for me to decide whether I wanted to live with my father in Delaware, or if I wanted to stay in Minnesota with Mom. The decision was tough, but I felt that I wanted a change and to see different things, so I decided to move to Delaware and take some time to be raised by a man. The experience that I would gain from the two and a half years I spent living with my father would definitely become one of the most important learning experiences in my life. When I got to Delaware, I had to adapt to a new set of circumstances. I had planned on living with my father, becoming closer, and catching up on the time we lost while I was growing up. When I arrived, I was greeted at my father's home by his "girlfriend." I was surprised to learn that she was living with us also. Initially, I was not happy to hear this because, as I had stated before, I wanted this time for me and my father to bond. But his girlfriend soon became a good resource since my father's work schedule didn't permit him to be around as much as we would have liked.

Actually, my father was not around much at all. In hindsight, I wonder why he wanted me to come and live with him at all when he did not have much time to spend with me. My father worked a very strange shift at the post office—from around 4 P.M. until 1 A.M.—and he had to commute 30 minutes both ways. On an average day, I would get on the bus around 7:15 in the morning, without seeing my father. After school, I would head home and grab some food before going out to play basketball. I would stay outside and play until it was dark, coming in to eat and do my homework. After finishing my homework, I would watch television until I went to bed. Because of his schedule and mine, it would not be uncommon for me to not see my father for three or four days in a row. Usually, on the weekend, I would see him on Saturday and Sunday. These days were the most important of the week for me because I could see him for an extended amount of time. He usually had a day off on the weekend, but only every other weekend. From this description, it is pretty easy to see that the dynamics of my relationship with my father were not exactly what I had expected before I moved to Delaware to be raised by him. I only lived with my father for two and a half years, but the brief time was enough to make an incredible impression on me.

There were many factors that eventually drove me away from my father's house. One factor was living with my father's girlfriend and her son. After I had been with my father for less than a month, they sent for her son, and we all lived together in my father's apartment. I had trouble dealing with the fact that I had moved from Minnesota to live with two other random people in my father's life. I had envisioned so much more. Living with my father's girlfriend and her son was miserable. She was a recluse and hardly ever left her room. She and I never had a conversation longer than two or three sentences for the whole two and a half years we lived together. Her son was just as weird as she was. They spent a lot of time together, which left me hanging out by myself. Very bitter about my predicament, I grew angry about my whole home situation. I never came home except to eat, and soon, I tried my best to get food elsewhere so I didn't have to go back to that uncomfortable house. The only thing I had to look forward to was the weekend when I could see my father. These were good times, spent playing basketball or just hanging out at the mall. These weekend times were what I was living for while I was staying with my father. But they weren't enough.

Times became too rough when my father began becoming paranoid about everything. I think his paranoia developed due to his relapse into drug abuse, even though I never saw him do it. My father began asking me in private whether I had slept with his girlfriend. She had become pregnant, and he thought the baby might be mine. He claimed that he knew that I had a strong sex drive and that I spent a lot of time with her. He figured that we had slept together, and he would reason with me that if I would just admit it to him, I wouldn't get in trouble (little did he know that I thought she was unattractive). He became paranoid about everything else as well. He thought that I had stolen money from him on numerous occasions. He also thought that other men had been coming over while he and I were not home.

Soon, his paranoia turned into violence. He would come home after work at two or three in the morning and come into my room and beat me if he thought I had been with his girlfriend. He soon became violent all the time and would hit me for almost any reason. Once, after receiving my report card, he sat his girlfriend, her son, and me down at the dinner table and read my report card. The card said I had received straight A's but that I was being too social in class. Upon reading that comment, he proceeded to punch me in the face in front of the whole "family." This was especially traumatic because my father was generally one of the sweetest and most compassionate men that I knew. I internalized this abuse and became deeply ashamed of all that I was doing. I vowed to get myself straight. But no matter what I tried, it didn't work. It was not destined to work. My father continued to come home from work, obviously frustrated at life, and take it out on me by waking me up and beating me. This was beginning to happen rather frequently, more than four times a week for a few months. This calmed down as the year progressed and I learned that my father's girlfriend was pregnant. Before she had the child, she and my father decided to get married. After their marriage, the beating began again. The premise for this new wave of beatings was that my father believed that he was sterile from repeated drug use. From this he concluded that the child that his wife was carrying was mine, since it had our mutual blood type. I think he was going to continue to beat me until he talked me into admitting that the child was mine. That was something that I would never admit because it wasn't true. I found it interesting that he took out his frustration and confusion on me and never on his wife, who would have been an adulteress according to his logic, or her son. Eventually, I became more and more scared by my father's accusations. I saw that he sometimes came home drunk, and I thought that he might eventually hurt me badly. I told my mother what my father was saying (but not what he was doing in terms of hitting me). She ordered me to move out of that house and got me to live with my aunt and uncle in Delaware.

Learning Disability

I was first diagnosed with dyslexia in college. Dyslexia comes in many different forms, and mine is auditory. The disability makes it difficult to hear and recite, read problems, and digest speech quickly. For me, Spanish recitation sessions were problematic because they involve call-and-response. I also had problems reading the language and comprehending at an acceptable rate. When I was first diagnosed with the disability, I felt that a weight had been lifted from my back. I had been having a terrible time in Spanish class, and I was becoming almost depressed with the thought of not being able to do well in language class. While trying to learn Spanish, I feared that perhaps I was not academically "up to par" with the rest of my classmates. But learning that many of the problems that I encountered were actually not caused by my lack of intelligence or lack of effort, but by a learning problem that I could not control, helped to alleviate some of my fears. Language learning was a stumbling block that I was not able to overcome until I was correctly diagnosed with dyslexia.

I remember sitting in a small office with the test administrator. I sat calmly as she explained to me all of the types of things that I would tend to have problems with due to my learning disability: reading quickly, learning languages, taking timed tests, remembering, hearing and responding in normal conversation. Honestly, I didn't think that all of the problems were applicable to me. I did have problems with languages, and I certainly did not read fast, but I didn't have all of the problems she listed. This made me ask her whether she had made the appropriate diagnosis. She made it clear to me that not all of the symptoms would present themselves in my life, but according to the tests, these were some of the things that I was likely to struggle with, and I accepted that analysis.

She then told me to meet with my academic advisor, Edith MacGill, who put me totally at ease. She described to me all of the things that come along with my learning disability, but she also told me about the things that it did not limit, such as computation, reading at a normal pace, and any form of comprehension. She made it clear that even with this diagnosis, I would have no problem leading a normal life and continuing with my education in any way that I saw fit. She told me about the various accommodations that can be made for people with learning disabilities. There was the extra time on timed tests. There were extensions that were sometimes given to students who had problems writing at a particularly high rate. There was also an opportunity for students with learning disabilities to come to the professor more often for help with comprehension. I did not like the image that these accommodations represented. The last thing that I wanted from the testing was to learn that I was needy. I did not want to seem different from any other student. In fact, it became my mission to be as good as any other student without accommodations until I found my learning disability too much of an obstacle. I did not want to be a needy student who used his learning disability as a crutch when times were hard or when there was something that I did not understand.

Once I was diagnosed with a learning disability, I found no reason to communicate this regularly, since I didn't feel it would play any tangible role in my life. I also associate some shame with having a learning disability. Even though I recognize that it is not a fault, nor does it reflect on the kind of person I am or on my intelligence, there is still a part of me that feels that telling people that I have a learning disability could shape the way they view me. This makes sense when I consider my own preconceived notions about disabilities. As a child, it was very shameful to be in the learning disabled classes or to be considered "retarded" in any form. Because of this, I feel that being diagnosed as learning disabled earlier in my life could have been more harmful than helpful. This is especially true since my disability did not drastically affect my academic achievement until I was in college. And even though I now know a lot more about learning disabilities and recognize that they are nothing to be ashamed of, I have a hard time explaining to people that I have a disability because of my own personal association with disabilities.

On the other hand, I am open to offering people my disability history when someone speaks about obstacles that they face. It feels good to let people know that there are sometimes invisible obstacles that can hold you back. At these times I like to let people, especially children or family, know that they can overcome any obstacle. People are often surprised when I tell them about my disability. But these opportunities to share are not frequent. I will use it sometimes when I am lecturing to children at basketball camps and clinics. In defining myself, I have never let the diagnosis of my learning disability play a role. Having a learning disability is only a small part of who I am. And even though the disability explains some of the frustrations that I have experienced academically, I refuse to let it stand in the way of my attempts to achieve success. Much more key to my self-identification are my achievements and my goals. I take pride in my athletic abilities and how far they have taken me, helping me to get into college and be successful. I am also equally proud of my academic achievements, which have allowed me to attend a prestigious school and reap the benefits and rewards of determination and hard work.

I put forth an honest effort and I try to do my best without succumbing to the obstacles. I think I can credit this attitude to how basketball has trained me to discipline myself and to only focus on weaknesses in order to improve them. As a junior high and high school student, I was not very good at using my right hand; I couldn't make lay-ups and couldn't dribble well with it. With that problem in mind, I spent one summer going to the park every morning before work and just dribbling full court with my right hand and making lay-ups. By the end of the summer, I could go full court and add two or three moves in between and still use my right hand to lay the ball in. From this persistence came an advantage: I could now use my right hand well enough to run fast and see my teammates open on the court. The ability to do that with both hands became quite a weapon. From that example and others, it is easy to see how my work ethic has carried over to my performance in the classroom. It is easy for me to gather inner strength and determination because I am used to pushing myself to work hard and be competitive. I try to be the best, which is why I have trouble accepting that a learning disability makes me worse off than another student. That is probably why I have not and will not take full advantage of any of the accommodations that have been made for me. That is almost like taking a head start in a game. I wouldn't feel comfortable doing such a thing.

Basketball is something that I hold very dear to my heart. Through my sport I have been able to work through various tough life situations. Having been born to a loving mother and an estranged father, basketball offered me the camaraderie and love that my life was sometimes lacking. It also offered me an opportunity to vent my life frustrations through immersing myself in competition, and that competitive spirit has carried me a long way. Through athletics, I have found a way to cope with frustration: by redirecting my focus and by learning to learn. Being a student of the game, you learn that sometimes you will win and sometimes you will lose. Most important is your reaction to competition: what you do next, what you take from the win or loss, how you learn from it. Learning to learn is important because once you can do that, improvement is virtually limitless. You may sometimes be disappointed, but you can always bounce back. From basketball I have learned to fight and to battle back from virtually any obstacle. I won't bow down to competition in any form, whether it is Michael Jordan on the basketball court or a learning disability in the classroom. My approach to these situations leaves me feeling confident that wherever life leads me, I will be just fine.

11

Learning to Raise My Hand

Kelly Miskell

Kelly is a 22-year-old, upper-middle-class, white woman, nearing the end of her senior year as a psychology major at a large northeastern state university. When tested for learning disabilities toward the end of her tenth grade year, the examining psychologist detected a language-based disability that limited her capacity to reason abstractly, to recall information she had learned, and to effectively process large amounts of new information, such as when reading from textbooks or attending lectures.

In this essay, Kelly tells an often painful—but clearly conceived and morally edifying—story of damaged self-esteem. This damage originated with her difficulties in learning, but eventually made her vulnerable to emotional abuse and sexual victimization. Kelly's voice is innocent, wise, and deeply familiar. She carefully examines the hurt she has suffered, distills from it a personal meaning, and outlines a future for herself grounded in a commitment to teaching others with learning disabilities.

To be completely honest, I did not want to continue my education any further than high school, up until the day I graduated. I simply wanted to become a hair dresser, get married, and have kids. I know it sounds pathetic, but I always loved doing my friends' hair and makeup, and I have always loved children. So I sort of had this plan that I could be happy doing those things for the rest of my life. Well, I had little or no chance of starting that plan right out of high school, because my family, friends, and teachers had higher expectations of me. So I gave into the pressure and applied to different colleges, and to my surprise I was actually accepted by a few.

As an LD student in college, I have had to work very hard to accept that I am different. I am not the average student, and definitely not an exceptional one. I study very hard for my exams, and very often don't get anything higher than C's. I look at other people in my classes who ace all the exams and make it seem so easy. This can be really upsetting, because people look at me like I didn't prepare myself, or I don't try hard enough. It is also discouraging because I know that when I graduate, employers are going to look at my transcript and think I'm a total slacker. This could not be further from the truth. I may not be a dean's list student, and I probably won't ever be that, but I know I try my best at things and that is worth something.

How do I feel about my learning disability? I was sitting in class today taking notes, and I found someone looking at my notebook. Then I found myself covering up my notes because I was embarrassed that my spelling was so poor, and I thought my notes were too in-depth. This is a pretty basic example of something I go through often, being a learning disabled person. When I am in class, I feel the need to write every little detail down, because I find it helps me recall the lecture better. Also I have a difficult time understanding text books, so if I don't have complete and accurate notes, I tend to doubt myself when studying. I guess you could say I am a very anxious student, and school does not come easy to me at all. For as long as I can remember, I have struggled with school. I feel that I am not within the "norm" and that if someone were to look at my notes, they would think I was strange.

I guess this leads to my insecurity, which is another huge issue for me, one that I feel directly stems from my learning disability. I know that it did not come from my family, for I have been blessed with a very loving and supportive family. The thing that affected me most negatively when I was growing up was my schooling and issues around school. This is not to say that these problems did not lead to other problems, but initially school was the major issue. At times, I've been afraid that the damage caused by my LD is almost irreversible. I was not diagnosed with an LD until my junior year in high school. Because I had been tested a number of times before without anything being detected, I believed that the only explanation for why I did badly in school was that I was just plain stupid. Perhaps a better term would be *not intelligent*. I mean, I knew I was not retarded, but I also knew I was not smart like my friends. Growing up believing that you are not as good as your peers, in any aspect, takes a toll on a person.

I can remember being in the first grade and getting moved into the "slow" class. At the time I did not know it was the slow class. I thought I was being moved because my teacher used to make me cry (she made everybody cry). Much later on, when I found out that I had been in slower classes in elementary school, I blamed the system for me being stupid and thought that if they had kept me in the faster classes I would never have had problems in school. Honestly, I feel that everything negative in my life is either directly or indirectly related to my learning disability, probably because it was detected so late in my life. All the bad feelings I had about myself were never challenged until I was 17 years old. I truly believed I was abnormal and that I was not going to make it in life.

Because I was so insecure, I allowed myself to accept second best in everything. I never had the self-esteem to stand up for myself, and make my feelings known. I felt like I was different, and I was lucky even to *have* friends and boyfriends. I can remember my parents telling me I was beautiful, and me thinking *Yeah, right, they're just saying that so I'll feel better about myself. I know I'm different.* My friends today tell me I am worth so much more than what I accept, but I do not see that. I still have to fight with myself about the fact that I am a good person and that I do have a lot to offer.

I can remember an incident in the twelfth grade, not long after I was diagnosed. It was a nice day in September, and it was the start of my final year in high school. The first bell rang, and I remember meeting up with my friends in the upstairs hallway so we could all walk to first period class together: psychology.

The room was packed with students. It was the first day of classes, so everybody was a little rambunctious and excited to see everyone. When the teacher, Mr. Peeps, walked in, the room quieted down, and the attention turned to him. He was a thin man, average in height, with dark gray hair and big blue droopy eyes. His face was a bit aged with wrinkles. I would guess he was probably in his late fifties or early sixties. When he spoke, his voice was raspy, like that of a smoker. He seemed like a "cool" teacher; I think he told a couple of jokes to break the ice. I remember him making degrading remarks about women, but he did so in a joking way, sort of to get a rise out of us.

About 15 minutes into the class, he was talking about *archetypes*. I really had no idea what it meant, because I had never heard the word before. That is when he walked up to me, in the front row, and asked me to give an example of a mother archetype. I thought he was kidding, and responded with a confused smile and said, "I don't know." It was then that he got in my face and started screaming at me. He was so close, I could feel his spit hit my face. He told me not to sit in his classroom and act like a typical blond bimbo. He told me not to embarrass him or the rest of his class with my lack of intelligence. I could feel my face get very hot and very red. I think that may have been the most embarrassing moment in my life. The entire classroom was dead silent, and Mr. Peeps went on to yell at me. When he was finished, I just sort of sat there and tried not to cry, while he went over to the window, I guess to cool down. I remember I would not turn around to face any of my friends or peers, because I was so completely mortified. I just kept thinking about what I could have done to deserve that. To this day I do not know what caused that episode, and I suppose I never will.

After the class was over and the bell rang, I went directly to my guidance counselor's office. I remember walking through the hallways, not stopping to say hello to anyone, fighting to hold back the tears. It was probably a 90-second walk to the guidance office, but it felt an hour. I just could not get there fast enough. I think I stopped in every bathroom I passed, just to catch my breath and try to calm down. When I finally reached the office, I went directly to my counselor and told her to get me out of that class. She asked what happened, but I refused to tell her. She could see how upset I was and did not really press me on the issue. She did act concerned, but told me I could not get out of the class because nothing else would fit my schedule. So I left that office with full intentions of never going back to Mr. Peep's class and taking an F in his course. I don't know exactly why I would not tell anyone about the incident, but I guess I thought it was my fault. I mean, I had never been yelled at like that. I think I was also very embarrassed and did not feel like discussing the whole thing.

I think it was about a week after the incident that I was called down to the principal's office. This was a huge deal, because nobody ever met with the principal, unless they did something very bad. I could not imagine what the principal would want to see me for, because by this time, I had pretty much forgotten about Mr. Peeps. I had not been back to his class and did not really care about it anymore. When I walked into Mr. Nixon's office, I remember feeling like I was going to throw up. I remember Mr. Nixon being sort of stern, and, yes, I was intimidated immediately. He sat behind his desk and never once cracked a smile; he simply kept a very neutral look on his face. So I remained paranoid, until he finally let me in on what was going on.

He asked me to tell him about an incident that had occurred with one of my teachers. I asked him what he was talking about. It was weird, like he knew what happened, but would not tell me so until I told him first. Well, after we played this little game for a while, I started to figure out that he was referring to Mr. Peeps, and he wanted the details. All I could think while I was sitting there, was *How the hell did he find out about this?* He knew word-for-word what was said to me in that classroom that day, and he was not pleased about it at all.

The confusing part comes in here. I am not clear as to whether he was pissed off that a student was treated that way, or if he was pissed off that the high school could get bad publicity for it. I mean, the way he handled the incident is definitely a little sketchy. There I was sitting in his office, trembling for Christ's sake, and he was bargaining with me. He told me, if I promised to keep the incident quiet, he would waive me from the five credit requirement, meaning he would let me out of psychology, and still let me graduate. He told me that Mr. Peeps would not return to the high school the following year, and that both he and the school offered their apologies. Whatever!!!

I accepted that offer, and walked away from the whole thing forever. Well, until I got a little older, and realized what bullshit it was. I've never done anything about the situation, but I have thought a great deal about it, and why it was so wrong. I mean, I was 16 years old at the time, and I was manipulated by a school principal, rather than helped.

You see, I had never had a positive self-image of myself, academically or in any other way. I thought I was stupid, fat, ugly, and worthless for a long time. So when Mr. Peeps told me I was a "typical blond bimbo," I guess he was confirming my negative view of myself. Then, when the principal of the school just sort of swept it under the rug, he made it all seem unimportant. Nobody once said to me that those things were not true, and nothing was done to show me that his actions were wrong. Therefore, I was allowed to accept that kind of treatment from a teacher. A Teacher! You know, those people who are smart, intelligent, and highly educated! Yes, that is who confirmed to me that I was worthless.

Later that year, I discussed the incident with my English teacher, Ms. Faskin, and she had some really interesting points to make about Mr. Peeps. She was a young, energetic, and creative teacher with a great deal of passion. I trusted her like I trusted my best friends, and I suppose that is why I talked with her about the many different problems I had in high school. She was always willing to listen and would do her best to help in any way she could. She never ever made me feel inferior or uncomfortable in any way. She looked at me like a person, not as some immature teenager.

Anyway, Ms. Faskin told me about an occasion when she was at a school committee meeting, and Mr. Peeps yelled at her and said something about her feminist opinions, and that they were ridiculous. I guess he really has a problem with women who stand up for themselves or their sex. Ms. Faskin had a theory about why Mr. Peeps exploded on me the way that he did. She felt it was probably because of my height (I am about six feet tall) and my appearance. She felt that I probably intimidated him, and he needed to feel superior right from the start.

Sick is the only word that comes to mind. I mean the fact that he made degrading remarks about feminists right in front of the school committee board says to me that the members of the education board had to have been aware of his views, and they still allowed him to teach young students. Perhaps, if actions were taken about his remarks at that meeting, I would have never been put in the position I was put in. I also heard rumors about other students making complaints about Mr. Peeps later on that year; to no surprise, they were all women.

It's funny, because I am a strong believer in the phrase "everything happens for a reason, and things works out for the best." So I sometimes wonder what good may have come out of this whole thing for me, and why it all may have happened. The only thing that I can come up with is that it taught me a lesson. I realize now how political school systems actually are. I mean, for a long time I really thought teachers and administrators were kind of "god" figures. I mean, here we have these people who get paid practically nothing, yet they put up with so much. I thought if you were a teacher, you really cared about kids and took a genuine interest in their well-being. Apparently, this is not so, in some cases.

I guess the most ironic thing about all of this is that when I went back to visit my high school the following year, I walked by Mr. Peeps in the hallway. I guess he did not leave after all!

Looking back on the whole incident, I wish I had made a bigger deal over it. It's just that, back then, I was unclear as to whether or not the whole thing was really that bad, and if it was worth making a big deal over. I honestly feel now that if I had fought back then, it would have helped me become a stronger person a whole lot sooner.

You see, I do not really know where I stand in the area of autonomy. I do know that I depend heavily on others in all areas of my life, and I seek approval in everything I do. I do not know if this means I lack a sense of autonomy, or if I am just extremely insecure. I guess it is a little bit of both, but I have trouble distinguishing between the two.

Because I am a learning disabled student and I have had a tremendous amount of difficulty in school, my parents have had to really push me and encourage me in life. I cannot give my parents enough credit for all the good that they have done. However, they have tried so very hard to boost my self-esteem and instill confidence in me, they have, in a way, been a crutch through my entire life. You see, I was always a very quiet girl, and I am still a very quiet young woman, and because of that, my parents have very often had to be my voice. They were and are the ones who speak up for me when I cannot do it myself. They, in a sense, control me, because I sometimes do not know how to control myself. I lack the confidence to make my own decisions, and depend heavily on them to guide me in the right direction. I am grateful for the motivation they give, as well as the confidence that they have in me, but I feel it is really starting to have a negative effect.

Now that I am 22 years old, I feel I should be making my own decisions and my own mistakes. I mean, I realize my parents are not going to be around forever, and I need to start functioning on my own. But, because my parents have always had a say in everything I do, it is really difficult for them to back off. I do not know how to make them understand where I am coming from. I know they are acting out of love. How can that be a bad thing?

I just feel like a little girl stuck inside of a big girl body. I want to be able to stand up for myself and speak my mind when I have something to say. But because I am so shy and insecure, I tend to keep my mouth shut. I really am pathetic in many ways, and I would like to change that about myself. But because I have never been pushed to solve a problem on my own, I lack the ability to know how to do so. My parents have always been there to help me through the problems I had with school, teachers, friends, or anything. It is like my parents have taken over for that little voice inside my head that wants to yell out. It doesn't yell out, because it has never had to. Mom and Dad always yelled out for it.

I'm certain that my insecurity has played a major role in my experiences with men. I feel these experiences have a great deal of significance in terms of who I am today. This is an extremely personal area of my life, which I do not share with just anyone. Through time and healing, I have come to accept the things that have happened to me. I do not know if I will ever be "normal" again, in terms of having a healthy relationship with a man, but I feel writing about it might be a helpful step. O.K., here goes!

It was a very exciting day for me, the day I entered junior high school. I had a new hairdo, a new outfit, and was about to meet lots of new friends. Well, it turns out I do not really remember much else about that day, except that it was the day I met Steven. Steven was a tall kid with blue eyes and blond hair. He was not your average-looking seventh grader, but then again, neither was I. We were both very mature-looking for our ages. It was seventh period English class. He sat diagonally in front of me, near my friends Mary and Cynthia. Shortly after class began, the teacher told us to look around and introduce ourselves to each other. Steven turned around, took one look at me, made a face, and told me I was not cool. He told Mary and Cynthia that they were cool. I know it sounds ridiculous, but that is what he did. I hated him. We hated each other. We fought pretty much every day for that entire year, and I mean *fought!* The worst thing was that we had a lot of common friends, and it was hard to avoid him. I really cannot explain why he hated me so much, because he did not even know me. Naturally I hated him because he was so mean to me.

So the end of the year came around, and for some odd reason, he started being nicer to me. I guess I liked his nice side, and I took to it very quickly. By the end of the summer, we were pretty good friends, and I had a total crush on him. Looking back on it now, I think I liked him because he was the only boy in the class who was taller than I was. I mean, all through elementary school, boys made fun of me because of my height, and none of them ever had any interest in me. So now I had finally met a guy who I did not have to look down on.

Anyway, the beginning of the school year rolled around, and everybody more or less knew that I liked Steven. I remember being at a school Halloween dance. My gym teacher got word that I had a crush on Steven and immediately tried to play matchmaker. He bought Steven a Pepsi, and in return, Steven had to ask me to dance. I can remember that dance as if it happened yesterday. My heart was pounding, and I could hardly breathe. It was the first time I had ever been asked to dance by a boy, let alone a boy I really liked. I can remember feeling so happy and so secure in his arms. I know it sounds pathetic, but it was just such a good feeling. Kind of like that feeling you only get a few times in your life—like a first kiss. You know, your stomach does like thirty thousand flips in .2 seconds, and your whole body just sort of goes numb. I remember that moment so well, because it was the first time I ever got that feeling, and I loved it.

Well, not much happened after that dance; we remained friends just as we had been before. I figured I had made a big deal out of nothing and continued having a secret crush on him. About a month after the dance, I was over at my friend Amy's house, and Steven was there with a few of his friends. We were all watching a movie, and Steven and I were sitting together on a small couch. He was being really flirtatious that night, and I remember feeling very anxious and wondering what it all meant.

Later that night, Steven went upstairs to Amy's room and did not come down. Amy asked me to go upstairs and retrieve him, and I did. Little did I know I was about to get my first kiss. Steven took my hand and stood really close to me. *Holy shit! He is going to kiss me! Oh my God, I don't know how to kiss! What the Hell am I going to do?* Once he started to kiss me, I had the same feeling I had at the dance, and I liked that feeling. I think we kissed for a while, a long while, and then went downstairs. He continued to be really nice all night, and it seemed as though he really might like me, and I felt like the luckiest girl in the world.

Monday morning came, and we were all back in school after a great weekend—or so I thought! Steven ignored me all day and ended up asking some other girl out. I was miserable for a while but still continued to like him. I do not know why I kept up this stupid infatuation. I think it was because of the rush I got when

I was with him. He was the first person who made me feel those lovey-dovey things, and I guess I thought he was the only person who ever could.

By the end of the year, he had broken up with his girlfriend, and I think I was again convenient for him. We spent a lot of time together and fooled around more than I care to remember. He was nice to me when he wanted to be, and he spent time with me when he wanted. He pretty much treated me like shit and took advantage of me in any way that he could.

The summer before the ninth grade, I really started to hate Steven. I was finally over my ridiculous obsession, and I had no need for him in my life. So, of course, he tried like hell to make me fall for him again. Well, it worked. At a school dance that year, he resurrected those feelings in me when he asked me to dance, and he held me tight. He asked me to be his girlfriend, and I melted.

Well, I had held him on a pedestal for so long, I imagined him to be so much more than he actually was. We dated for about two months, and I broke up with him. I think I enjoyed the games and the excitement more than I enjoyed the relationship that was forming. About a month after we broke up, I began to miss him and tried to win him back. He made it very difficult for me and really showed no interest until springtime. We ended up dating again and got very close during the summer. Things were absolutely wonderful. We really cared about one another and for the first time ever, treated each other with real respect.

When we entered high school, the real heartache started. About three weeks after school began, Steven broke up with me and started dating another girl. I was completely devastated and could not understand why he would do such a thing.

As the year went on, I continued to like Steven and remained depressed about losing him. I tried to move on. I remember one time that a senior guy, Tom, asked me out, and I accepted. It was really quite exciting, because he was so much older, and he was very good looking. I remember I really kind of liked him, and for the first time since Steven broke up with me, I felt really good. Tom and I dated a few times, and we had a great time together. He was not only tall, dark, and handsome, he was curious and thoughtful. The last time Tom and I went out, he tried to go a little further than kiss me, and I was not comfortable with that. Although Tom apologized time and time again, I could not go back to him. You see, I had found out that Steven told Tom I was easy, and he could get a piece of ass from me.

I really do not know why Steven would say something like that—he was the only person I had ever been with, and he certainly did not even come close to sleeping with me. Anyway, Steven told me that Tom did not really like me, and I was making an ass out of myself by dating him. Steven remained involved in my life and everything I did. Despite the fact that he had girlfriends, he would always find time to call me and fool around with me and convince me that he cared for me.

Well, I guess it was inevitable that Steven would be "my first" and God, do I regret that. Things progressively got worse. Because I allowed Steven to treat me like a piece of shit, that is exactly what he did. If I ever tried to stand up for myself and get away from him, he would convince me that I was overreacting, and he would tell me that I meant something to him. He used to say that our relationship was special, because we were friends first and then lovers. God, it makes me sick to think back on the whole thing.

Well, as time went on, not much changed. I remained obsessed with him, and he continued to play his game with me. He would date other girls, but I could not date any other guys. He stuck his nose into every relationship I ever tried to have with another guy and made sure that I would always be there for him to fall back on. He cheated on every girlfriend he ever had, and I waited around for him to do it. I know in my heart that he was not good for me, but whenever I got the strength to move on he would sweet-talk his way back. It was like a bad sickness that I would not get rid of.

Because I was not familiar with being treated with respect, I did not know what it took to get respect. All I wanted was for a guy to like me and care about me. I had such a poor view of myself. I got hurt a lot by other guys, who listened to Steven's stories about me. Because Steven made everybody aware of how painfully easy and pathetically unstable I was, a lot of guys did their best to get what Steven was getting.

Well, after a while, I gave up on the idea of ever having a real boyfriend and just, sort of, stuck with Steven. I figured, when I got out of high school, I would meet someone else. Wrong!

When I went off to college, Steven initiated us keeping in touch. My junior year of college, I transferred to his school, and that is when things got absolutely terrible. He treated me like an absolute whore, worse than he ever did in the past. He would call my friends in the middle of the night to find out where I was, and then he would come drag me out of my friends' houses. It was ridiculous; he was acting like a complete jealous boyfriend, only he and I were not a couple. I cannot lie, I did allow it because I still really cared for him. I guess I was happy with any sort of attention from him, even if it was negative. It was the same old, same old, until finally, one day, he just stopped calling. Nothing happened to make him stop calling—he just did. I would call him and he would tell his roommates to say he was not there. And he would never call back.

I was devastated. I could not understand why he was avoiding me. I went into a major state of depression and would only leave my bed to go to the bathroom or to vomit. I was not eating, not sleeping, not going to class, nothing. I thought about killing myself quite often during that semester, and it is really quite scary to think back on. I cannot blame all that depression on Steven, but he was a definite part of it.

In a nutshell, my relationship with Steven lasted about eight years. During that time, I allowed him to control and dominate me. He did a great job at making me believe I was not worth anything. He had all the confidence, and I had none. I would like to blame the whole thing on immaturity and naiveté, but it goes deeper than that. Steven was such a huge part of my life for so long, and my relationship with him will always affect me. For eight crucial years, I was treated like shit. I had no self-respect or self-esteem, and I am still dealing with those issues today.

But there's more to my bad experience with men than just Steven. Probably the worst of it happened during the summer before my senior year in high school.

There was a party at my friend Jennifer's house, and some other friends and I decided to go. Jennifer had an older brother named Rick. He was a year older than us, and he was the captain of our high school football team. I had always had a little crush on him—I guess everybody knew it. It was really quite stupid, because he did not even know who I was. He was like a god at our high school and probably the cockiest kid you could ever meet. But I, for some reason, liked that. I think, because Steven was such an asshole, I learned to like assholes.

Everyone was drinking and having a good time. Rick was really nice that night, and I remember talking with him a lot. As the night went on, Rick started acting a little weird, and he was really drunk. I remember standing at the top of the stairs that lead down to his bedroom, and him asking me if he could see my breasts. I laughed and thought he was kidding, then walked away.

A little bit later, I was upstairs in Jennifer's room, talking with some people. Rick came upstairs and asked me what I was doing. I made a joke about what he said before about looking at my breasts, and he got angry. He told me he knew that I liked him and that I wanted him. Then he grabbed my arm and dragged me down the stairs to his room. He kept yelling about how he could get any girl he wanted and that I should not pass him up.

When we were down in his room, I was really scared. I told him I did not care if he could get any girl, and that I was not one of those girls. He was holding on to me really tightly, and he would not let go. He was forcing himself on me, and I could not get away from him. He threw me down on his waterbed and got on top of me. All I kept saying was *"Why are you doing this?"* I was yelling for help. Because his room was in the basement, and the music was playing loud, no one could hear me. Well, at least my friends could not hear me.

After a few minutes, Rick had ripped my clothes off, and five of his friends were on the floor next to the bed laughing and trying to touch me. I was crying and begging them to stop. I could not see anything, because the lights were off, and I do not know whose hands were touching me. I just kept saying over and over, *"Why are you doing this to me?"*

After Rick raped me, he asked the guys on the floor who wanted to go next. I was starting to go numb and yelled out for one last time for help. I could hear people on the stairs laughing, and I knew that no one was going to help me.

Then all of a sudden, I heard the door to his room fly open and a voice say, "Her sister is here! Everyone get out, her sister is here!" I just lay there, while everyone in the room, including Rick, ran. I could not move. The kid that saved me, Chad, was one of Rick's friends, and cocaptain of the football team. I had never talked to him before and knew very little about him. He came downstairs and gave me my clothes, and helped me up. He had lied about my sister being there, but he knew that was a way to get them away from me. Chad wanted to take me upstairs, but I would not go. I was afraid, and I asked him to just find my friends for me. Apparently, the two girls I had gone to the party with had left, so Chad called a friend to come get me.

While I was waiting for my ride, Jennifer was apologizing to me, and told me that Rick was upstairs having sex with his girlfriend. She wanted me to tell his girlfriend what he did to me. So I went upstairs and screamed and yelled and promised he would pay for what he did. His girlfriend jumped away from him and seemed really confused. I guess she learned the truth later. From what I heard, that was her first time having sex. God, he is such a pig.

The day after the rape, my friend Beth took me to the hospital. I did not want to go, but I knew I had to go. My friend Beth held my hand through the whole thing. They had to do a rape kit on me, in case I pressed charges. The whole experience was an absolute nightmare, and each day it got worse and worse.

It was five days after the rape that my mother found out about it. My mom was very supportive and allowed me to make the decision not to press charges. To this day, she feels that at that time in my life I could not have handled going to court and fighting. She was also fearful about what my father would do if he knew. He still does not know. I feel guilty that we have kept it from him, but I believe it is something he could not handle knowing.

It was not long before the entire town knew about the incident, and I mean the entire town. My teachers, the police, my peers, and everyone else. I must say I received a great deal of support from so many people, and so many people were behind me. But, regardless of that support, I would not press charges. I just wanted the whole thing to go away, and I desperately wanted to forget about it and just be normal again. I hated being looked at as "the girl who was raped." In so many ways I felt responsible for what happened to me. The fact that I always had a crush on him made me think that, in some way, I asked for it.

At the end of the summer, Rick left for college on a full football scholarship. All I could do to find peace of mind was to remind myself that what goes around comes around. It did come around for Rick, but unfortunately it was at the expense of others. It turns out he was thrown out of college for raping two other girls. I had a really hard time dealing with that because I thought if I had pressed charges on him, he would not have gotten the chance to rape another girl. I just wish I knew then what I know now.

Now that I am coming to the end of my story, I would like to write about who I feel I am today, and what my goals are for the future. I must admit, if it were not for this autobiography, I would not be as clear on my thoughts as to who I am today. I have come to realize where my weaknesses and strengths lie. In writing this essay, I began to understand just how much my past experiences have affected who I am today. I have never looked so closely at myself, and now that I have, my life makes much more sense to me. Over the past six or seven years, I have tried very hard to put my past behind me and to become a new person. I realize now that I cannot do that. My past is a part of who I am, as well as who I will become. I need to accept my bad experiences and deal with them on a daily basis, and keep learning from my mistakes.

I have been through some pretty shitty stuff, and I have had to deal with some critical issues at a pretty young age. I have had to work extra hard at my education, at my personal/emotional health, and more or less at a social level. I always felt so cheated in life and wondered why I could not just be normal. Well, I no longer feel cheated, I honestly feel lucky. I feel like I was faced with difficulties for a reason, and it has ultimately made me stronger. Yes, it took me 22 years to realize and accept it, but it happened. Maybe because of my past experiences, I will be able to help young adolescents or others like myself, or maybe I will be a speaker about rape, or politics in the school system, or peer pressure. There are just so many things that I have to say about these issues because I have personal experience with each and every one. I strongly feel that I can help prevent such experiences for others.

Finally, this leads me to my conclusion about what this essay has done for me. I used to think about becoming a teacher, but because of my grades, I felt it would never be a reality for me. Well, after figuring out that I am a good strong person, with excellent qualities, and extreme determination, I have decided that I am going to teach and I am going to do whatever it takes to make that dream come true. I have too much to offer as a person in the field of education not to. I feel that if I give up on my dream of teaching, I would not only be letting myself down, I would also be letting a lot of children down as well.

Now I realize that I might be able to make a difference for students like myself. I know from experience how it feels to have difficulty with school, and because of that experience, I would be more sensitive with my students. I would help them become more self-confident and ultimately better learners. I have not yet decided whether I want to teach special education, but I do know I would do well in it.

I feel a huge part of my lack of confidence stems from my disability. I never raised my hand in class because I did not have the confidence to do so. I was so used to getting things wrong on tests and papers, I would never risk embarrassing myself by getting things wrong out loud in front of a classroom full of my peers. I am still this way today. As a teacher, I would encourage all my students to raise their hands, and I would appreciate any answer given. Even if the answer was wrong, I would explain the wrong answer, and commend them for trying. Too many teachers today respond to wrong answers with a "No, that is not it, anyone else?" Why not tell students why "that is not it" and clear up their confusion about why they may have answered in that way? As a teacher, I would work hard to treat each child as an individual and give students the respect that they deserve. I would not act like I was the dominating superior person in the situation, but rather as a guide for them to discover themselves and their strengths. I know school can be a very positive experience, but we need to start educating teachers about what kids face in and outside the classroom. Times are changing quite rapidly, and unless teachers are forced to continue their own education, the children are going to suffer a great deal.

12

Riding the Drug and Alcohol Train

Nelson Vee

Nelson is a 33-year-old white man who is currently studying at a community college, where he is pursuing a degree in elementary education. In a voice that alternates between fury and a yearning for reconciliation, Nelson describes the way that his problems with auditory discrimination—the ability to discern, process, and recall the sounds used in the production of speech—first caused him to feel misunderstood and rejected as a young child, and then led him to abuse drugs and alcohol as a young adolescent. Nelson's substance abuse continued throughout most of his adult life. When he entered a drug rehabilitation clinic at the age of 30, he began to confront the life issues underlying his substance abuse. In this essay, as he uncovers the feelings of rage and brokenness that have beset him for most of his life, he remains doggedly committed to the goal of self-healing. Key to the realization of this goal is the testimonial process itself, a process that allows him to say the things that he could not say—or that others refused to hear—earlier in life.

So you want to know about the LD? Do you really want to know? Can you read between the lines? Have you got the time? If you don't, fuck it, put the book down and take a walk or catch a movie.

I'm fucking 33 years old. I've been fighting this shit all my life. I'm pissed, but I'm not looking for pity. The search is about life. I've been in the dark a long time. One doesn't emerge from the darkness to suddenly receive total enlightenment. Not here. Maybe in that movie.

This morning, there is a sense of chaos, the semester's walls are closing in around me. I'm in college, studying—of all things—to be a teacher. I've got shit going on in 3D. Scheduling for January and the spring semester, auditory testing, student teaching possibilities. Jesus Christ, which way is up?

The question for discussion is *"Where is the LD?"* That's just it! I've been looking all my life. It's inside of me, a part of who I am. It is the part I wasn't allowed to be as a child. It gets confusing before we even begin. Was I not allowed, or was I ignorant and unaware? What role did my teachers and parents play? How much of it has to do with communication difficulties? Did those difficulties not, in fact, lead to emotional battlefields? There are more questions than answers. At 33, I don't really understand my LD.

The struggle to uncover the workings of my LD comes from a deep inner desire to give voice to all that went on, get at the real issues, to get them out and dissect them. In the end, it is about arriving at a place of healing. The wounds are so very deep. Even in the midst of writing this essay, I find the obstacles that stand in the way to be plentiful and insidious in nature. There are no easy answers, no quick fixes, no battery of tests standing in the wings. The answers primarily lie within.

When I was four, I was treated for a severe speech impediment and major auditory perception problems. I couldn't discern certain vowel and consonant sounds. To this day, I can't hear certain sounds. Just yesterday, I wrote a letter to a professor asking for a recommendation. He later commented on my terrible spelling. There are reoccurring words that cause me trouble. Oftentimes, even words I know how to spell stymie me. For some reason, I can't hear all the sounds, and it causes me major frustration. My stutter disappeared after two years of treatment, and my parents were obviously relieved and wanted to put the memory of it behind them. I am angry and bitter about the denial.

As I kid I don't recall difficulties learning to read, but that's not to say I didn't have them. What I do remember is scoring low in comprehension on the numerous standardized tests I took in the New Jersey school systems. Last summer I was surprised to find that in the placement test at my college I scored high on comprehension. I attribute that to two things: First, I have developed survival strategies, like reading text slowly and carefully, and rereading sections and whole text. Second, I suspect the test was watered down and meant to serve as a general sampling.

Overall, school was a negative experience for me. Somehow I never got what was needed, and I got a lot of what I didn't need. Children and teachers are often very quick to label. I was so insecure, unsure, and afraid. I remember being laughed at for mistakes in pronunciation, which still happens to this day. Somewhere, I took this as a message that I was dumb and didn't have anything worthwhile to say. I really internalized it, believed it whole hog. The voice is still very loud and is an obstacle to me being open with others.

On the teacher side, I heard from an early age: "Nelson is careless." "Nelson is lazy." "Nelson could do it if he wanted." All were things that blamed. This had a terminal effect on me. It was the opposite of what I needed, which was to be built up. I wonder if public schools can build up children with LDs or special needs? Do they have the resources? Do they want to do it? Does society want to build up those who are less than perfect? Competition was so much a part of my learning experience. It was like a food chain kind of thing. Kill or be killed. I felt like a ball rolling along through the system. Bounced here and there. It wasn't long before I shut down. School didn't feel real, pertinent. Oh, there was always the line: "What will you do?" "You need to learn a skill." Okay, teach me one! I came to discredit authority at an early age. There was no other choice: It was a matter of survival.

When my stutter disappeared, so did my parents' willingness to face my learning problems. I know it isn't politically correct to call an LD a problem, but that's what it was. That's what it still is. Through denial, that problem only grew bigger. It festered to the point that it really stunk. Overtook the host.

Add to the toxic cocktail a father who loved his boys, but did not know how to accept them for who they were. A father who grew up in Brooklyn and later Long Island in a house of privilege (whatever the hell that means!). The house was right on the water, a mansion. I can't fathom this, but he was raised mostly by a nanny. I don't think his parents had too much involvement in the daily stuff of life. Did it make him bitter?

I remember him chasing me in the yard. I was maybe ten. He chased me in anger, clearly frustrated that I was fleeing. I don't remember my infraction. Most likely it was a job not started or finished. Jobs were given first priority in that house. They came before all else. Why? I think it was because it is how he defines himself, and how his father and his father's father defined themselves. Don't get me wrong; he was committed to raising his children the best way he knew how. He just hadn't been given much to work with. My brothers and I were the training ground, and he hit the ground running.

Here we are talking about a man who worked all his life in the field of education. He seemed to say, "Look around you, perfection is everywhere." "You are expected to deliver." "My colleagues are watching." Maybe he was driven by an intense need for perfection. Maybe children were seen as an extension of himself. Teachers were put into a narrow mold. They must be from the same place, speaking the same language. Was he trying to prove something to his folks through the kids? He wasn't perfect, even though he is still trying like crazy. But there were these three boys, a sort of second, third, and fourth chance for him. So he couldn't be passive. He was an in-your-face dad. Everything had to be a lesson. All of it seemed to be a push. "Be all that you can be." That's what Dad and the Army said. He was a member of the Army Reserves for nearly thirty years. He went after it with serious intensity. It was his only gear, and it remains so.

I wasn't aware of my LD until I was in seventh grade. When I was made aware, it was not a fuzzy, happy kind of event. I had failed French. It was an embarrassing occurrence. I couldn't reproduce the sounds. I was back to toddlerhood, even as I was entering puberty. Along came Marsha Lewis, a learning disabilities specialist, riding a white Cadillac, offering quick, easy, drive-up diagnosis, one size fits all. The year was 1976. The word *dyslexia* was into its early stages of growth toward major "buzz word status." Even now, parents and children alike will take the label if it doesn't quite fit, out of desperation. I didn't see too many other specialists. The one other, a year later, was a complete quack. Marsha Lewis had a genuine concern for children. I felt that in her intensity. I think she was trying to help. She was the wife of an orthopedic surgeon in Princeton. I was brought there for testing following the French episode. It was the beginning of a painful cycle, one in which I was dealt with in the disaster mode time and time again, until I became a total disaster myself. Send in the professionals. Jesus, I really grew to despise that. The difficulties were always there, but only got attention when they went red line. Well, things don't pan out so well when you wait for panic to react. It's a little bit late. I think I was late for years. I missed the bus, baby! I never had a fucking schedule. Well, I did, but it was discontinued.

At 13, I was sad, afraid, and isolated. After having failed French, I was taken out of public schools and placed in the prep school in town. This was a difficult event. I protested to no avail. The response was "We're doing what's best for you." That was always the response. How did they fucking know? Did they stop to ask? The script felt like it was written before I even had a chance to work it out. I never had a say. What happened was that I came to believe I didn't have anything to say. This led me down a dark road.

The Pennington School. I hated the sound of it. It was a nasty place, one that I did not want to have anything to do with. Yet, there I was, thrust upon the scene, forced to adjust. In the wink of an eye, I had become a dreaded "preppy."

It was very shortly after arriving there that I got drunk for the first time. Gennesse Cream Ale by the pond. I got stumbling drunk, tripped on the railroad tracks, and got a huge bruise on my shin. I think it was the beginning of really losing myself.

It was here at Pennington that my attitude went south. It got really ugly. I tried to float between the worlds. That of the partying and the other one I guess I thought I should be in, the sports world. I played golf, soccer, basketball, and hockey. I also remember many hours sitting off by myself, lost in books. I think it was the only time in my two years at Pennington that I felt somewhat happy. I goofed off in class. I got the old line of "Nelson could do it if he applied himself, if he wasn't lazy." I resent that statement. I couldn't break free into a place where I was heard and seen. Looking back on it, being heard and being seen was what I longed for. The whole shit of growing up was, in many ways, a strange, long, holding period as I waited to break free of these horrible conditions.

In 1978, while I was away at summer camp, came the move to northern New Jersey. My parents' geographic cure. Escape. Panic. The results? Escalation of my difficulties. I became even angrier and felt more unseen. I didn't even feel a part of a family there.

I lived in the basement, had my own entrance. We didn't eat together as a family anymore. My parents dined with the troubled rich girls. I was given a plate, brought down by my mom, wrapped in cellophane, warmed to staleness in the oven. The isolation built. My parents and I lived in two opposing worlds. They were helping maladjusted teens. I was becoming more maladjusted at an alarming rate.

Their world was a country prep school in a lovely valley. It was a farm-like setting, with very posh facilities. They got a huge new house, free of charge. They were the prep school instructors. I weeded the grounds and mowed the lawn in the summers, shoveled horse shit in the winter, and there in the barn felt up a few of the troubled girls who roamed this peaceful place, adding to their troubles.

In the beginning, I took the bus 20 miles to Bernardsville where I went to school. This was the corporate home of AT&T, and Jackie'O and Malcolm Forbes lived in the area. I rode the bus with seven others from the outskirts of the district. There was Frank Hall, Bob and John O'Rourke, Blair Wotton, Joy Jefferson, Lori somebody, and one other person whose name I don't remember. Joy killed herself in tenth grade. I hardly felt it. I was right there on the verge myself for those two years. Blair's a hippie in the mountains of Colorado. Bobbo ended up fine, I'm sure, but I remember him being crushed by Joy's death. Frank and John both ended up in prison. Both were hardcore alcoholics. I once saw John wake up around noon after drinking till the point of passing out the night before, drink a quart of Miller straight down, and puke on the lawn. Frank, John, Bob, and I played hockey for the Essex Hunt Club Foxes. Yes, they did hunt foxes. We would steal Heinekens from the club bar after games. Drink down three straight when your body was dehydrated, and you were flying. I remember drinking with Frank and John numerous times.

After a while I didn't take the bus. I'd catch a ride with Frank in his old Chevy that had a Dead tape glued to the deck. The song "Trucking" was always playing. Some days, I hitched to the train station in Peapack, and rode the Erie Lackawana to school. We called it the Erie Marijuana.

As you can see, school wasn't so important. Mostly it was a hindrance. When I did go, I was good and stoned. If I didn't get stoned on the way, I'd cut first period and get stoned for second. I still tried to keep one foot in the sports world. Varsity soccer and golf in tenth grade. I wasn't alone. There were plenty of other partiers, at least on the soccer field.

My parents never entered my world and I barely entered theirs. One day, Blair and I had just scored a case of Schmidt's tall-boys, the official beer of that little valley. Blair had a shack on the Black River. We sat by the wood stove and wasted the hours away. It was a place where we could escape. It was our world. We were marching up the road on this school day afternoon with the case, and my dad jogs by. He just shook his head and kept running.

I think all you have to do is read this shit to understand why I was so pissed. So I caught the drug and alcohol train out of there. I didn't stop to question where it was headed. I didn't need to know. I was pissed off for so long I forgot I was pissed. It became part of my being. No matter how far I rode the train, that anger stayed within me.

At age 16, I was out of control, depressed, angry, confused, scared, and suicidal. I was smoking three joints a day, and occasionally even drinking at school. I don't think I could have made it through my senior year of high school.

In the midst of the darkness, an opportunity arose. Tim Ellis, the director of the Maine Reach School, came and talked about his school, showed a movie. I wanted in. I knew it was what I needed. It offered choice, the one thing that had eluded me all my years.

I went and it was great. The program was called Applied Academics. We, the students, chose our fields of study. We went on wilderness trips to Baxter State, the White Mountains, the Allagash, and Acadia. For the only time as a teenager, I was loving life. The school had an alcohol and drug policy, so for the most part I was clean for nine months. Who needed to escape in that environment?

It was here that I met Julia, my first wife. We married when I was 20, green as can be, ready to settle blissfully down and repeat my parents' legacy. Five years later, Julia and I parted ways, me after hitting the bottom on crack and heroin. I got treatment and stayed clean for nine months, but then relapsed on New Year's 1988. I did convince Julia to give it a second try. She knew I wasn't ready to clean up, but she wanted to believe my lies. Our reunion lasted all of five months.

That's when I met Erin. She was this crazy, mixed-up, young chick. I hate that word, but that's what Erin was. It was delusion at blurred sight. I was 27. Erin was dating Ernie, the guy who lived below Julia and me on Maple Ave. Maybe it wasn't dating. I don't know. She gazed deep into my eyes and seemed to forget about Ernie. The next time I saw her, she was partying at Ernie's. Halfway through the night, she remembered me. She had her tongue in my mouth on my porch, her leather jacket with her firm tits underneath grinding against me. I was desperate just like her. So for three years we ignored our many differences and sick behaviors as best we could.

She knew I was road kill. She saw it everyday. Finally she couldn't stand it, and she called the shrink for me. I went. I knew she was right. I thought, *Oh, my sweet little Erin! You'll be so happy when I clean up.* Yeah, right.

The shrink, her name was Barbara, said she'd be happy to sit there, but first I had a job. I had to pack my bags and check out of the real world for a little while. I said, "I can do that." After all, somebody else could pump and order the gas down at the Mobil station for a while. I called Mike, my boss, up at his house one night. Told him I was headed to the treatment center to get some help with what had been a lifelong self-medicating ritual. That ritual was keeping me from having a life and not making me such a good petrol distribution technician. He was probably into his second six pack of the night.

The day I checked in, I had been told not to expect to get in. Oh great, send a pot head up the road to Vermont in desperate need of help and nowhere else to go. The shrink, her name is still Barbara, said something about how the insurance companies needed the fucked-up, desperate people to be drunks, not druggies. But in the end, the folks at the center saw I qualified and adjusted the language.

It was June 18th, 1993. Barbara set me up with Jill. Jill was a substance abuse counselor for a local outpatient outfit. Jill said, "Can you stay clean for a couple of days till we get you in somewhere?" I said I thought I could. I had just got back from what I hoped was the last bender of my life. It was my fifteenth million Dead Show. I had stumbled off to Buffalo with my buddy, Kenny. I wondered what

Kenny was thinking about my sorry ass the entire three days. The show sucked. What I was looking for wasn't in Buffalo.

When I got to the center, I walked through the automatic doors. Strangely, I felt a sense of relief being there. I had gotten myself in there. Now, I'd sit back and let them take over.

On that particular Tuesday morning, the admitting department had some visitors. Dr. What's-His-Name asked me if I minded if these two visitors observed my admitting process. It was fine with me. I was there to get in; I wasn't going to make any obstacles. So all together there were six of us in the director's posh office suite. I remember the director's desk: polished hardwood, maybe cherry. I think it had some plants. I was right in front of him at his desk. The observers and two other staff members were lined up behind me. The office seemed to go on behind them indefinitely, but then again I wasn't looking that way. I bet that is where the lush green plants were. I wasn't feeling alive. I wanted life. I was there to fight for it. The sense I had of that was incredibly clear, which is funny because I was in a fog. The director told me a little about the process. The staff would ask me some questions, and afterwards they would discuss my case in private and then call me back in to hear the results.

I began doubting if I would be admitted. Maybe I wasn't quite fucked up enough. Well, once he started firing those questions, my pain and hurt came rushing out into that room. I was sobbing uncontrolled for close to two hours. All those years of running from myself had led me there to that room. I had nothing, and I let them see that. I saw it, too, and for one of the first times, I really felt it.

That voice inside of me that has brought me through so much darkness was present. It said, *You are going to make it.* Not only did it come from inside, it came from outside, too. During the break, when the staff was discussing admitting me, one of the observers came out to use the can. He came up to me and held my shoulder. His words of hope still ring in my head today. He said, "You'll be fine. You're going to make it, I can tell!" God, it was so beautiful in that moment of desperation to hear those words. In the program of AA, they call coming in all beat-up and ready for sobriety "the gift of desperation."

Well, I had a big old gift. It dragged me into Barbara's, Jill's, and What's-His-Name's without even a fight. It led me through the two weeks at the treatment center and beyond.

Beyond was where the real pain and loneliness was. I got out on July 1, and on the weekend of the fourth, I went with Erin to her family reunion. There was drinking and pot smoking, just what I was told to steer clear of. But I had the curse. I was riding a dead horse. For the next two months, I tried to remount many times only to be thrown. Again it was only when I fell that the movement toward myself could begin.

Drunks are known for their uncontrolled rage. I guess I was more the stereotypical pot head. The only thing that got me pissed was not having my green dope. At least that's what I thought. Mostly my anger was directed within, toward me. It had always been there, boiling below the surface. Pot was a good pacifier, and I just couldn't stop smoking it. I had tried to stop so many times, probably once a month since I was 21. Sometimes I did for a while, but the moods got too much for me, the loneliness too intense. Pot was my lover, friend, mother, and companion.

After the treatment center, I started going to a weekly group for men in early recovery. We started to talk about anger issues. I was confused. I knew I had some anger, I just wasn't sure where it was. Couldn't quite access it. I also thought it meant I had to rage at someone. Gee, I thought, Erin's a perfect target. One day I was at the house of some mutual friends, and in she walked. I had been working on feeling some anger that very day. I lay on the couch, breathing hard. The silence seemed to hang in the air. Erin was in the bedroom, quietly talking. Suddenly, I was in there hitting her and screaming at her. She was shocked and started screaming and calling me an asshole. Luckily, my friend Nav was there, and he pulled me away. I don't think I would have stopped. He was laughing at me, shaking his head, saying I was fucked up. A half hour later, at his suggestion, I apologized. He said she could press charges. I was shocked; I had never done anything to harm her or anybody else physically. That night I lay in bed alone, feeling suicidal.

I can't point to one place and say that's where the loneliness began. I think I have always had a sense of it in this world. But anyway, the loneliness was thick that night, and for the following days and nights. I had been in a live together relationship with a woman since I was 18. That was 12 straight years. So, when I woke up alone on those long, quiet Sunday mornings, it was slow going. As those days grew more familiar, something changed. I got comfortable being with me. I started to learn who I was for the first time in my adult life.

As I approached my first year of sobriety, a single mom with a four-month-old child moved into the cooperative house I would soon be moving out of. I fell in love with the child first and then his beautiful mother. I was much more cautious around getting involved with Amy. She had just ended a long and difficult relationship. I didn't want to get involved. Maybe she'd be going back. But I had become a different person, and Amy was attracted to the person she saw. This woman is strong. She is very alive. She was the first person of complete integrity who wanted to be with me. She was also reserved, so it took some time, but finally I got around to telling her I was nuts for her. She replied that the feeling was mutual. So now we two nuts live together, are married, and have a second child due soon.

Recently, I went with my wife and our three-year-old son, Brennan, to visit relatives on my mom's side in Virginia and North Carolina. I shared with them the places where, as a child, I spent joyous summers. Then came a quick stopover at Mom and Dad's at the end of the weeklong journey. Mom had just had the first of five chemotherapy treatments. She was feeling awful. We were road weary. My dad was in pain.

The morning that we were supposed to head back to Massachusetts, he attempted to reach out to me. He did it in a typical, indirect, controlling way. He mumbled something about needing to talk with me, and he asked me to give him two hours of my time. Did I have anything planned? "Yes." I said. I had promised Brennan a soak in the hot tub after breakfast. "Can you put that aside? This is important." "No," I said "He's been waiting, and no one else can take him. I'll take him for ten minutes." "Okay," he says. Suddenly, he wants to go out to see what the fence needs for repairs. I followed him out to the yard. It felt very familiar. I felt instantly disgusted. Why was he doing this? Suddenly words came flying out from inside of my being. "Dad, what's going on here? Instead of pulling me around, why don't you say what's on your mind? I've got a family ready to get home. You say you've got something important, yet you're talking about fixing a fence. Can't we just stop with this crap and talk?" He instantly exploded. "Look, Nels, I've been sitting on information here that no one knows, not even your mother. Your mother has a 20–25 percent chance of living beyond five years. I wanted to just spend a little bit of time with you. I didn't want it to come out like this. But it has, so there, it's out." Then he walked away.

After a while, he came back and we had a talk. It lasted about an hour on the front porch in the sun under the wisteria. Truth flowed at moments. This man, my father, is facing the hardest struggle of his life. He needs support, he longs for it. Yet he is entrenched by a legacy of fear and hard-nosed self-sufficiency. He is torn up inside, as anyone would be, facing the mystery of cancer. He spoke of plans: retirement, health insurance, building a new home, or maybe a vacation home. He said he had reached the end of his rope with his job. He couldn't care for Mom and do the job. The job was so detailed, it couldn't be done half-assed. The talk ended by me saying, "Let's go look at the fence." He said, "No. But when I say that I need a little of your time and you turn around and get defensive, it hurts. It really hurts." I sat and stared off toward the sun, soaking it all in. A few minutes later, he came out with a chair for my mom. We all sat quietly. I said, "Come on, Dad, let's go do those things." He said, "No, I've got to go to the office." A few minutes later he was gone, knowing we would be gone when he returned. The job that he couldn't do any more was once again a place of retreat.

As I drove north my head was spinning.

What enrages me about the LD is the fact that he never saw me, never accepted me as I was. But I learned the hard way that an LD can't be corrected by looking past it. The opposite tack is the only way. His pushing took me miles from the help I needed. So far away that I couldn't see or feel. What the hell do you do with that?

Maybe, faced with this life change, I can move. Life is so amazing. The most amazing thing is how we all need each other. That's just it: I need my dad, just as he needs me. Confusion? Rage? Anger? How do you sort all this shit out? Does an answer or true healing exist? Whatever happens with him in the future will happen. I can't change him. Not by raging, not by bitching. The same is true for my childhood. Yes, he was an asshole. Yes, he did push, but the asshole loved me.

What more could the schools have done? I really don't think they could have done much. If a child's parents aren't able to truly see and accept a problem, if they are stuck in denial, how can any professional effect any major movement toward learning? God knows they were summoned. So that brings me back around to anger. I can just say it's all my parents' fault. They suck! They blew it! What the hell were they thinking? How could they miss it? All the signs were there and then some. But you know what? Even though the anger is real and justified, it doesn't in itself lead to any significant answers. No, it seems to just keep me spinning my wheels, much like I did when I checked out with drugs and alcohol. Even at this very moment, when I remain much in the dark about my LD, I see that acceptance is a must. My parents didn't create the LD. I was blessed and cursed by it. It is part of me.

13

Figuring Out
My World

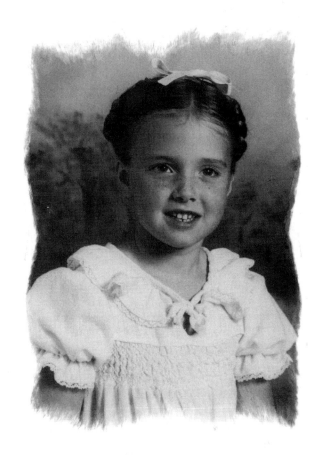

Alison May

Despite undiagnosed learning disabilities in childhood, the 21-year-old, upper-middle-class, white author of this essay describes a highly successful school career. Alison's success, which masks a vulnerable sense of self-esteem, is attributable in large part to hard work and explicit compensations for what was diagnosed as visual and auditory dyslexia prior to her freshman year at college. A strong work ethic and brightness are not, however, sufficient to earn Alison the grades she strives for and believes she merits. Despondent about her failure and the "unfairness of the world," she seeks advice and encouragement from the college's LD services coordinator, who is herself learning disabled. Supported by family and friends, and with a new sense of assurance, Alison commits herself to a future career as a clinical psychologist who will relieve the emotional toll learning disabilities exact on others.

It was the summer of 1993. I had just graduated third in my class of 237 from high school. During this final year of high school, I was accepted at a college in New England, and my classmates had voted me "Most Intelligent" and "Most Likely to Succeed." Although honored, I felt misunderstood by my classmates, and I entered the summer before my freshman year of college feeling alone, scared, and confused.

Although I had become close to a lot of my classmates, I felt that I had not established any true friendships because I had hidden who I really was. Nobody knew how much I had struggled to make the grade. Nobody knew how many times I had thought luck was the only thing I had going for me. And nobody knew how scared I was of being found out to be as incompetent as I thought I was.

I tried to take comfort in what was to come—a new life away from home—but I wasn't sure I could be as successful in college as I had been in high school. In college, I feared I'd be the one who'd let everyone in her hometown down. I knew hard work and motivation had been a part of my prior success, and that I would continue my work ethic in college, but what if it wasn't enough to succeed? I had had to work so hard in order to understand even simple things, so I thought I couldn't possibly be intelligent. How could I rely on a trait I didn't have to get me through college? "Oh well," I thought, "I can't keep up this charade forever." I tried to resign myself to an empty peace by thinking, "It's out of my control."

Among the many letters I received from the college that summer was one from Mary Fox, the Student Disabilities Coordinator. It asked, "Do you have, or have you ever had any learning disabilities?" That one question began a new chapter in my life.

I hadn't been prepared for such a question, but I quickly armed myself against this absurd inquiry. Sure, many of my elementary school teachers had wanted to put me in special education classes because I had more difficulty understanding than my classmates. One of the child psychologists that I saw even diagnosed me as mentally retarded! But I defensively answered that though I had apparently had some undiagnosed learning disabilities early on, I was fine now, and I did not want anybody "nagging me." I was threatened by the implications of this question, fearing that anything I achieved at college would be invalidated if I were offered special treatment. In the letter I received in response from Mary, she promised not to "nag" me; she only asked if we had documentation of any of the learning disabilities.

Mom decided to talk with Mary. She explained that it was my older sister Jennifer's kindergarten teacher, Mrs. Lin, who had first made Mom aware that I might be having problems understanding. Mrs. Lin had observed my habit of repeating slightly incorrectly the things Mom said to me. For example, Mom once asked me to get my brush, but I looked baffled and asked, "my braid?" Mom thought I was playing word games, but Mrs. Lin suggested that I could be suffering from a learning disability. Little was known at the time about learning disabilities, and they were diagnosed only in children who were severely affected.

Though perplexed, Mom acted on Mrs. Lin's suggestion. She began to analyze our conversations and noted that the problem practically disappeared when she made sure my full attention was focused on her, when she made tactile cues (when asking me to get my brush, she would pretend to brush my hair with her hand), and/or when she had me repeat back to her what she had said.

Once in Mrs. Lin's kindergarten class, however, I was still having obvious difficulty understanding what she said to me. When she noticed my anxiety and helplessness, she would gently ask if I understood. But I often felt so overwhelmed that all I could do was hide behind a charming, bewildered smile, or go to the corner and lie down on my mat. I learned helplessness at a very young age.

Mrs. Lin recommended that I be tested for learning disabilities. Unfortunately, the psychologists who tested me had no idea what my problem was. One said I was just being stubborn or disobedient, but Mom and Dad understood the great need for harmony in our family, so they immediately knew his findings must be wrong. Other psychologists thought I was deaf, or too disabled to read, so my parents finally gave up on having me tested. They decided to rely instead on a more reliable psychologist's advice (my great uncle's), who told them not to worry, saying, "She's so bright that she will grow out of, or compensate for, her learning difficulties."

But now, 13 years later, Mom and Mary decided it would be wise to have me tested again. So, I found myself on my way to Dr. Milton's office. During that long car ride I recalled my school-age experiences of hearing teachers talk and feeling as if they were speaking in a foreign language. I seldom understood my assignments, and what was worse was that I didn't *know* I didn't understand, so I couldn't ask for help. Instead, I developed a hypersensitivity to the cues of those around me, and observing my classmates and the reactions of my teachers, I was usually able to piece together my assignments.

I still remembered the pain I suffered over one assignment I couldn't piece together, though it was 12 years earlier. Mrs. Escher was glancing at the exercises my class had just completed as we lined up for recess. When she got to mine, her face clouded over with anger, and she ripped me from the line of boisterous kids, who suddenly became very quiet. "What is *this*?" she demanded. I hadn't understood the assignment in the first place, so how could I understand the question she was asking now? She took my inability to understand as a sign of defiance, and bellowed at me, enraged, "You will stay in for recess and do this assignment correctly!" As my classmates filed out of the room to recess, I sat crying at my desk, wondering why I was isolated from everyone in my class. I felt not only the pain of my failure to understand, but also that I was a bad person for not understanding. Carrying all this emotional baggage into Dr. Milton's office, I kept thinking, "They couldn't find an excuse for my stupidity all those years ago, so why should they now?"

The testing was intensive. During several visits, I took a variety of tests, including the *Wechsler Adult Intelligent Scale* and the *Woodcock-Johnson Psycho-Educational Battery: Tests of Achievement and Cognitive Ability.* The tests were fairly straightforward, though certain ones really gave me a hard time. I couldn't hear the stopwatch ticking, but I knew I was taking quite a bit of time to complete some of the tests. At one point, when struggling with a motor-skills exercise, I said flat out, "I know it's wrong, but I don't know how to correct it." Although I felt a little embarrassed by the fact that Dr. Milton had probably seen some seven-year-olds sail through this activity, I had been prepared for my difficulty by low scores in prior motor-skills tests. Though I would've loved to ace this test, Mom had long ago helped me to understand that we all have different gifts.

Some of the tasks I found to be easy actually indicated a learning disability. For example, on a simple word-matching task, I scored perfectly when not looking at Dr. Milton, but when I looked at him, I answered incorrectly three times. This made sense to me: I had always listened without looking at someone when trying hard to understand what they were saying. It hadn't struck me up to now that this behavior might be unusual.

Throughout the testing, I was preoccupied by the fear that I was going to let everyone down. When I was little, I felt I had disappointed my parents when I didn't pick up on things as fast as other kids my age. I remember many times sitting in class concentrating hard on what my teachers were saying, but still often being unable to understand their questions while my classmates' hands waved wildly in the air. Some of my most vivid memories of such failures occurred as recently as my senior year in high school. In those uncomfortable moments, I became the kid who didn't want to be called on. It was especially frustrating because I had done my work, I had been paying attention, and I had been taking notes like a madwoman. I just needed more time than everyone else to process ideas.

My parents never in any way fostered my feelings that I was a disappointment. On the contrary, they made it obvious how bright they thought I was, and often said, "We feel like the most blessed parents in the world." Still, my insecurity seemed to go hand-in-hand with my learning difficulties, and I struggled to fulfill what I perceived to be my parents' expectations for me. I thought they expected this latest round of testing to verify that I had some learning disability—and perhaps would confirm that my difficulties had not been due to their neglect. I desperately wanted to absolve them of any concerns over their parenting. They had been wonderful parents—I was the faulty one!

When the testing was over, I was prepared to disappoint everyone—again. And now there was one more person I valued who I expected to let down—Dr. Milton. When my parents and I met with him to discuss the test results, I sat with the same pleasant smile that I had always hidden behind, feeling inadequate and only half-listening as Dr. Milton explained my test results. We all understood that I often had trouble calculating the higher levels of abstraction between objects. For example, I had stated the major relationship between table and chair as "they are both necessary to eat dinner." When Mom and Dad commented that they would have said "both are pieces of furniture," or "both have four legs," I responded with a look that said "I never would've thought of that!" We all enjoyed a big laugh because our family relishes creative, innovative responses to things.

When Dr. Milton finished talking, Mom asked, "Is this anything like dyslexia?" Dr. Milton confirmed that I did, indeed, have visual and auditory dyslexia. I practically yelled, "I did it? I got what we came for?" I was thrilled; I hadn't let anybody down.

I left the testing feeling the same as always. I didn't believe attaching the words "visual and auditory dyslexia" to me would change my life, though I did recognize that they affected my parents. Mom seemed transformed by what she had just learned. She could hardly talk about our visit without getting teary-eyed. I guess finding out that your eighteen-year-old is visually processing as an eight-year-old and auditorially processing at an even lower level would make any parent wonder what emotional price her child had been paying. Still, I felt I had fulfilled my part of the bargain, and that these so-called learning disabilities were in my past. I did not realize then that they would not only affect my future, but also serve as a new vantage point from which I would have to reinterpret my entire past. I was oblivious to the heart-wrenching feelings of inadequacy, inferiority, and alienation that would come later.

The rest of the summer and my freshman fall at college were times of discovery for me. I explored which of my behaviors, thought processes, slips of the tongue, etc., were due to my learning disabilities, and which were just normal mistakes. My family members became my test subjects, and they were eager to help me in my quest. They were also appropriate test subjects because we had established long before that each of us had very different ways of thinking.

Having already laid this groundwork, we began to determine how I, the visually and auditorially dyslexic, processed differently from everyone else in the family. A few major differences emerged immediately. For example, Mom recalled a time when she had asked me to get something from the bottom, left drawer of the secretary. I stood there for about three seconds, appearing as if I hadn't heard a thing, but then I whipped down the stairs to the living room and came back with what Mom had asked for. Mom laughed with joy and wonder at the realization that she had seen me thinking in those few seconds. "Doesn't everybody do that?" I asked. It became clear to me that no, everybody does not do that. In fact, having great difficulty understanding and following sequences of instructions, even simple ones, had been one of the earliest signs of my disabilities.

Moreover, I realized that in all my auditory understanding of verbal material, there is an element of hesitation. When people speak to me, about half the time I must repeat to myself (often several times) what they have said before I can understand it. This repetition can help keep what has been said to me fresher in what seems to be my deficient memory, and, more importantly, acts to fill in the holes in my auditory processing. I have become skilled and efficient at using phonological and contextual cues from the conversation to fill in the gaps, little by little, each time I repeat the sentence to myself. Ninety-nine percent of the time, this process enables me to offer an appropriate response in a socially acceptable amount of time, so that the other person doesn't suspect that I am having difficulty understanding them.

That one percent of the time that my compensation process doesn't work, however, has caused some confusion to those I'm speaking with. This occurs most often when I'm preoccupied with another activity. For example, filling up the car at a gas station, my boyfriend Mark was going inside to pay, and he stopped to ask me, "Do you want anything when I go in?" Here's what happened inside my head: I heard, "Do you want anything," but I knew he had said more than that. I had grasped the approximate length of the sentence, and even the general syllable structure, but that wasn't enough. I quickly thought back to the last time we went into a gas station together and remembered that there had been "Slim Jims" on the counter. Mark had picked one up and had done a hysterical impersonation of the professional wrestler in their advertisements. I therefore concluded that his question had been, "Do you want anything, like a Slim Jim?" so I answered, "You know I don't like Slim Jims." (Note that the sentence I came up with had the same number of syllables as, and practically rhymed with, Mark's question.) Needless to say, Mark was confused. I have no name for these mental events I experience, but they present a wonderful opportunity for me and those close to me to enjoy a good laugh, and to appreciate how even learning disabled minds work so extraordinarily, if at times incorrectly.

My auditory glitches weren't always so funny, and I find humor in them now only because it is so obvious how far I have come since my major breakthrough at age seven. Before I was seven, I had felt comfortable conversing with any adult, yet when it came to understanding directions, I felt everyone was suddenly talking in a different language. This made me feel lost, scared, and helpless all the time. I never knew what was going on, while all the other kids seemed to know. I was also scared of being left behind, and of making those I looked up to unhappy with me. I felt the world around me was putting pressure on me to act, yet I did not know what it wanted from me. I was like a message decoder who never got a break: As soon as I broke one code, the next would be waiting on my desk.

Somehow I survived until my big breakthrough at age seven, when I began to understand that I wasn't understanding. This realization allowed me to ask others to repeat and clarify their directions, spoken or written. Suddenly, I could do the assignments that had seemed so confusing and was spared my futile attempts to do the work without understanding it. Nonetheless, my low self-esteem reminds me that I am still paying a price for all those years of not understanding

Though my auditory processes for language were disrupted, my ability to perceive music was intact from the beginning. Mom and Dad were astounded when, at less than a year old, I could finish the tune of "You Are My Sunshine" after my music box had stopped. Hoping that the structure of the Suzuki method would help me learn sequences and patterns, Mom got me started on the violin at age two. In fourth grade, I switched over to the cello, and in fifth grade, picked up the flute. I now play the cello only sporadically, and my family is amazed that I maintain my skill as if I had just played yesterday. Still, there seem to be some glitches in my playing. For example, I play notes in the bass clef while thinking of the names of the notes in treble clef, essentially playing one note while thinking of another. Apparently, I rely upon the position, rather than the name, of the note to read music.

I began to understand more about the effects of my learning disabilities when I got to college. I was shocked that Dr. Milton had recommended that I receive a waiver of the language requirement because I might have difficulty with the Rassias method, which emphasizes speed and oral communication. After all, I had always been one of the top students in my French and Latin high school classes. I decided to give French a try, and was placed in French 2, which was mostly a review for me.

I had some difficulty with the drills, during which my instructor fired rapid questions in French and demanded an immediate response. If I thought about what the instructor had said, that is, attempted to translate it into English, I became completely confused and responded incorrectly. But, if I blurted out the first French sentence that came to mind, I was almost always right. The drill instructor was impressed with my performance, and said he never would have guessed that I was dyslexic.

A lot of the non-dyslexic people to whom I've described my difficulties with reading have noted that they, too, have some of the same problems, though my difficulties seem more extreme. For example, one common problem I have is that I "read" a whole passage and realize that I haven't understood or remembered a single word. I commonly forget the beginning of a long sentence by the time I reach the end and have to read it three or four times to grasp the whole thing. This forces me to read very slowly.

I agree with those psychologists who feel that word-retrieval is the basis for dyslexics' difficulty with reading. In other words, though I have a vocabulary in the 99th percentile, I hesitate each time I look at a word. The word is not backwards or scrambled (a common myth about all dyslexics), but I have a lag between seeing and recognizing familiar words in the context of a sentence. Sometimes, reading out loud helps to eliminate some of the difficulties, but because of my auditory dyslexia, the benefits are often minimal. No matter what strategies I try, reading is laborious and physically exhausting. Yet despite my hardships, I love to read: With each word I understand, I feel I reaffirm my parents' faith in me, and prove wrong all the doctors and psychologists who gave up on me.

Another area in which dyslexia affects me is in writing. I don't write letters backwards, but when I write by hand, I have to pay close attention to the formation of each letter. At the same time I must think about spelling. It is as if my memory has not properly encoded what each letter looks like, so each time I try to write one, I have to wrack my brain for a template. My motor functions hamper me even more, which makes writing very involved and exhausting for me, not to mention extremely slow!

Adding comprehension to writing creates a whole new problem. When I am listening to a lecture, it is impossible for me to both take and understand my notes. Because I can't always rely on my auditory processes, I really need to have notes. Moreover, to get the gist of a lecture without repeatedly hearing or studying it, I have to write the notes down verbatim. Since I can't write very quickly, however, I'm at a stalemate. Luckily, my advisors recommended that I buy a portable computer for note-taking, and my laptop has been my savior.

Typing seemed to compensate for my encoding difficulties because letters were no longer letters, but positions on a keyboard. I use my laptop to take notes mainly in lecture-based classes. Even so, I still do not do as well in pure lecture classes as in those that bring in discussion or use other media such as video clips. My repeated difficulties in lecture-based classes make me feel unwelcome in college, as if I don't belong. I've often cried to Mom and Dad that I shouldn't be in college, that college is an institution made for learning, not learning disabilities.

The limitations of the help my laptop can give me is revealed in paper-writing. Although typing helps me produce papers that are far better than I could handwrite, I still have trouble with structure and organization. Of course, it helps that I can cut and paste paragraphs in different places, but if I have no idea *where* to paste them, these functions are of only limited value. It's frustrating to know that all the elements are in my paper, but that poor organization and difficulty with sentence structure might obscure the quality of my product. Equally upsetting is my tendency to lose trains of thought: Often I have the perfect sentence and then suddenly lose it.

Like my writing, my speech is hampered by structural, organizational, and what I call memory difficulties. I have to concentrate very hard on what I say. When I don't, I tend to transpose letters and words. I often start speaking before I've had time to think through what I want to say. I will start the sentence, realize that it is not the best way to express what I'm thinking, then start it again, maybe even a few times, before I actually finish. This makes me sound like somebody trying to get out of a punishment: "She was . . . we were . . . it wasn't my . . . all right, I hit her first!" I also often switch sounds or words—for example, "Could you get me some poilet taper?"

I often don't realize that I've made such verbal slips until the person with me chuckles about them. Although I once would have been mortified to make such mistakes, I take them in stride now. It would be debilitating to handle them any other way! Still, I'd be fooling myself to say my verbal slips and organizational difficulties don't inhibit me. I have always preferred small groups of close friends and avoid large groups where the additional noise and confusion make it impossible for me to concentrate. Besides, parties are full of people who don't know me, and they might think I'm dumb, not learning disabled. I believe it is this distinction that gets every learning disabled person out of bed in the morning.

My verbal organizational difficulties affect me most when arguing or debating, which may be why I have always had an innate need for harmony. Besides having to think hard about what I'm saying, the stress of knowing that someone is angry with me is overwhelming. In addition, the interruptions that typically occur during arguments completely destroy my train of thought. When arguing with my boyfriend, for example, I quite literally can't keep up. I am still trying to respond to his first sentence as he argues on. And I can't share in the emotional aspect of the argument because I am so busy trying to analyze and remember what I want to say. Oh, I do cry when I argue, but I never know whether I am crying because of the emotions the argument has aroused or because I feel mentally incapable of arguing. I think crying is my grown-up way of exhibiting learned helplessness, although if there were a mat to lie down on when I felt lost, I probably still would.

I hear many people say they wish they could be kids again, to return to a time of less responsibility, with time to go out and play, and to be carefree—or so I've been told. When I look back at my life, I don't ever remember feeling like a kid, and I certainly don't remember the blissful harmony that everyone else seems to. What happened to my childhood? I'll tell you what happened: I was forced to grow up more quickly than other kids in order to make it in this world. At a young age, I learned that I had to figure out my world, and myself, or be left behind. I became highly introspective, always trying to figure out how to make myself learn at a rate commensurate with my classmates.

By the third grade, I blended in pretty well academically, but I never felt that I did socially. I felt distant and detached from everyone else my age, and a lot older. Aware that school was easier for my classmates, I spent a lot of time worrying that not only school, but life in general, would be more difficult for me. While my friends were wondering whether to invite boys to their parties, I was understanding what my Dad was going through as he battled depression.

I was also physically more adult than my classmates. I was tied for the tallest in my second grade class, was chubby, asthmatic, and early to develop. I remember feeling envious of the smaller girls, but I didn't start thinking about fairness until third grade. Once I did, my world became even more bleak. How could others be cuter, smarter, and more athletic, while I was only bigger, dumber, and slower?

Nevertheless, I never had trouble making friends because I was always kind to everybody, even to classmates who treated me like a doormat. I did have a few close friends, but I still felt alone, even when spending time with them. Gwynn was one such friend. We often played together after school, but I constantly worried that her next-door neighbor would come over to join us. I never understood that she could be good friends with me and with someone else: I thought someone had to lose out, and it would naturally be me.

By the eighth grade, I avoided joining cliques. Though I did this in part to stop worrying so much about what others thought of me, it differentiated me even more from my classmates. I got along well with everyone, but I did not feel I was part of a loop. I became wrapped up in trying to figure out where I did fit in, but this just made me an observer of everyone else's behavior. I began to focus almost entirely on academics, especially psychology.

My studies in psychology helped me to realize that I was delayed in reaching adolescence. Knowing this helps me to understand the increasing numbers of arguments I've had with Mom and Dad since I've started dating and gone off to college. Mom admits that part of the problem is that she and Dad are very protective of me. "After all," she argues, "when you're dealing with someone whose childhood was so painful that you're not sure she has any self-esteem intact, you have to watch out for her!"

More a problem than my parents' overprotectiveness, however, is *my* unreadiness to assert my independence from them. I realize that I ask Mom and Dad's advice in a lot of arenas that most 20 year olds wouldn't even mention to their parents, but I don't think it's fair to judge me by the standards of the average 20 year old. Because I was born with an unusual set of circumstances that prevented my life experience from being average, it has been a lot harder for my parents to let me spread my own wounded, little wings and fly. Maybe I am the one most afraid of falling if they let go, however.

With so many obstacles to overcome and so many new insights to consider, my first quarter at college was grueling. Although I felt sure that I would be doomed in all of my classes, my love for learning and my desire to know I was doing my best kept me getting up every morning for class. I had developed a labor-intensive work ethic over my high school years: I simply worked on something until I understood it, which meant I often worked a lot harder on my studies than others. Still, I didn't attribute my success to intelligence; a nagging inner voice told me I couldn't possibly be smart if I needed so much more time to understand what my classmates got almost immediately.

My nagging voice began to get louder at college where I was always surrounded by other students. I observed their casual study habits and easy comings and goings. I, on the other hand, sat in my room working, taking breaks for only food, bathroom, sleep, or class. This really did not bother me: I was motivated by fear of failure to work my hardest. I thought I was doing fine—until I got my first-quarter grades.

They arrived and I was devastated: a 3.0 GPA. Granted, this is a great GPA, especially at a selective college, but I had put absolutely all of my time, effort, and heart into my studies. Was this a gauge of how the next four years of my life would go? Even worse, I had gotten a "C+" in my Data Analysis class, my first "C" ever. Though I had spent hours with the professor outside of class and I had done and redone almost all of the assignments, it had all been for nothing. But it wasn't just the grades that upset me. It was that I now knew I was working harder than other people who were making the same or better grades than I was. It was the fact that the work ethic that I had labored so long and hard to perfect had failed me. It was the fact that I felt I wasn't good enough for the college now and never would be.

On the Saturday night after I returned to New England from Christmas break, as the others in the dorm headed out to have fun, I was ready to call it quits. I called Mom and Dad for what I thought would be a routine call, but as soon as Mom answered, I began to sob uncontrollably. All the frustration of not being rewarded for my hard work last term overwhelmed me, as did the thought of changing my now-discredited work habits. I feared if I modified my work ethic, I might return to the confusing world of childhood. I felt doomed to bang my head against the wall again by repeating last term: work ethic, failure, and all. I was so hysterical that my parents feared I might try to harm myself; Mom was prepared to make the 520-mile drive here in a severe snowstorm. But after a long conversation, I finally stabilized, exhausted from all the pain and tears. I fell asleep that night feeling that I had the love of my family, but definitely nothing else.

Although I never again hit a point that low, I spent the first few weeks of my winter term merely existing. I lost my appetite, my enjoyment of academia, and my faith that the world could be fair. I spent about a month in counseling, which I didn't find that helpful except that I started to talk out my feelings. The counselor couldn't grasp the extent to which my learning disabilities had affected and were still affecting me, which was the heart of my problem.

I found much more comfort talking with the woman whom I'd once thought of as a meddling troublemaker, who had now become a dear, understanding friend: Mary Fox. The time we spent together was extremely productive and meaningful. Mary has learning and hearing disabilities herself, which helped her get right to the heart of the things that were bothering me. She knew that just because

I'd been able to compensate for my disabilities didn't mean I hadn't suffered in the process. She also realized that being at college meant a lot less to me than actually being happy with myself for one moment in my life, and she thought these values were in the right place. One might say that Mary and I couldn't help but bond because of our similarities, but people with learning disabilities are just as different from one another as those without. And no, the term *learning disabled* doesn't bother me; I think if you make the term too euphemistic, people won't realize how hard you've had to work to achieve your goals. By talking with Mary, I gained such pride in myself in terms of dealing with my learning disabilities, and she will always be a pivotal person in my life.

I have often wondered what kind of person I would have become had my learning disabilities been diagnosed earlier. My first instinct is to think that an early diagnosis would have been detrimental because I would have known that I had a legitimate excuse not to excel academically, and I would likely not be so motivated to learn. It is, after all, this attribute that I take the most pride in. My motivation makes me my own hero, for I've never met anyone willing to struggle as long or hard on anything as I am. With an early diagnosis, I would also likely have been placed in special education classes. As it was, some of my teachers wanted to put me in special education, but Mom and Dad resisted the suggestion. I needed the push of a regular curriculum and later a gifted-and-talented program to achieve what I have today. Without the challenge of these classes, I could not possibly have qualified for the opportunity that I have at college today.

Nevertheless, I can't deny the emotional cost of being diagnosed late. Mom often cries about the fact that it took us so long to recognize my learning disabilities, as well as the related psychological costs. Had we known earlier, a psychologist could have helped me combat some of the painful realities I'm facing now, which are much bigger and more impenetrable than they would have been as a child. Though it's so frustrating to think I might have been helped earlier, I simply have to exert myself to bring my self-esteem up to the point my success says it deserves to be.

I have known since the fifth grade that I wanted to be a clinical psychologist. I sometimes worry that my interest in psychology is a way to avoid dealing with my own emotional problems; it is certainly much less painful to deal with others' problems than my own. Still, I am actively engaged enough in helping myself and having others help me, and I feel I am ready to be a helper as well. My family and I only recently realized the emotional toll my learning disabilities have taken on me, and if I can prevent that pain from afflicting one other person, I will have done the job I feel destined to do.

I believe being intelligent and learning disabled is one of the hardest predicaments a person can find herself in: to have trouble understanding, but also to *know* that you're not understanding. The worst part is that other people can't see that something is different about you. They can't understand why you're preoccupied with self-esteem and happiness. I have cried out many times to this world that may never understand me, "If I have to be learning disabled, I'd rather be stupid!"

In retrospect, however, I feel that I have been very lucky. Being learning disabled and intelligent presents a precarious paradox. Well-intentioned experts who don't know the best way to help people struggling with such a paradox could destroy hopes and dreams. I hate to imagine how much less I would be without parents who refused to give up on me, even after so many doctors did. I thank God that each event in my life has occurred as it has, for I fear that one slight change in the decisions my family and I have made might have rendered me anything but a survivor. My confidence hasn't caught up yet, but with my motivation and the support of my family and friends, I believe I just might make it.

Scholarly Perspectives

"Skin-Deep" Learning

Lisa Delpit

Eyes wide with wonder, nine-year-old Maya stared at me. "Gee, Mom," she whispered in an awed voice, "that sounds just like me!" After having read Gretchen O'Connor's essay myself, I was struck by so much that was familiar that I decided to share it with Maya. She was right; it did sound just like her. Although she has never been formally diagnosed with any learning or attentional differences, I have long suspected that her mind works in unique ways.

I admit I am sometimes frustrated with her disorganization, the hours it takes her to complete the simplest tasks, her handwriting difficulties, her apparent inability to keep track of any of her belongings, or to finish the many projects she begins. However, I would trade none of those traits if it meant I would lose her poetry (one poem refers to daffodils as "those flowers that stick out their big noses to sniff for spring"), her ability to play anything by ear on the violin (or almost any other instrument she picks up), her letters to the fairies, the amazing costumes she designs for the various characters she creates, her visionary artwork (when asked to draw a picture of her room, she represented what I saw fairly well, and then drew flocks of multicolored birds all over the floor), her kindness to younger children, her ability to entertain herself with even the simplest of artifacts—an odd-shaped stick, a flattened stone, or an old tarnished fork—or the vibrant energy that she brings to every act of living.

I have always known her to be special, but schools have sometimes seen her only as a bundle of problems to be solved. After a happy kindergarten year, Maya was so excited about going into first grade that when she woke up on Sunday morning she wondered if there were any way I could make her sleep until Monday so she wouldn't have to wait another day! When Monday morning finally came, she sang and skipped and danced her way to school, so happy she was about to burst. By Friday, she cried in the mornings saying she had a stomachache and didn't want to go to school anymore. Every day she brought home packs of worksheets, marked with big red letters "INCOMPLETE." Wanting to give the teacher and the school time, I decided to wait and see if things would settle down. By the end of the next week, she was still crying, still bringing home uncompleted worksheets, and, by Wednesday, sobbed that she wasn't going to get a treat on Friday because she had too many checks by her name. I knew I had to go in. When I entered the cramped classroom (the school was overcrowded so the school system rented several small rooms from a church next door), I almost started sobbing myself. Her classmates were seated in very closely placed desks facing the blackboard. Her desk was at the back of the room facing a window. What I saw in my brief visit was a disaster for any child with attentional issues. While the children were supposed to be working on a worksheet copying words from the board to complete sentences from a three-lined "story" they had earlier reviewed, the teacher first discussed the lunch procedure and then welcomed another adult who presented the class with a caterpillar in a jar. After pondering aloud about the differences in the developmental stages of moths and butterflies, the teacher told the children to continue working on their worksheets while she read to them about caterpillars from the encyclopedia. I quickly realized why I saw so many unfinished worksheets coming home. Trying to fight back my own tears, I asked the teacher if I might be able to talk to her after school.

While waiting for the end of school, I secured the curriculum guides for first grade from the office. From these I learned that the district embraced a "whole language, literature-based, integrated curriculum." When I was able to speak with the teacher, I asked first about the curriculum. She informed me that "whole language" meant that "the whole class reads from the basals at the same time"; that I had seen an example of integrating science and language arts when she read about butterflies as the children were completing an unrelated reading worksheet; and that "literature-based" meant that when the children finished all their worksheets they could go out into the hall and read a book. I was dumbfounded at her interpretations of the curricular guide and was hardly hearing when she went on to complain specifically about Maya. "She daydreams all the time, she won't finish her work, she doesn't pay attention, and she talks to her neighbors." Mrs. White went on to say that her job was to train Maya to be a student. I tried not to sound as upset as I felt when I told her that if she wanted Maya to pay attention she might want to reconsider having her facing a window. Since I knew all of the children from the previous year, I suggested a possible seating arrangement that could minimize inappropriate talking. I also tried to explain that Maya was a very competent reader and could read all of the worksheets without difficulty. Her challenge was that she could not easily copy from the board or write quickly because her motor skills were slower. I wondered if she might be able to read more books and copy less as her motor skills were developing. The teacher told me that no, she knew what she was doing and that I needed to "trust" her. After all, she had been teaching for 15 years and she knew what was best. The next day I spoke to the principal about my concerns. She told me that "the purpose of first grade was to learn to sit in a desk," that Mrs. White was one of the best teachers in the school, and that I should "just learn to trust her."

By the time I made it to the district office, with no hope of a different perspective in sight, Maya was still bringing home packs of uncompleted worksheets on a daily basis. I was at my wit's end. I had tried "trusting" everyone else, thinking that maybe I couldn't trust myself. Was I too emotional? Was I too overprotective of my child? Were they right to try to make her conform and I wrong to try to get them to change? As the first six-week grading period neared, Maya had begun to say she was dumber than everyone else in the class because she couldn't finish her work. She had not gotten to read one book in school. She started wetting her pants and sticking holes in her clothes with scissors. On the day before the parent-teacher conferences, I got a call from the teacher saying that Maya had cut up the teacher's basal sentence strips and was in big trouble. I then knew that I had to act. Clearly the entire district's philosophy ran counter to anything I believed to be in my child's best interest. I used my connections to find someone in a neighboring school district who might be able to help me locate a more appropriate school. Even though I had to pay for Maya to attend, I found a first grade teacher who understood children's needs for movement and appreciated divergent thinking. Indeed, at the end of the year all children got awards, but Maya's was "for the having of wonderful ideas." Once more she flourished, and once more she looked forward to the following school year.

Unfortunately, second grade brought a teacher much like Mrs. White in philosophy, if much more effective in execution. Again faced with sitting in a desk all day and listening to the teacher talk, Maya once more shut down. When I discovered that we might have to return to our home district the following year because of overcrowding, I agonized over what to do. Finally, after long discussions with friends who had older children and much heartache over "abandoning" public schools, I enrolled Maya that October in a very small private school with a diverse student body and teachers who truly integrated the curriculum, focused on children's strengths, and demanded hard work.

Maya is now in fourth grade and is very happy. She recently informed me she was writing the story of her life. Yesterday she wrote, "If I could do one thing for the rest of my life, I would go to my school. I love school." Not that she hasn't had challenges—her handwriting is still tortured, but she's learning to type; with her teacher's help, she's learning to stay focused; with posted reminder lists, repetition, and contracts, she's learning to be more organized. And her teachers love and comment on her creativity, push her to write more poetry, let her interpret social studies through dance, and repeat math concepts as often as it takes for her to "get it."

At this point, we have not sought further testing since the school is meeting her needs, but I often wonder, "what if." What if I had not had the background to know her first grade teacher's understanding of curriculum was flawed? What if I didn't know how to interpret curriculum guides? What if I didn't know the "right people" to talk to to find an appropriate school? What if I didn't have the money or the resources to find the right private school?

What would have happened is exactly what happened to many of the writers in this book, and to thousands upon thousands of other children every year— especially children of color and children who live in poverty. Their schools, unable to accommodate any behavior or learning style outside a narrow range of that deemed acceptable, taught them a lifelong lesson. They have learned that they are incompetent, inadequate, damaged. As Nelson Vee's saga of pain and substance abuse portrays, they have been left with a sense of rage and brokenness. As Lynn Pelkey says, "I was taught to hate myself."

One of the major factors that has allowed Maya to flourish is that both her present teachers and I concentrate on her gifts, on those things she does well. Many children identified with learning disabilities do not get such treatment:

Gretchen O'Connor: My teachers and parents overlooked all the areas in my life where I was succeeding and instead concentrated on my faults.

Lynn Pelkey: Why must the learning disability categories be classified around negative attributes? Can we not focus on strengths and positive attributes?

Velvet Cunningham: I was judged for what I could not do and not for what I could do.

They became packages of pathologies to be "fixed," or maybe tolerated, or maybe rejected. They felt stupid, unacceptable to the school. The result is that, unless unusually supported outside of school, they reject the school environment. They, like Aaron Piziali and Oliver Queen, withdraw from caring, like Velvet Cunningham, they use anger as a defense, or like Nelson Vee, they turn to drugs or alcohol as they attempt to numb their pain.

As hard as things are for these children with learning disabilities, poor African American and other children of color with learning problems are even more likely to face psychological trauma. First, the schools often do not identify their learning problems. When these children have trouble learning, it is assumed that it's only because they are less intelligent. When put into special education classrooms, they are most frequently labeled, not as having a learning disability, but as educable mentally retarded or behavior disordered (Artiles & Trent, 1994; Heller, Holtzman, & Messick, 1982; Mercer, 1972). In other words, those children or young adults from middle-class families who are classified as learning disabled are often told that they are intelligent, but that there's a part of their brain that works differently. If their parents locate supportive professionals, they are told that their children can learn just like everyone else, but that they must find settings that meet their specific learning styles. By contrast, many African American children and their parents are told that they are unable to learn, are intrinsically less intelligent, and must be isolated because they cannot be trusted to act like civilized human beings.

The results are predictable. Just as many of the authors in this volume did, these youngsters reject the school environment, they withdraw from caring about themselves and others, they use anger as a defense, or they turn to drugs or alcohol to numb the pain. After an article about my work appeared in a local paper, I received a letter from an African American man who was in prison for life. He was a very thoughtful man who was concerned about the young men who were regularly imprisoned. He felt that these young men were full of rage, cared little about themselves or each other, and had very little academic knowledge. He had become a father figure to many of them. He wrote about what he perceived to be their major problem—the school systems that had shunted them aside and refused to educate them. He was especially concerned with the "special remedial" programs, which, for these young men, seemed to him to be a specialized track to prison.

Almost everyone he encountered had been in "special" classes for much of his life. Given the overrepresentation of African American boys identified as behavior disordered or mentally retarded in special education classes, the impact on African American communities seems inevitable.

Yet many of the teachers in special education classes are committed educators. They want to teach, and they want children to learn. Why are the results often so problematic? In Claude Steele's groundbreaking research in which he attempts to identify factors that cause gaps in performance between various stigmatized groups and the "mainstream," he identifies a significant factor he refers to as "stereotype threat" (Steele, 1992). This he defines in part as individuals internalizing the negative stereotypes held about them by the larger society. Stereotype threat, for example, could affect African Americans attempting to take standardized tests or women attempting an advanced math course by creating a state of anxiety that artificially depresses their performance. In other words, when people are in settings in which they feel stereotyped as less competent, their performance tends to bear out the stereotype.

Perhaps Steele's research might help to explain not only why many African American students fare poorly in special remedial classrooms, but also why the writers in this volume who were placed at the youngest ages in special education classes seemed to have sustained the most damage from their school experiences. It is not necessarily the teachers or the classes themselves that cause the problem, but the early labeling as "less than." One is struck by the number of these writers who were not identified as having a learning disability until college. Did those who are diagnosed—and consequently, labeled—early, learn to believe, as did Lynn Pelkey and Nelson Vee for such a long time, that they were not college material?

Certainly some students need specialized assistance, but why must a school brand them with labels that only cause their teachers, their peers, and ultimately they themselves to focus on their weaknesses rather than on nurturing their strengths? At Renfroe Middle School special education classes, known as "Critical Thinking" courses, are fully integrated into the general curriculum. They are scheduled during an elective block, and because of the name chosen to appear on the rosters, there are always requests from students at all performance levels to enroll.

Steele's research also found that identifiable remedial programs for societally stigmatized groups exacerbate the problem, causing them to perform even worse by possibly reinforcing the belief that they are less capable than others. He suggests instead that such students receive the necessary support to succeed in a challenging curriculum that also provides instruction in areas in which they need extra help. One example is what Uri Treisman accomplished with a group of "remedial" African American college students (1992). By presenting them with a challenging calculus course, letting them know that he knew they could succeed, providing them with extra help and teaching them to problem solve collaboratively, these "remedial" students outperformed their white counterparts in advanced classes. I also know of a university professor and a teacher who worked with a group of remedial students at McKinley High School in Baton Rouge, Louisiana, to research their school's long and illustrious history. In doing the research (which the instructors stressed was usually done by people in graduate school), these high school students researched archival data, interviewed former teachers and students, and recorded and transcribed audiotapes, all of which of course meant that they had to read complex material, learn punctuation and spelling, and study copyediting. They eventually presented their research to a standing ovation at a national educational research conference.

By contrast, I am haunted by Lynn Pelkey's description of the "retard room." It was bright and colorful—like a kindergarten—and without the accoutrements of an age-appropriate learning environment, like maps, because, the unspoken message said loudly and clearly, learning disabled kids didn't need to learn "that kind of stuff." But even more troubling for me is her description of the teaching and learning within those classrooms:

> *The teachers were very kind, but I believe now that they underestimated me. I would do what they told me to do, recite what they told me to recite, but I was rarely asked to really think, and I almost never experienced those moments when something I was learning came together and made sense.*

As hard as it is to comprehend that in the name of "helping" children with special needs, they are sometimes being confused with disconnected knowledge bites and made to feel stupid because nothing makes sense, it is even more difficult for me to fathom how this kind of teaching has become commonplace in "regular" education in many inner-city schools. When I go into my daughter's school—a well-worn building rented from a church with children's artwork all over the walls and few resources (only one Internet-capable computer for the entire school, for example), the children run up to me with great excitement. The littlest ones, the three- and four-year-olds, tell me about their studies of the ear canal or show me their portraits of Thelonius Monk and Miles Davis and ask me to listen to the blues songs they created. The second and third graders rush to tell me about what they found out in their study of the history of medicine (the Babylonians used mallets instead of anesthesia), explain the ecosystem they're creating, show me their drawings of constellations they've studied, and act out the myths from different cultures they represent, or describe the play, novel, or book series they're writing.

When I first entered some of the inner-city schools I work with—worn buildings with teacher-created bulletin boards all around and few resources—the children would run up to me with equal excitement. When asked to share what they're learning, these children would proudly present their neat handwriting or their latest worksheet. Although there is absolutely nothing wrong with neat handwriting and worksheets, there is a problem when these represent the limits of the teaching and learning taking place in a classroom, when isolated bits and pieces are presented to students without the "big stories" that make the pieces make sense. As surely as the children in Lynn Pelkey's special education class, these children were being robbed of a connected, comprehensible education.

Of course, neither all special education nor all inner-city classrooms are like that. Amanda Branscombe's ninth grade special education English class studied Shakespeare by first discovering the "rules" of rap and then looking for similar rules in sonnets. They became pen pals to older students at another school, and communicated by letter to researcher Shirley Brice Heath about research the students and Heath were conducting into language and language structure (Heath & Branscombe, 1985). By the end of the year, all but one of the students tested out of special education and one tested into honors English!

Lita Sanford's special education classroom at Oakhurst Elementary in Decatur, Georgia, is frequently mistaken for the "gifted" class by short-term visitors, as children use computers to solve complex problems and create science reports with sound tracks and scanned-in photographs. And I am privileged to know many teachers in inner-city schools, like Elizabeth Bland, Deborah Mills, Najiyyah Nashid, Deborah Mitchell, Lynn Simpson, and Chinwe Obijifor, among many others, who create magical classrooms that surround children with excitement and learning. The problem is that these classrooms are still the exceptions.

Several of the authors in this volume equate having a learning disability with how it might feel to be gay—you know you're different, but you can choose to hide the fact if you decide to. Others have equated the oppression experienced with having a learning disability with being a person of color in a predominantly white society. While both analogies hold some truth, African American Michael Sanders resists the latter analogy, stating that although the learning disabled and racial minorities both encounter discrimination, there ends the similarity. Because racial status is visible, people of color have a greater chance of bearing the brunt of bias. He adds, "I've never heard of anyone with dyslexia being lynched, burned, or beaten."

Michael Sander's explanation alludes to another difference between those with learning disabilities and racial minorities. Those in the former group are largely isolated in their struggles. The pain, the oppression, the attacks on self-esteem are very real, but are very personalized at the level of the individual and his or her family. By contrast, although the oppression of people of color is also experienced personally, it exists in the world as discrimination toward a group. Those so inclined may not even know the individual and yet respond to his or her group membership with negative stereotypes or overt hostility.

Oliver Queen describes his community's response to two local institutions for children with special needs. Whereas Greenfield, the institution housing an almost exclusively white population, was embraced, Dixon Valley, a school populated by primarily African American students with learning problems, also identified as "behavior disordered," was quite another story:

> *Contempt and hostility toward Dixon Valley was as much a factor in my development as television, comic books, and action figures. I had been surrounded . . . by the notion that Dixon was a malignant tumor on the otherwise healthy, happy Springfield body. . . .The community . . . espoused that all blacks were trouble and brought only disease and chaos wherever they went.*

Such are the attitudes many African Americans must contend with. Without knowing even one of the Dixon Valley students, the community rejects all of them. African Americans in this country continue to experience discrimination, poor African Americans even more so. If our educational practice is ever to meld with our rhetoric, we must first cease to categorize people into the worthy and the unworthy. Historian and psychologist, Asa Hilliard, says that we in the United

States believe that people are born into three categories—the low, the average, and the high—and that our job as educators is to reveal the category into which they were born and to keep them in it.

Those who are white and from middle- and upper-middle-class families are assumed deserving of membership in the top two categories. When these children exhibit learning challenges, they and their parents are told that they don't try hard enough, that they're lazy, that they could do the work, but just want to be disruptive. Because this often robs them of attention being paid to their particular learning challenges, that is problematic. On the other hand, those who are poor and come from families of color are assumed to belong in the shallow end of the intelligence pool. Should they exhibit difficulty learning, the system tends to regard them as merely fulfilling their limited potential. That is even more problematic. A year or so ago, a psychologist at my university made some preliminary assessments of my daughter. Her initial scores on several subtests were very low. Because the professor knew me and had come to know Maya, he decided to retest her on that and several other subtests two days later. Upon retesting, her score on one subtest moved from the 8th percentile to the 89th percentile, and jumped equally dramatically on the others. In schools, children who are poor and who belong to racial minorities are almost never retested. Even though the tester may have caught the child on a bad day, or did not consider the differences in the child's culture and the assessment tool, the low score meets with the school's expectation of their group ability. We all mouth the mantra, "All children can learn." I would modify the chant to "All children *do* learn." It's just that some of them learn that we expect them to be successful, and some learn from us that they are dumb. Whatever we believe, they learn.

The reality is that all children have much greater potential than we ever imagine, but our rigid educational system that assumes that some children are incapable of achieving academically and that one model of instruction fits all does many a disservice. Schooling that recognizes differences without negatively stereotyping children, believes in all children's potential, and implements challenging instruction that embraces children in all their splendid variety, can, as Maya's school does, teach to and develop children's strengths. Schooling that labels children as broken or tries to "fix" them to match the school's limited models is doomed to failure. A colleague and I are presently working on a book about language and identity with the working title *The Skin That I Speak.* If language is as intimate and tied to one's identity as is one's skin, then surely our ways of learning and living in the world are equally enmeshed in who we are. Learning styles, like the language we speak and the skin we wear, are not separate entities to be "fixed," but an integral part of the essential nature of any human being. "LD," says Christie Jackson, "is a label, . . . [b]ut that label is also a part of me. It's as much a part of me as my middle name, as my smile, as my love for lilacs." If we can see all of the children we teach—color, culture, learning styles, income level, notwithstanding—as complete, deserving, brilliant human beings, then perhaps we will manage to create the educational system we need. Education for all children should be "special"—especially designed to discover the strengths and accommodate the needs of each child.

15

"Shimmers of Delight and Intellect"

Building Learning Communities of Promise and Possibility

Carol S. Witherell

Pano Rodis

This is Simple
Power is mute (the trees tell me)
and so is profundity (say the roots)
and purity too (says the grain).
No tree ever said:
"I'm the tallest!"
No root ever said:
"I come from deeper down!"
And bread never said:
"What is better than bread!"

—Pablo Neruda

The Scope of the Challenge: The Landscape and Some Guiding Questions

Stories, as an Apache elder has reminded us, can work on us like arrows. They can find their way to the very core of our being, stunning us without warning, halting our gait, asking of us a very deep attention. They can pierce our armor, disturb our comfort, expand our vision, and call us to know more about who we are and who we might become. They can lead us to see in new ways that which we encounter every day. Through the leap of imagination and empathy that authentic narratives provide, we can enter the experiences of others, even when these are vastly different from our own.

As we read the autobiographical narratives collected in this volume, we were struck by how difficult it is for so many classrooms to become places where individuals with learning disabilities—whatever their assets and challenges—can thrive. The lines of Pablo Neruda's poem quoted at the beginning of this chapter kept ringing in the background as we read, for they seemed to capture the heart of the challenge facing educators and communities today: How can we create learning communities that recognize and nourish the strengths and talents of children and adolescents who learn differently? How can we teach in ways that convey an understanding of the fact that human beings learn, perform, and excel in different ways, and that it is this very diversity that makes life interesting, even wonderful? Neruda's poem reminds us that neither trees nor roots nor bread are known to us along a single hierarchy or dimension: Should it be any different with human beings, who are infinitely more complex and varied?

The autobiographers' personal stories that form the cornerstone of this book offer a rich and radiant response to these questions. They demand of us a very deep moral as well as strategic attention, so that we might begin to understand what it was in these writers' educational experience that affirmed them as persons of worth, that recognized their various strengths, and that focused on these strengths as scaffolds for meeting new expectations and challenges. It is neither effective nor respectful, our autobiographers and commentators reveal, for educators to focus primarily on students' "deficiencies" through disparaging labels and through extensive use of discrete and repetitive drills, whether in the regular or special education classroom. Nor is it effective or respectful to set aside appropriately high expectations for learning in the areas that are most difficult for these students. Rather, the environments in which students experience the greatest educational fulfillment are those wherein their teachers set high but achievable expectations, wherein teaching and curricula are culturally, linguistically, and developmentally responsive, and wherein all students are able to become successful participants in the discourses valued by their school and society. Such teachers hold their students to these expectations in honest and caring ways without neglecting opportunities for them to further develop their unique strengths and talents—what Mel Levine calls their "islands of competency" (1994).

Accordingly, we will develop in this chapter the stance that classrooms can become cultures of promise and possibility for students with learning disabilities when their participants grasp an essential, double-pronged premise: *Students with learning disabilities are most likely to thrive educationally when teachers affirm in meaningful ways the talents and interests these students already possess and, at the same time, address seriously their need to develop fluency in all primary academic discourses, including those that are most challenging to them.* In order to actualize this premise, we propose that teachers must have not only a clear understanding of the individual capacities of each of their students, but also a socially responsible, pedagogically sound model for shaping classroom culture. As will be explored later in this chapter, we believe that the foundation for such a model may be found in the notion of *intellectual diversity,* by which we mean a respect for and an investment in the precious uniqueness of every mind, as well as a commitment to forming from this uniqueness a genuine community.

The community of participants we refer to includes other students, parents, regular classroom and special education teachers, school psychologists, counselors, instructional assistants, child development specialists, administrators, and the students with learning disabilities themselves. However, in this chapter we are most centrally concerned with speaking to regular classroom teachers. It is strikingly clear from the autobiographies that the education of students who have learning disabilities is shaped at least as much by what transpires in the regular classroom as by their experiences in special education. With the current emphasis on inclusion, the great majority of students who have learning disabilities spend at least part of their day in the regular classroom. Yet, as the testimonies of the student writers also make vivid, having a learning disability often creates for children a sometimes terrible sense of division between "us" (those who have learning disabilities) and "them" (those who don't), together with a constant, appropriate longing for community membership. Regular education teachers able to offer students who have learning disabilities this kind of membership make an inestimable contribution to their lives.

Truly, regular education teachers are essential partners in the education of students with learning disabilities. Yet, a great many of us were never given specific training in how to work with students who have learning disabilities, nor have we discovered that such training is likely to come to us once we start teaching. It is hoped, then, that this chapter can be of use both to teachers in training and teachers in the field, offering each group a general framework for creating classroom cultures of promise and possibility.

A Framework for Understanding and Teaching Students Who Have Learning Disabilities

The lines from Pablo Neruda's poem point to an idea that has been steadily gaining currency in educational circles over the last 15 years: This is the idea that teachers need to appreciate not only their students' cultural and ethnic diversity, but also their *intellectual diversity,* which is to say their "differences of mind."

The notion of intellectual diversity arises when we ask the simple but ever so important question "Are all minds the same?" If the answer is "no," then shouldn't we, as educators, orient ourselves toward appreciating this lack of sameness, varying our teaching practices in appropriate and responsive ways?

Rather than starting with a preconceived notion of how students ought to learn, teachers sensitive to intellectual diversity start by investigating how their students actually *do* learn. As teachers actively partner with their students in this investigation, they also seek out ways of teaching that truly fit their students' capabilities and needs. The result is a classroom culture in which learning differences are viewed neither as bizarre, nor embarrassing, nor unduly burdensome, but rather as natural, expected, even welcomed. In such a climate, intellectual prejudices (overtly expressed, for example, in epithets such as "stupid," "disabled," and "retarded") are challenged just as directly as racial or socioeconomic prejudices. And, most importantly, because the actual daily practices of such teachers radiate a continuous curiosity about and respect for intellectual differences, students are less apt to fall behind academically, to become demoralized about their capacity to learn, or to be socially marginalized by their peers.

In a nutshell, the invitation here is to understand the unique intellectual styles or *modi operandi* of each of our students, using this understanding as a basis for crafting a fulfilling, generous, and useful education for them. Responding to this invitation can help to ensure the formation of a classroom culture far more likely to inspire in each of our students what Christie Jackson calls

> *that shimmer of delight*
> *and intellect*
> *the impressionable wonderment*

that emerges only when students are authentically engaged with learning.

While the concept of intellectual diversity is of great value to teachers regardless of who their students are, it has special relevance to the task of creating a fair and enriching climate in the regular classroom for students who have learning disabilities. We know that many factors—biological, cultural, psychological, and experiential—interact in creating the intellectual diversity we see in each classroom. Teaching—as the art most directly committed to the influencing of minds—often flourishes when it takes stock of and responds constructively to each of these factors.

When it comes to learning disabilities, however, much of the current research suggests that neurology—or the given structure and operations of the mind's "machinery"—is often the primary root of the matter. Persons with dyslexia (i.e., reading difficulty), for example, appear to have a brain-based difficulty distinguishing, processing, and manipulating the discrete sounds that make up human speech. Because alphabetic letters depict sounds, most children with dyslexia may encounter much more difficulty "breaking the code" than other children. Similarly, many children who experience great difficulty learning mathematics, understanding the meaning of words and text, sustaining attention during certain tasks, or carrying out the many demands involved in writing are discovered to have specific neurological differences from most of their peers.

All the same, it is very rare that a learning disability renders a person unable to learn. Instead, in the vast majority of cases, it means that a person will need to learn via routes more carefully planned, structured, and demanding than the ones most other students have the option of using. Children and adults with dyslexia, for example, can make excellent progress in reading when offered systematic study in such areas as auditory discrimination, phonology, morphology, and grammar, especially when instruction occurs in learning contexts that have high meaning for them (e.g., contexts connected to stories they have read, heard, told, or written). If students with learning disabilities are not offered access to learning modalities that can work for them, school can become an ongoing torment. While it is often through special education that students with learning disabilities obtain access to such modalities, their educational experience is immeasurably enhanced if general education teachers follow suit, deriving from the notion of intellectual diversity a model for both classroom culture and pedagogy.

To this end, it is valuable to further explore the notion of intellectual diversity in two directions, both of which may help us grasp the experience and needs of persons with learning disabilities.

The first of these focuses on intellectual diversity within the individual. As psychologists and neurologists have studied the human brain, they have found that it houses a wide array of distinct capacities, ranging from those which allow us to process sensory input to those which allow us to conceptualize and act upon complex symbolic codes (e.g., language, numbers). Scientists interested in tracing intellectual functions to precise locales in the brain have been somewhat frustrated by the brain's tremendous complexity, but they have been able to confidently establish certain general patterns, such as the association of the left hemisphere with speech apprehension and production, and the prefrontal cortex with decision making (Luria, 1973). Howard Gardner—one of the most widely read advocates of intellectual diversity—has entreated educators to "try to forget that you have ever heard of the concept of intelligence as a single property of the human mind" (Gardner, 1983, x). Instead, he suggests, consider the proposition that "At the level of the individual, it is proper to speak about one or more human intelligences, or human intellectual proclivities, that are part of our birthright" (ibid., xvi). Gardner's division of the human intelligences into seven species (linguistic, logical-mathematical, musical, spatial, bodily-kinesthetic, interpersonal, and intrapersonal) has provided an important basis for many educators committed to developing a truly fair and nourishing pedagogy for all students. For such educators, it seems increasingly clear that sound educational programming must acknowledge the fullest range of student potentialities, leaving behind the narrow, "one-size-fits-all" pedagogy of earlier times. A challenge clearly before us, as schools are asked to establish clear and common standards of educational performance, is to assure that the assessment of students' learning also reflects this diversity.

According to this expanded notion of intelligence, then, the mind is not *monolithic*—a single, unitary organ, but *pluralistic*—a collection of quite various capacities and functions. If each of our brains performs a wide variety of functions, it stands to reason that many of us, if not all, find that we are better at some of these functions than we are at others. One child, for example, will seem to have a marvelous ability to quickly process visual information (thus making him or her a top-notch video game player) but have a miserable time trying to distinguish between different musical notes. Another child will demonstrate an admirable capacity to produce poems and stories that capture the imagination, yet his or her spelling remains what some might call "atrocious." Such discrepancies within individual intelligence(s) are at the core of what it means to have a learning disability. Indeed, to be diagnosed with a learning disability in the United States, a person must demonstrate a greater-than-expected discrepancy between what is deemed by standardized testing to be one's "native, raw intellectual capacity" (i.e., one's IQ) and one's proven ability to carry out the functions involved in reading, writing, and/or mathematics. (That such an approach to conceptualizing and measuring human intelligence and learning potential is reductionistic and outdated is an ancillary topic of much importance, one that has been addressed eloquently by cognitive psychologists and biologists such as Howard Gardner [1983] and Stephen Jay Gould [1981] in much of their writing.) Students who are found by intellectual testing to be low "across the board" on such a regimen of tests are not typically classified as having a learning disability. Instead, this diagnosis is reserved for persons who are found by psychometric testing to be unusually low *as compared to themselves* in one or more areas of academic functioning. Naturally, persons who manifest such unexpected difficulties are often surprised by themselves; worse yet, they may be ashamed of or even angry at themselves. It is not easy to be "different-minded" when academic struggle and even failure are involved. But from a wider perspective, we are all stewards of diverse intelligences, and we must all exert ourselves to learn what we do well and to capitalize on these talents, even as we learn what is hard for us and devise strategies for developing greater strength in those areas. For the person who has a learning disability, it is simply all this but more so. One of the foremost moral and strategic tasks of teachers is to help persons with learning disabilities and their peers grasp this philosophy of cognitive self-acceptance and use it to good mutual benefit.

The second direction in which we may explore the concept of intellectual diversity focuses on differences *between* persons. Human beings have long been preoccupied with comparing themselves and others in terms of intellectual prowess, often with a destructive result. Although we may wish to create classrooms in which such quantitative comparisons never occur, these hopes are difficult to realize. Not only does Western culture in general place a deep and constant emphasis on measurement and comparison—on being bigger, stronger, faster, smarter, richer, and so forth—but also schools seem to have been increasingly pulled into the same habit by widespread social demands that they continuously monitor student achievement. As a result, following both the wider culture and the school culture, children seem often to take the measure of themselves and others: Worse yet, they can be merciless in their assignation of a set "value" to a person. Thus, a person who does not read well might be called "dumb," and a person who struggles with writing may consider herself to be "worthless." For persons who have learning disabilities, life itself can be impoverished by this sort of reasoning. Having difficulties (or as kids often say, "being bad") at a key academic skill such as reading out loud means, at the very least, having to work harder than one's peers. It may also mean having to attend special classes, being excluded from intriguing courses or projects, or having to rely on special accommodations (e.g., books on tape) in order to meet the demands of the curriculum. But it may also come to mean a lowered social status, an injured sense of self-worth, or the feeling that school and learning "just aren't for me." Consider that only about 48 percent of students with learning disabilities graduate from high school or secure a GED, and only about 9 percent earn either a two- or four-year college degree (Vogel & Reder, 1998).

Thus, as so many of the autobiographers remind us, being different from other children can eventually be the equivalent of feeling "less than" others. Velvet Cunningham, for example, was diagnosed in the fourth or fifth grade, a time when many girls begin to experience something of a crisis of confidence in their intellectual capabilities (Brown & Gilligan, 1992): Interpreting her LD diagnosis as a declaration of her uneducability, she writes, "I thought that was it. I was never going to learn anything again." She describes her stealthy approach to her special education resource room each day: "I could always time it perfectly so I was always five minutes late, so the other (smart) kids would not see me going into the SPED class." For her part, Gretchen O'Connor interpreted her differences from other children as a reflection of her moral inferiority: "I feel like a really bad kid." Gretchen echoes countless other individuals with special needs when she states that she would have had a more positive image of herself growing up had she been taught that ADHD made her a *different* learner rather than a *disabled* learner. And Oliver Queen writes of his school district's decision to track him with "the lowest track students": "Their logic was simple enough—in an environment of idiots I would quickly blend in . . . and no longer feel the oppression that so tortured me in the mainstream."

Certainly, all of us who work with students who have learning disabilities (or any other kind of difference) wish that such comparisons—and the pain that they cause—could be just brushed away. If, however, we want really to understand and improve the experiences of students with learning disabilities, we must confront this pain, understanding that it is rooted in real intellectual differences that have somehow been improperly responded to. While much unhealthy distortion can come into the picture, a basic reality is that in the "community of minds" that is the classroom, students who have learning disabilities may often be the least "able" students in the performance of some academic skill. In order to keep the intellectual differences between students from leading to the caste-based classroom society described by Oliver Queen in his autobiography, teachers are challenged to do a great deal, ranging from openly deconstructing notions of "ablism" and "disability" to educating all students in a "frame of mind" that encourages self-knowledge, self-belief, a vigorous work ethic, and a clear sense of their right to a nourishing, substantive education.

It is equally important to remember that these same students may stand out as extraordinarily competent in any number of other areas. If we are to compare students with learning disabilities to other students, it is only fair to look also for the ways in which they are more able, wise, passionate, knowledgeable, and skilled than their peers. If we do not search, affirm, and celebrate these strengths, we constrain students' opportunities for using their islands of competency as springboards for academic success and self-esteem. As substantial research has shown, these strengths are often key to students' forming a future sense of identity. To have a learning disability is to be *both* able and obstructed, bright and bewildered. If students are essentially taught to think of themselves only in terms of their limitations, what a betrayal this is! By contrast, if students are encouraged to root their sense of self in what they enjoy and do well, and are guided to use these strengths as they approach tasks difficult for them, how much more likely they are to thrive in their learning and to become full participants in classroom community membership! Teachers who work with students to discover and nurture their strengths, allowing them ample opportunity for affirmation from the entire learning community, will notice gains for all of their students.

It is also important to note that the "bright" areas for students with learning disabilities often serve as the source for solutions to the puzzle of how to learn in the areas of their disability. Students, for example, who have impaired visual-spatial processing problems are likely to have a terrible time learning mathematics the way most students do; that is, by using manipulatives and drawing visual diagrams. If, however, such students have good verbal reasoning skills, the resourceful teacher can teach mathematics by playing to this strength. What special educators call "compensatory strategies" for learning in the area of one's disability are most often ingenious uses of a student's existing strengths.

The same claims can often be made when a student has a clear passion or an area of well-developed knowledge. The student who struggles with math might, for example, have a cultivated fascination with World War II. Could a sense for history—an appreciation, that is, for the sequencing of events and for cause-and-effect relations—help a student to cope with algebra? It most certainly could, especially if a teacher helps to connect these assets with other approaches found useful to students with difficulties in this area. Conversely, a teacher who inadvertently squelches a student's capacities either by failing to recognize them or by assuming an overly critical posture toward them does that student a major disservice. If, for example, a teacher responds to an eager young writer's compositions only by pointing out the mistakes in spelling and grammar, that teacher risks damaging the writer's creativity and feelings of accomplishment as a writer.

Of crucial importance in these writers' educational histories are those moments in which someone—often a teacher—recognized and supported their abilities. Lynn Pelkey, for example, describes her special education teachers as generally very kind, but believes that they underestimated her:

> I would do what they told me to do . . . but I was rarely asked to really think and I almost never experienced those moments when something I was learning came together and made sense.

In striking contrast, she describes one event during junior high school that has stayed with her over the years. Peter, her friends' algebra teacher, invited Lynn into his class—"a 'real' class with normal students!" She began skipping her officially scheduled class so that she could remain—illicitly but thrillingly—in the class taught by Peter. "Something magical happened to me . . . I wasn't memorizing, I was thinking." This experience of having a teacher believe in her intellectual potential and being in a regular classroom (an advanced class, at that) has remained with her over the years. Sadly, this experience was a notable exception in Lynn's educational career:

> *I expected to fail, so I set no goals, believing my ability was set . . . Thus, I learned helplessness . . . I hid who I was out of shame.*

Ten years after "flunking out" of the community college she attended, Lynn returned to complete her studies. As a result of her honest and persistent requests of her teachers to allow accommodations on assignments and tests because of her dyslexia, she developed a feeling of personal efficacy and resourcefulness, completing her associate's degree with honors.

In his autobiography, Aaron Piziali identifies David, a university writing tutor, as a strong source of support and guidance as he struggled to meet academic challenges: "Working with David was a bright moment in my educational career and one that reverberates across all spheres of my life." David helped Aaron identify his strengths as well as his challenges. In his letter to David, Aaron writes: "You were more concerned about getting me to recognize the ways in which I could do the work that best matched my developed skills." Our experience observing teachers who are successful with students with special needs confirms Aaron's testimony: They begin with a child's strengths, talents, and interests, making them visible and accessible to the student; then they help the child put his or her powers to work in meeting the challenges of the academic and social arenas.

To recap, then, it would seem that appreciating intellectual diversity begins with accepting the variegated, heterogeneous character of the human mind; teaching can only succeed when it is in touch with reality, and there is no escaping the fact that all minds are different. From one perspective, homogeneity would be convenient: How much easier it would be to teach! But there is little in nature to suggest that such a picture jibes with reality, regardless of whether one is talking about snowflakes or persons. In fact, learners flourish when their intellectual variousness is celebrated and even cultivated, when it leads to the formation of a culture in the classroom that actively seeks to be responsive to and affirming of the different ways that people discover, know, and articulate their knowing. It is this kind of classroom culture that Gardner and others hope to encourage; it is also the kind of classroom that the autobiographies collected here morally oblige schools to provide. Given that students comprise a "plurality of minds," it follows that education, too, should be pluralistic, affirming the manifold possibilities of each learner. Good teaching is not defined by unwavering commitment to a single pedagogy, but by the capacity to flexibly alter one's teaching in order to meet the community of individual, unique minds where they live.

In so doing, we cannot emphasize strongly enough that it is *not* all right to so dilute or shift expectations for students with learning disabilities that they are exempted from the opportunity to learn to read, write, speak, and perform mathematical operations with power and fluency. This is not "exemption," but rather constitutes *exclusion* from the rights and opportunities of sound educational practice. Students for whom expectations are so lowered that they fail to learn the arts and skills associated with the wider culture are, in fact, victims of educational neglect. Our job as educators, rather, is to see that students with learning disabilities develop proficiency in the "power discourses" of this society, recognizing that—in order to achieve this goal—we and our students may need to travel learning routes rarely taken. Indeed, the honoring of intellectual diversity does *not* mean abandoning the goal of assisting students to acquire competence in stock discourses; it means, rather, being willing to recognize, discover, and celebrate the many and various pathways to learning that can carry students to such competence. It also means being willing to shoulder the burden of providing students with the emotional and psychological encouragement that is essential to success. As these life stories testify, when an individual has a learning disability, learning is *hard.* Sometimes it takes a very long time to see the hoped for results. Educators, then, must accept that assisting a student who has a learning disability to gain academic proficiency involves attention to his or her whole person. If we educators fail to do these things, we may be complicit in leaving these students of ours to lives far less satisfactory than they might have been, and to the prospect that as adults they will be plagued by the problems commonly associated with social and economic marginalization.

Naturally, whenever we discuss the perils of *exclusion*, we inevitably enter into the discussions that currently surround the notion of *inclusion*. Several different meanings are associated with the term "inclusive schools and classrooms." Most commonly, however, the phrase refers to the notion that schools and classrooms will strive to help all students feel included as full members of the community, whatever their personal strengths and needs, language, or ethnic identity. The essential concept of inclusion not only possesses a clear, undergirding moral logic, but also (a) is supported by extensive research on the well-being of students with special needs and (b) is one of the principal emphases of the Individuals with Disabilities Education Act of 1997 (IDEA 97), the federal legislation that establishes guidelines for special education services.

For a long while, many teachers have been painfully aware of the "disconnected" students who are only partially included in regular classrooms. Nancie Atwell (1988) calls these students her "ghost students"; they were rarely in her classes because they were in the special education resource room "being remediated." Once she included them fully in the connected literacy activities of her own classroom, she found they set higher academic expectations for themselves, often reaching far beyond those discrete goals and objectives recorded on their individualized education programs (IEPs) to more complex, integrative competencies that were firmly connected to the academic activities of the regular classroom (Sustein, 1991).

Atwell's expertise joins with that of our autobiographers in affirming that, if teachers wish to achieve meaningful inclusion for their students, they must fully acknowledge students' needs to act willfully and creatively in the shaping of their own education. Models of classroom practice that place students in an essentially *passive* role are always problematic. This is perhaps especially true for students who have learning disabilities, for these students are more likely to be (a) subjected to purely directive instruction while in special education classes and (b) vulnerable to increasingly toxic levels of self-doubt regarding their own creative abilities.

Teachers committed to working within the intellectual diversity framework will naturally see the value of encouraging students to discover fulfilling and effective routes toward personal expression. Teachers must intervene to prevent students from feeling silenced or unimportant and from equating a difficulty with standard literacy practices with no longer having the "right" to express themselves as individuals. Indeed, teachers who give students ample encouragement to express their personal experiences, ambitions, and feelings, and who then show responsiveness to these expressions (whatever form they take) can do a great deal to keep alive students' interest and sense of ownership in both essential literacy and in lifelong education. As Aaron Piziali noted, the education of persons who have learning disabilities "is self-destructive and alienating if it is not approached from a point of respect and non-paternalism."

For all students—including students with some form of disability—"respect and non-paternalism" in schooling are exemplified in what can be called *dialogic* or collaborative practices. The testimonials gathered in this volume again and again offer at least two central criticisms of traditional schooling: (1) It is silencing and disempowering, failing to affirm the wisdom and creativity of students with learning differences. (2) It is noncollaborative, failing to engage diverse learners in designing and executing their own educations. A dialogic approach to schooling, in contrast, exudes interest, curiosity, and confidence in students as partners and co-citizens in the learning community of the classroom. It asks, "Who are you? What is the nature of your experience? What are your learning goals and aspirations? Will you work together with me in finding ways to realize these goals? And will you consider the goals that the wider community has for you and by what pathways we might reach them?"

Of course, the answers to such questions are never final. There is always more to be said or discovered, much that will require negotiation or reconsideration, and also much that may need to change in the students' worlds or worldviews before truly promising answers can emerge. But in a world in which individuals think and learn in unique ways, *not* asking these questions is tantamount to the disrespect and paternalism that Aaron Piziali instructs us to reject.

All in all, what the eloquent autobiographers gathered here suggest is that meeting the needs of students with learning disabilities requires a coherent *moral*— as well as *strategic*—framework for the classroom. This framework encompasses the *reality* of intellectual diversity, the *necessity* of providing effective, responsive instruction, and the *will* to collaborate with students in building learning communities of genuine promise and possibility.

Stories can, indeed, work on us like arrows. These stories offer us the opportunity to respond to a moral call to action on behalf of persons with learning disabilities and other special needs, engaging them as fully advantaged participants in our educational communities—participants who will not have to live and learn in the margins but who are met with a sense of wonder and responsible caring, with *"that shimmer of delight and intellect, the impressionable wonderment,"* that Christie Jackson captured so luminously in her poem.

What Works? Specific Recommendations for Those Who Teach and Live with Youth with Learning Disabilities

- Create inclusive classroom communities where all forms of diversity are valued.
- Explicitly teach intellectual diversity, making it one of the foundations of the classroom's culture.
- Honor and celebrate different approaches to learning.
- Support students in learning about their own minds and learning styles.
- Incorporate as many of Gardner's seven intelligences into teaching as possible.
- Teach in ways that are culturally, linguistically, and developmentally responsive to all students.
- Establish a clear community identity in the classroom, emphasizing commonality of mission and purpose.
- Recognize and affirm the "islands of competency" that reside in every student.
- Affirm the importance of students' feelings and attitudes toward learning.
- Honor hard work.
- Maintain high expectations in a climate of caring and responsibility, discussing frequently with students what will be needed to meet these expectations.
- Support copious and yet nonpunitive practice in basic literacy skills.
- Provide the structure, specific guidance, and opportunity for practice that students need to be successful.
- Develop collaborative relationships with students with learning disabilities.
- Involve students in setting specific goals and responsibilities at school and at home.
- Encourage autobiographical and journal writing, storytelling, artistic/media expression, or other activities that will enable students to affirm their life stories and further their creative expression.
- Create classrooms of promise and possibility for all students. Love the questions and challenges that come with the territory.

16

The Educational Lives of Students with Learning Disabilities

Harold McGrady

Janet Lerner

Mary Lynn Boscardin

In this chapter, we discuss what might be considered *best practice* in the education of students with learning disabilities. Although the primary grounds for this discussion are the 13 autobiographies gathered in this volume, we also draw upon relevant publications in the field of special education and upon our own experiences as researchers and teachers. Unlike many discussions of best practice in education that offer a unitary set of recommendations, here we hope to impress on both preservice and inservice educators the need to consider approaching instruction from a multiplicity of perspectives. Accordingly, we openly confront and debate each major theme voiced by the autobiographers, through this strategy sometimes affirming and sometimes challenging traditional approaches to instruction. Readers will notice that we sometimes raise questions for which there are no simple answers and that we sometimes embark on explorations of topics that are not brought to comfortable closure. By this strategy, we hope to suggest to readers the value and importance of an inquisitive, critical, and individualized mode of response to students with learning disabilities (LD) and the stories they tell.

This chapter is divided into two broad sections. The first of these is devoted primarily to a review of the autobiographers' statements concerning key areas of practice and policy in special education. Additionally, we use this first section to provide nonspecialists with information about many of the laws, techniques, and concepts that have played an important role in shaping special education in the

United States. While some important lessons for best instructional practice are unquestionably present in this first section, we reserve outright discussion and debate of best practice recommendations for the second section.

The Role of Special Education

Labeling and Classification

We begin this chapter by speaking to the most contentious and controversial of issues: labeling. Labeling in education often occurs primarily to marshal resources. Without the categorical label *learning disability*, most persons with significant learning needs would be denied access to special education services in all but two states. There is a certain comfort in having a readily available label for a given malady. It is perhaps assumed that if something can be labeled, then a cure must certainly exist. This misconception has led to confusion and disappointment in the field of education. Even though an educational difficulty can be labeled, labeling rarely leads to universal success as the polio vaccine did in the field of medicine. When it comes to student learning, the acquisition of knowledge is an individualized process, and a "one size fits all" principle is rarely successful.

Labeling had both positive and negative effects on our writers. For some, the label categorized and stigmatized them. It drew negative and demeaning comments from fellow students and even from teachers. The negative implications of the separation from other "normal" students were far-reaching. Nelson Vee, for example, mentioned that other children were quick to label him, and they laughed at him for his mistakes in pronunciation. Kevin Marshall Jr. associated learning disabilities with "shame":

> *Even though I recognize that it is not a fault (nor does it reflect on the kind of person I am or on my intelligence), there is still a part of me that feels that telling people that I have a learning disability could shape the way they view me.*

Velvet Cunningham was labeled with "dyslexia" at around age eight. Her mother reported that, "After she was diagnosed, she turned into a troubled, upset child." Velvet said she thought that she "was never going to learn anything again." She saw herself as being "stupid, dumb, and incompetent."

Some of the other life stories reflect the *positive* aspects of having a label. Alison May describes herself as "thrilled" when she was told that she had "visual and auditory dyslexia." She thought the labeling and diagnostic process had brought her greater self-evaluation, in that she could better assess her abilities or at least recognize when she was having difficulty learning. Additionally, she noted that the diagnosis positively affected her parents, prompting them to realize what a struggle it had been for their daughter to do as well as she had in school. Christie Jackson also found value in her diagnosis, saying that it gave her, "a feeling of peace and assurance that I wasn't an oddity." Claiming that diagnosis was "painful, yet calming," she explained:

LD is a label and, as a label, stereotypes will always surface. But that label is also a part of me. It's as much a part of me as my middle name, as my smile, as my love of lilacs.

Lynn Pelkey experienced *both* positive and negative effects of being labeled. She noted that the label *dyslexia* caused her to be set apart from others and designated as "different" or "less than." She asked, "Why must the learning disability categories be classified around negative attributes? Can we not focus on strengths or positive attributes?" On the other hand, she also felt some comfort when she was found to be "dyslexic," because, as she wrote, "Then you know it won't go away." The implication is that, once given a label, a student can then accept the disability, deal with it, and work harder to overcome it.

Labeling for these students, whether positive or negative or both, served as a sort of reality check. In other words, it placed them in a position where they not only had to confront their learning disabilities, but also develop constructive ways of dealing with the pressures of their environments. From these responses to diagnosis, we are able to extract a meaningful lesson about labeling: It has value only if it allows persons to acquire an accurate understanding of their learning difficulties and to develop effective strategies for meeting the educational, psychological, and social challenges that face them. These essayists discovered that simply knowing in a generic sense that they had a learning disability was not enough; they also had to be able to communicate to their teachers and professors how they learned and what they needed in order to be most successful in the classroom. Garett Day, for example, was able to describe the exact nature of his disability, while Alison May provided a detailed analysis of methods she used to compensate successfully for her disability.

Additionally, many of the writers talked about the basic fact that some people learn in a different manner. Acknowledging this fact, they say, should be the guiding principle for everyone who interacts with individuals who have learning disabilities. Christie Jackson put it simply, "Some people just learn differently." Or, as Gretchen O'Connor stated:

If I had been taught to believe that ADHD was a learning difference rather than a learning disability, I feel I would have had a more positive view of myself while growing up . . . I just do not learn the same way other people do.

Classroom Accommodations

A common practice today is to place students with learning disabilities in the general education classroom along with recommendations that accommodations be made by the teacher or special educator. This practice—known as *inclusion*—is consistent with the federal requirement that "to the maximum extent appropriate, children with disabilities [should be] educated with children who are nondisabled" (PL 105-17). This is sometimes referred to as the *least restrictive environment* or LRE. The 1997 Individuals with Disabilities Education Act (IDEA) amendments guarantee access to the curriculum for students with disabilities. How access is obtained is determined by assessing present levels of performance, including how the student's disability affects involvement in the general curriculum. As part of the Individual Education Program (IEP), goals and benchmarks, supplementary aids, and services are developed to enable the student to access and progress in the general curriculum. When most of the autobiographers attended elementary school, the term *mainstreaming* was in vogue. Although students with learning disabilities were mainstreamed into the classroom, this practice did not ensure that teachers would modify the curriculum so that it would be accessible to them.

Only two writers commented about their experiences in regular classrooms. Lynn Pelkey recalled joining a junior high school algebra class on a full-time basis, which she said was a positive learning experience. Garett Day, a young man who now holds a bachelor's and two master's degrees, reported a mismatch between his disability and classroom placement due to his teachers not making the appropriate accommodations. Attending an elementary school that had been built in the 1960s, he was enrolled in an "open classroom." He described this arrangement as "the worst design I can think of for a person with a hearing deficit or a learning disability," both of which he had. He said that no one from the special education department, or any other part of the school system, made an attempt to make accommodations for his identified problems. Though Garett spoke positively of his high school experiences in regular classes, he decried the lack of academic support from the special education department.

Alison May's story, on the other hand, shows how valuable appropriate accommodations can be. She recounted, for example, how her kindergarten teacher, after analyzing Alison's listening problems, instinctively made appropriate adjustments when giving directions. Good teaching paired with appropriate accommodations helped delay Alison's eventual diagnosis until her freshman year in college.

It is one thing to desire accommodations and not receive them, but it is another for students in this group to want to avail themselves of them, even though their teachers are willing to implement the necessary interventions to help. Kevin Marshall Jr., who is dyslexic, did not request accommodations when he had difficulty with Spanish in college. He said he "did not like the image that these accommodations represented" and that he did not want to use his learning disability as a "crutch."

Individualized Instruction

A large misconception among educators is that merely assigning a student to a placement such as a resource room constitutes an individualized educational program. IDEA is very clear about the need to provide IEPs to students with disabilities. It maintains that the concept of individualized instruction is key to the teaching of students with disabilities. Note that the initial word of the acronym IEP is *individualized;* however, according to our writers, the concept of individualized instruction was not always practiced by their teachers. Garett Day, Gretchen O'Connor, Aaron Piziali, and Michael Sanders each said their teachers failed to practice this concept. Some teachers were not flexible about finding strategies to meet the needs of individual students or matching their instruction to the unique capabilities of the student. As summarized by Gretchen: "Most schools have a set curriculum and routine method . . . but it is ridiculous to believe that all children will be stimulated by the same things."

Additionally, their remarks suggest that one-to-one instruction, or tutoring, alone does not guarantee successful learning experiences for students with learning disabilities. What may be more important is the *nature* of the instruction through such relationships. *Individual* instruction is not the same as *individualized* instruction. These writers argued persuasively that instruction must be attuned to a student's specific abilities. They said they failed when their instructors did not take into consideration their learning strengths and weaknesses.

While some of these authors wrote of their successes and failures with IEPs, others referred only to their educational placements. Some wrote of experiences in the general classroom, and others referred to being "pulled out" and placed in a resource room. For many years, it was thought that students with learning disabilities could not be adequately educated by classroom teachers because these teachers did not have the "specialized" skills to teach these students. No one considered that it was possible to train teachers through professional development so students with learning disabilities could remain in the general classroom. It was also believed during the 1960s, 1970s, and into the early 1980s that the only place a special educator worked was in the resource room or a self-contained classroom. These writers' stories contain strong memories of the resource room. Many felt that placement in the resource room was stigmatizing; other writers thought it was helpful, a quiet refuge. Based on the information gleaned from these authors, it is difficult to know how any student will react to a resource room placement.

Garett Day liked the resource room in elementary and junior high school. To him it was a haven from the "slings and arrows" that arose in interactions with his peers outside of that protected environment. In the classroom Garett was often the target of ridicule delivered by his classmates. He liked the intimacy of the resource room setting where he developed confidence working with other students, some of whom were better and some worse than he academically. Garett liked the resource room better in junior high school than elementary school because he could disappear into the resource room while changing classes, making it less noticeable. However, the resource room placement made it obvious to Garett that he had learning disabilities. When he went to high school and was no longer in special education classes, he decided not to tell his new friends about his disability because he was not sure how they would react. He noted that students have no choice about divulging their disability when they make the obvious trek to the resource room from their general classroom.

Several writers reported that the stigma of going to the resource room had a profound impact on them. They said that the name of the resource room was sometimes changed to make it more pleasing, but as Lynn Pelkey noted, "a rose is a rose is a rose is a rose." She said that, although the sign on the resource room door said, "RR," for "Remedial Reading," she (and everyone else in the school) thought the letters stood for "Retard Room." The ambiance and arrangement of that room merely fortified Lynn's feelings that she was "dumb." Her brother, also diagnosed with learning disabilities, was placed in the "Learning Community," which Lynn concluded was the same as her "Retard Room."

Lynn complained of another problem that often occurs in resource rooms: She was the only girl in her junior high school resource room. She described the effect of being in the room with a group of very active adolescent boys as a frightening experience, but the most significant effect of this placement was her interpretation that she was "the only girl in the whole school that was stupid." Because females tend to withdraw, determining if they are having problems learning is that much more difficult (Anderson, 1997; Kaye, LaPlante, Carlson, & Wenger, 1994; Lerner, 1993; McLesky, 1997; Shaywitz & Shaywitz, 1988; Vogel, 1990). Lynn's feelings were validated by the statistics that show boys are more frequently identified with learning disabilities than girls.

Aaron Piziali was outwardly angry about his experiences in resource rooms. He said about his four years of attending a learning center daily, "Over that time, I learned the most disabling skills ever." The resource room was a place where a multitude of techniques were taught (e.g., note-taking skills, keys to comprehension), but Aaron said that there was no attempt to help the students "gain an insight into our learning style and our relationship to [our disability] . . . [or] the psychological impact of the learning disabled identity." The consequences of this omission were revealed in diminished social success for students who were taught in the RR. For example, Aaron felt that the skills learned in the center were not "adequate enough to support and enable myself and my comrades for the terrain of classroom, school work, and school halls. . . . The social impact of learning disabilities," he warned, "is self-destructive and alienating if it is not approached from a point of respect and nonpaternalism."

Even if the room is not called the resource room and the "LD" label has not been formally assigned, placement in any program other than the general education classroom has a stigmatizing effect. Kelly Miskell was transferred into the "slow class" during first grade because the teacher "made me cry." Later, Kelly blamed the system for her language-based learning disability, which interfered with her ability to reason abstractly, retain information, and process new information because she was placed in "slow" classes. This placement contributed to what has become a lifelong battle with low self-esteem.

The goal of individualized instruction is not to abandon the curriculum, but to make the curriculum accessible to those with disabilities so they can enjoy the same benefits as their classmates without disabilities. To achieve this level of accessibility, teachers are not asked to alter what they teach as much as how they teach it. The instructional material maintains its integrity with a classroom-based intervention approach. Garett Day discovered, for example, that he was able to develop a deeper understanding of literature through music.

Early Identification and Intervention

The merits of early intervention as opposed to letting children outgrow their disabilities is still a topic debated among scholars, educators, physicians, and parents.

It harkens back to the nature versus nurture debates. One of the tenets of helping children with learning disabilities is that the earlier the detection, the more likely that intervention will yield success (Lerner, Lowenthal, & Egan, 1998). Few would argue against the value of early intervention, and many support the idea that it is easier to prevent the problem than to try to remediate a problem. From these student essays, however, it is clear that students rarely outgrow a disability.

Most students with learning disabilities are initially identified in the second or third grade, because it is generally believed that children should be reading by then. Children who are identified earlier usually have a speech and/or language disorder, a developmental disability, an emotional/behavior disorder, or fall under some other label (Lerner, 1993; Wiig & Semel, 1984). Difficulties arise in identifying disabilities earlier because parents do not bring their children in for preschool screening, pediatricians are not adequately trained to refer students for further assessments that fall outside the medical realm, and a general belief persists that the child will outgrow the problem. Some writers recalled that early identification and services were helpful, whereas others reported that early signs of their problems were ignored or misunderstood. These latter students had cognitive issues, such as coding, sequencing, categorizing, organizing, and memorizing, which were not necessarily identified at this age. This failure to identify learning disabilities came about because the students were either able to develop their own compensatory strategies or were in unfortunate situations in which the educators were not skilled enough to recognize learning problems.

Because his disability was detected early, Garett Day received early intervention services. Nelson Vee, Gretchen O'Connor, Kelly Miskell, Alison May, Christie Jackson, Oliver Queen, and Kevin Marshall Jr. reported that their early symptoms went undetected or were ignored. The resultant delay in receiving special help created serious difficulties in school and in life. For example, several of the authors reported the cumulative emotional effects and resultant lack of self-esteem, which we discuss later in this chapter. Advice such as "She'll grow out of it," or statements suggesting that the child was simply undisciplined, stubborn, or disobedient were sometimes contributing factors to the delays. As Gretchen explained, "If I had some help, I could have accomplished so much more and been spared the humiliation I felt when I was kicked out of school."

Several writers thought that early detection would have helped them avoid some of their learning problems, and that it might have eased their problems with self-esteem and emotional well-being. These stories tell us that early identification leads to better understanding of one's learning problems. The message the writers send us is "Don't ignore the early signs."

According to Maria Montessori, the famed physician and educator, there are critical periods of learning, and when these stages are missed, they can never be recovered. E. M. Standing (1998) recounts Montessori's analogy of the lady knitting on the bus: When the bus hits a bump she misses a stitch, and the only way to recover that stitch is to completely unravel the completed work. As educators we must be careful not to miss opportunities for helping students learn at critical periods of their lives, particularly in the early years, because, unlike the sweater, we cannot unravel time.

Measures of Success

The discussion around assessment practices has shifted over the last decade with the introduction of assessment-linked classroom interventions and mandatory statewide large-scale assessments as a way of measuring the progress of students with and without disabilities. Prior to this time, the primary emphasis was on formal standardized assessment measures such as the Wechsler Intelligence Scale for Children (WISC)–Third Edition (WISC-III), Peabody Picture Vocabulary Test-Revised (PPVT-R), and Woodcock-Johnson Psychoeducational Battery-Revised (WJ-R) as a means of identifying individuals with disabilities and determining progress. While these psycho-educational assessments yield important information about receptive and expressive language, short-term and long-term memory, sequencing, visual-motor skills, and so forth, they are not directly linked to instructional practice. The information yielded from these instruments is rarely helpful to teachers who must modify curriculum content to accommodate student learning needs.

Another difficulty is that these measures produce normative scores. As such, these scores indicate whether or not a student is performing at grade or age level but do not by themselves offer any indication of progress made in learning the curriculum. Criterion-referenced scoring, on the other hand, offers an opportunity to determine how much of the instructional material a student has actually mastered. Many states are moving away from requiring IQ scores for the purpose of identification and placement of individuals with disabilities in favor of measures more directly tied to the curriculum.

As educators look to improve instructional practices, states have introduced curriculum frameworks to which large-scale assessments are tied. The 1997 IDEA Amendments require that students with disabilities be included in state- and districtwide assessments with appropriate accommodations. For those students with disabilities who cannot participate in general assessments, alternate assessments must be developed. Within the IEP, any exemptions, accommodations, or modifications related to the state or district must be specified along with the appropriate rationale. In response to the need for accommodations or modifications, curriculum-based measures are being implemented by teachers and special educators alike. With greater emphasis placed on functional forms of assessment that are closely linked to student instructional needs, teachers can be fairly certain about the progress a student is making in the classroom and whether students with disabilities are actually accessing the curriculum.

Aaron Piziali spoke directly to that point: "I shouldn't be compared to anyone else. My evolution is the only standard against which to check my progress." While Aaron's desire to focus solely on his own progress should be taken into consideration whenever educators measure a student's progress on IEP objectives, it is important that Aaron be able to accurately assess his abilities in comparison not to other students but to grade-level expectations.

Lynn Pelkey was particularly upset with the "state tests"; she gave a heartrending account of what persons with learning disabilities might feel and how they might react when faced with mandated, high-stakes testing. Lynn noted that her performance was always at the bottom of the class, and the gap grew over the years. Perhaps the worry, anxiety, confusion, panic, and anger she suffered—as well as the strategies that she used to hide her failure— were the same as students without LDs, but their impact and consequences were much more severe.

Nelson Vee had a similar bad taste from state testing, and recalled always scoring low in comprehension on the numerous standardized tests he was required to take in his state. The good news is that he developed survival strategies, such as reading text slowly and carefully and rereading sections and whole text, which allowed him to pass the comprehension test for college placement.

These life stories reveal the worry and anxiety students with learning disabilities experience when they are subjected to testing. Their stories should make us think about the value and purpose of such testing for those who are challenged with learning disabilities.

Psychological, Social, and Emotional Consequences

There is debate within education regarding whether or not the educational needs of students with learning disabilities can be separated from their emotional and psychological needs (Adelman & Taylor, 1984, 1994; Kazdin & Kagan, 1994; Reynolds, 1984, 1991). In emphasizing the psychological and emotional impacts of their learning disabilities, the autobiographers suggest that such a separation may be dangerous. They spoke repeatedly about the complex effects of their learning disabilities, including behavior problems, low self-esteem, poor interpersonal relationships, drug and alcohol abuse, anger, depression, and job failure. Unfortunately, most of the autobiographers echo Garett Day's criticism that "The school system never felt compelled to educate me on how having a LD would impact on my life."

The authors of these stories also stressed the importance of learning to *accept* their own disability and, thus, who they are. Velvet Cunningham wrote:

> *The hardest thing was owning my difference and incorporating it into who I was instead of trying to hide it. I am a good person, and I can be loved and accepted for who I am and not hated for who I am not.*

Nelson Vee added, "I see that acceptance is a must. I was blessed and cursed by it. It is part of me." Oliver Queen also recognized the importance of acceptance:

> *I refuse to make excuses, refuse to blame. My learning disability and ADD are a pervading factor of my life. Though burdensome, they are no longer intrusive.*

True acceptance of a learning disability includes the knowledge that life will be harder for the person living with it. As Garett Day noted, a person with learning disabilities must work harder than a nondisabled peer to accomplish the same learning. These students acknowledged the value of developing a realistic understanding of their own limits and abilities and of encouraging others to understand their individual uniqueness. Acceptance of the uniqueness of their own learning problems seems to have been an essential ingredient to their success in life.

Despite these successful examples, each writer experienced some level of emotional difficulty related to their learning disability. Alison May lamented a lost childhood. Oliver Queen felt bedeviled by intense pressure from his parents to succeed academically. Kelly Miskell described long battles with low self-esteem, which led to sexual assault and abuse, resulting in serious suicidal ideation. Lynn Pelkey and Oliver Queen pointed to the creation of a subculture of students with learning disabilities, and Christie Jackson described how she abandoned her career goal. Several authors commented on "learned helplessness," and "acceptance of failure," while others, like Velvet Cunningham, went "bad," acting out their despair through behavior problems and/or addictions.

The emotional well-being of individuals with learning disabilities is constantly threatened. Educators need to consider Aaron Piziali's desperate question: "What do I do to survive emotionally, and how do I go about it?" and then ask ourselves how we can help individuals with LD survive emotionally—not just academically. The writers spoke repeatedly about the need for teachers to "understand" and "care." They vividly recalled their teachers' negative attitudes as well as incidents in which teachers blamed them, making them feel "ashamed" or "embarrassed," or destroyed their hopes and dreams. How many lives have educators failed to the degree that their students' lives have been less fulfilled? A teacher's positive impact on academics may be overshadowed by the emotional legacy: Good teaching may, in fact, go unrecognized and unappreciated, whereas bad teaching may live long in the memories and futures of individuals with disabilities.

Although Garett Day, Aaron Piziali, and others remembered some teachers as being positive and caring, the writers overall provided many more examples of teachers' negative attitudes and behaviors, which led to serious psychological consequences for these students. Oliver Queen became a discipline problem as a young child. He said his teachers did little more than offer special techniques, that they failed to "understand" his learning disabilities. Velvet Cunningham spoke of a particular teacher who "always snaps at me." Alison May related the pain of repeatedly failing to understand assignments, saying she "felt not only the pain of my failure to understand, but also that I was a bad person for not understanding." Nelson Vee described school as a negative experience, suggesting he never got what he needed and got a lot of what he didn't need. His teachers always seemed to "blame" him, calling him lazy or careless or telling him that he could do things if he wanted to, which eventually made him angry about having a learning disability. Lynn Pelkey felt that teachers underestimated her and rarely asked her to think. She said, "I did a lot of memorizing, but not much understanding."

Gretchen O'Connor, as a child with inattentive and disorganized behaviors, described the wrath of teachers or other authority figures when she failed to heed a direction given by a coach or a teacher. It was not her behaviors per se that seemed to be the problem, but rather that the roots of her behaviors were misunderstood by teachers and other adults in her life; she noted that her teachers "overlooked all the areas of my life where I was succeeding and instead concentrated on my faults. Because of all the people telling me there was something wrong with me, I was unable to recognize any part of myself as positive and 'normal.'"

By contrast, Kelly Miskell described at least one supportive relationship with a teacher and offered the following advice to other teachers: "Work hard to treat each child as an individual, and give them the respect they deserve." She said that teacher trainers "need to start educating teachers more about what kids face in and outside the classroom."

These writers repeatedly talked about the way they were treated by teachers and how teachers' attitudes affected their emotional well-being. Their stories demonstrate the power of the self-fulfilling prophecy and the powerful impact, positive and negative, of teachers' expectations of their students. Teachers who care, accept, and understand may be just as important as educational methodology and techniques.

Administrative Support and Advocacy

The context of special education administration also has evolved with time. With the advent of site-based school management, many principals find themselves in the dual position of their buildings' general education administrator and director of special education services. Many are ill-equipped for the challenges associated with these positions. Special education directors no longer find themselves functioning primarily as advocates of children's rights but as gatekeepers for school district budgets.

Given the contemporary trend to create unified school districts, it is important to train educational leaders so that they possess a complete understanding of the critical linkages between general and special education, as well as the potential benefits these linkages offer the entire school community. Understanding these linkages, as well as the overall effect of diversity, is essential in providing effective services to students with disabilities. Special and general education administrators need additional training in the skills necessary to deal with the increasingly complex demands and diversity of the students with disabilities in order to be effective advocates for these students.

Sometimes inadvertent administrative failings have effects that go unnoticed but have long-term consequences. Oliver Queen described the struggle he experienced when the school system decided to provide special education services by sending him to a private school, ostensibly because they did not have an appropriate program for his combination of learning and behavioral problems. He felt that the school system was happy to get rid of him.

Kelly Miskell still harbors intense feelings against her school system—feelings that climaxed following an incident in a twelfth grade class. When Kelly replied to a teacher that she didn't know the answer to his question, he screamed at her, called her a "typical blond bimbo," and told her not to embarrass his class by her lack of intelligence. Kelly never returned to the class. When the principal called her to discuss the matter, he said that if she promised to keep the incident quiet, he would waive the course requirement. He also assured her that the teacher would not return the following year. Kelly felt that she had been manipulated by the principal and blamed the school board for not dismissing the teacher earlier, even though such incidents had been reported before. This incident merely confirmed her feelings of low self-esteem.

These stories remind us that school systems need to provide adequate training so that key administrators develop an understanding and appreciation of effective programs for students with learning disabilities.

Personal Insights and Best Practices

From the personal insights offered here, educators can learn much about how to help students with learning disabilities understand and accept their disabilities and how to develop effective instructional interventions. In this section, we focus on the knowledge and skills these writers suggest are important in providing a positive learning environment for students with learning disabilities.

Labeling

Do students need to be labeled as learning disabled in order to receive effective interventions? As we learned in these stories, some of the writers stated that the process of labeling was actually helpful to them in that it identified their problem, while others were troubled by being labeled and thought it was stigmatizing. These two views reflect the controversy surrounding labeling in the field of education. Is it the label that is stigmatizing or the student's academic failure that causes the stigma? While not wanting to diminish the significance of this question, we would argue that the answer is nevertheless unimportant. We find that labeling does not always result in appropriate interventions and sometimes leads people to believe these students are not intelligent. A label in and of itself does not help students, or their teachers and parents, to clearly understand the nature of their learning disability and how it affects their learning. If a label does not help a student, then its utility must be questioned. Conversely, these stories demonstrate that some students are empowered and able to control their learning environment once they are able to self-evaluate accurately the effects of their learning disability and communicate those effects to others. Teachers and parents play a critical role in helping students understand their learning disabilities and in helping them articulate their learning needs, both in the educational and affective domains, in order to obtain the necessary accommodations.

Accommodations

Over the course of our collective careers we have seen accommodations interpreted to mean simply reducing the amount of work assigned to students with learning disabilities or asking them to redo an assignment that was not completed correctly. Both of these approaches demonstrate a failure to fully understand how students with learning disabilities approach their learning. We suggest that it is essential that educators be given the knowledge and skills to develop alternative teaching strategies. Educators must learn what questions to ask and how to assess student performance in order to devise interventions that help all students, not just students with disabilities, access the curriculum.

Garett Day and Gretchen O'Connor, in their stories, provided examples of what happens to students when classroom accommodations are not responsive to student learning needs. For an accommodation to be successful, it must be not only appropriate, but also comfortable so the student does not feel stigmatized in any way. Sometimes students give up when the accommodation is not appropriate or, if, when asking for an accommodation, students feel singled out as being different.

While some students learn to ask for accommodations, at times this may not be enough, particularly at the secondary and postsecondary levels. Many teachers and professors are not trained to design and implement accommodations, while others feign ignorance to avoid having to make changes. A common misconception is that an accommodation is an excuse for the student not to work hard. Regardless, students must learn that accommodations are a right afforded to them through their IEP and assistance from others must be sought when teachers and professors do not cooperate.

Teachers must sometimes step beyond their comfort zones and be innovative and creative. Not thinking necessarily of altering what is taught as much as how it is taught is a form of human engineering. Teachers are simply being asked to figure out how to convey the same information to the student but through varied pedagogical approaches that ultimately make the information more accessible. There are several models from which to draw (Reid, Hresko, & Swanson, 1996): medical, perceptual, sensory, kinesthetic, behavioral, developmental, and cognitive. Some of these models are more helpful than others. Much depends on the individual needs of the student with learning disabilities.

Individualized Instruction

These life stories demonstrate the need for individualized instruction and for teachers to understand each student's unique needs. Giving a student a placement was not synonymous with giving them an individualized education. Sometimes particular placements provide a safe haven from the "slings and arrows" of the general education classroom, as Garett Day acknowledged. But other writers addressed the stigma of being assigned to resource rooms, the segregation such a placement created, and their awareness of the lowered expectancies such a placement entailed.

Aaron Piziali put placements in perspective when he said their purpose is to help students understand their own learning patterns and their own relationship to their disability. Although students will infrequently express that they are often hesitant to ask for individualized instruction for fear of rocking the boat, there is no room for placements that simply warehouse students with disabilities. When these writers were in elementary and secondary school, the *inclusion* movement had not yet taken hold. These were students of the *mainstreaming* movement, where the goal was simply to place students with disabilities in the general classroom with little concern about their ability to access the curriculum.

These writers had little uniform experience in their education, bolstering the argument for individualized educational programs. Often one writer liked a practice and found it helpful, while others found it had little value. Educators must understand that learning disabilities extend beyond a label, that what works and is useful for one student will not necessarily work for another. This supports the basic philosophy that instruction must be tailored to the needs of the individual student and not to the needs of the teacher. Teachers must be taught to isolate student learning difficulties at an individual rather than a group level, through collaboration with special educators and other involved personnel. Together they must identify a student's learning problem and determine what strategies will help that student access the curriculum within the context of the general classroom.

The ability to problem solve using a strong analytical approach is often key to developing a responsive individualized educational program. It is not unusual to review an IEP for a student with learning disabilities only to discover that most of the interventions recommended are behavioral rather than instructional. Trying to alter behavior is sometimes perceived as less onerous than trying to develop responsive instructional interventions. Also, by focusing on behavior, it is easier to place the responsibility for change on the student. Certainly, for a student whose disability is word recognition, even the most thoughtful accommodations are no substitute for a sound reading intervention program that offers systematic training in word-attack strategies, phonemic awareness, and auditory discrimination.

Early Identification

The stories show clearly that early and accurate identification of learning disabilities is essential. The value of early identification varies with the type of learning disability. While early diagnosis of learning disabilities related to reading is desirable, it is not always possible because this skill is not acquired until later in the developmental cycle. Writers who were not identified as learning disabled until later in their school careers said that many years were lost because their problems were not accurately diagnosed. Early identification is critical to establishing learning skills and strategies important to future academic success. This was best illustrated in the case of Gretchen O'Connor: If she had been identified early as needing accommodations, the magnitude of her organizational and sequencing difficulties could have been dramatically reduced, potentially eliminating her later problems with self-concept and self-esteem.

The cases of Gretchen O'Connor and Lynn Pelkey illustrate the role sex differences play in early identification. Boys are two and one-half times more likely to be identified as having a learning disability than girls (U.S. General Accounting Office, 1981). According to Lerner (1993), the reasons for this discrepancy remain speculative. It is possible that boys are more biologically vulnerable (Lerner, 1993); boys exhibit more disruptive and physically aggressive behavior, signaling a loss of control when they are troubled (Shaywitz & Shaywitz, 1988); and boys have more difficulty with visual motor abilities, spelling, and written language mechanics (Vogel, 1990). Girls' difficulties, however, are often confined to the cognitive, language, and social realm (Shaywitz & Shaywitz, 1988) and some aspects of reading and math

(Vogel, 1990). It is these more visible learning difficulties in boys that make them more likely to be identified. Teachers must be particularly vigilant of bias when it comes to recognizing learning difficulties in girls and be more astute in recognizing the less visible characteristics of all children with learning disabilities if these children are to benefit from early identification.

Early identification is associated with testing. This perspective needs to change; early identification needs to be thought of as ongoing and as something that can be done by all educators working with students. A student not performing according to teacher expectations raises an early flag for concern. At this critical juncture, a teacher should stop, ask why performance is not meeting expectations, and seek assistance from others in making modifications to the student's educational program. Modifications in the form of performance-based assessments can be directly linked to the curriculum, providing a more objective approach to designing interventions. In many instances, teachers already know what a student can and cannot do, and it is unlikely that a standardized test is going to provide them with significant pieces of information that will help them design effective classroom interventions.

Testing

Testing and assessment practices are undergoing critical review. The continued use of standard protocols is no longer acceptable and has been deemed outmoded because the protocols are unresponsive to student instructional needs. While those who provide these assessments may feel uncomfortable with this new stance, we must remind ourselves that our purpose is to engage in best practices that meet student needs. Using assessment instruments for the sole purpose of labeling students is no longer acceptable. As mentioned earlier, many states are recognizing this as they rewrite their rules and regulations governing special education.

Some students, such as Aaron Piziali, will always feel comparison to other students is unnecessary. A good compromise is a curriculum-based measurement program that allows for both self-comparison and group-level comparison to maintain a balanced evaluation program. This provides the student with a sense of progress measured against different realities. Lynn Pelkey and Nelson Vee were not pleased about having to participate in statewide assessment tests. States and school districts must be able to provide students with valid and reliable modified forms of these tests, recognizing that a particular test modification for one student might not work for another student.

Teachers will need to be trained to provide students like Lynn and Nelson access to their state's curriculum frameworks and to the necessary testing accommodations that help students approach academic requirements prepared and with hope rather than with futility and despair.

Social and Emotional Consequences

All of our essayists talked about the deep social and emotional effects of having learning disabilities. A revealing finding from these life stories is the pervasiveness of the psychological and emotional consequences of their learning disabilities. Many of the authors reported a lack of understanding by their teachers and parents about how their learning disabilities affected them emotionally and psychologically. The memories of specific negative experiences were painful and long lasting. What teachers do and say makes an enormous difference in the lives of students with learning disabilities. Students are very sensitive to whether teachers believe in them, are supportive of their efforts, and are able to adjust their teaching to their unique learning differences. Some of the essayists felt that their behavioral problems were misunderstood. The following factors (McGrady, 1983) have been known to contribute to the strong relationship between behavioral problems and learning disabilities:

- the reductions in both academic and social skills, which have accumulated over the years
- the student's own reactions and responses to consequent successes/failures in attempting to cope with learning problems
- the effects of reactions from others to their past failures and low levels of functioning

It is important that teachers possess skills in managing behavior, social interactions that include relationships with others, and anger. In addition, training in substance abuse is critical, as drugs and alcohol are frequently misused by those with learning disabilities to bolster self-esteem and self-confidence.

Oliver Queen also cited the necessity for students with learning disabilities to develop an internal locus of control and take responsibility for their actions rather than blame others. Students with learning disabilities tend to develop a learned helplessness that is reinforced by others. Often students will hear others say to them, "You have a learning disability, poor thing" or "I am sorry to hear you have a learning disability." To assist with the development of an internal locus of control, parents and teachers must work with the student to develop realistic, achievable goals while not confusing the importance of caring (Noddings, 1992) with the reinforcement of debilitating behaviors.

Administrative Strategies

Administrative support and advocacy is critical to the overall success of students with learning disabilities. Administrators cannot respond only to crises as they strike. Students with disabilities must be considered as valued members of the educational community. This attitude must emanate from the top of the administrative hierarchy. Administrators must create *inclusive* school environments. The term *inclusive* is used in a manner that encompasses the term *inclusion* commonly used in special education, but it is conceptually more far-reaching. Whereas *inclusion* is most often used by special educators to describe students brought back from pull-out programs or separate placements, the term *inclusive* embraces and accepts students from the moment their educational careers commence. The inclusive school is supported by the concepts of community (where diversity and solidarity coexist and complement one another) and contiguity-based solidarity (where, unlike organizations, there is a natural interdependence based on a shared sense of belonging). Sergiovanni's (1993) organization-community continuum supports the structure of schooling, and Maxwell's (1994) contrastive elements of similarity-based and contiguity-based solidarity are used to convey the purpose of schooling. (See Boscardin & Jacobson, 1997 and Jacobson & Boscardin, 1996 for a more detailed explanation.)

Students with disabilities in an inclusive school are viewed as valued, integral members of the school community, not as expendable commodities or individuals who detract from the school setting, as was the case of Kelly Miskell, where the administration swept an incident of abusive behavior by a teacher under the rug, pretending it never occurred. Although students with learning disabilities are not always the easiest ones to teach, administrators must make every effort to reinforce attitudes that embrace all forms of diversity and create a school culture that is positive for both students and staff. Administrators need to advocate for appropriate programs, encouraging communication and collaboration among special education and general education personnel in order to build a school community in which the learning differences among all students are embraced, not just those with disabilities.

Conclusions

We analyzed 13 autobiographical essays of individuals with learning disabilities to determine the effects of their educational experiences within the context of ongoing debates within education and special education. These stories poignantly document the writers' struggles in school with labeling, placements, educational programming, early identification, assessment and testing, administrative support, and advocacy; they show also the students' unsuccessful social experiences and the difficulty they encountered in coping with accompanying psychological and emotional problems. In planning educational interventions, it is of paramount importance to consider the cumulative effects of learning disabilities on the social and emotional lives of these individuals, especially during adolescence and beyond.

We believe that good teaching in a caring environment is necessary for the maximum development and life success of all students. However, for students with learning disabilities, it is *imperative.*

17

Easing a World of Pain

Learning Disabilities and the Psychology of Self-Understanding

Robert Kegan

"It is a common trait among the LD to know how to endure hardship and keep dark secrets."

—Oliver Queen

I doubt that anyone can come away from the eloquent testimonies to personal courage in this book without feeling some sense of outrage at the worlds of pain their authors have had to endure. In nearly every account, we learn that this pain can be dramatically reduced by a new understanding of oneself, one's past experience, and one's present possibilities. In some accounts, that new understanding is actually assisted by the rendering of a diagnosis of a learning disability (LD), which makes comprehensible the unacknowledged burdens under which one has been toiling for a long time. This itself is a notable finding in this book, suggesting that sometimes diagnostic labels are liberating rather than stigmatizing and demeaning. In other accounts, the new understanding is afforded by the empathic company of a good listener—someone "trained though human," in psychologist William Perry's words. By seeing a way of learning that is "different rather than dumb," such persons may help those with learning disabilities to extend to themselves a form of respect and regard they have not felt before. It is not necessary, in other words, for magic pills to be dispensed or wands to be waved for worlds of pain to be greatly diminished. A person's learning disability itself does not need to vanish for the person to feel liberated from an imprisoning situation.

Such a finding makes clear how important it is to reconsider the usual way that psychology is joined to the subject of learning disabilities. A "psychology of self-understanding" may be as important (or more important) to the consideration of learning disabilities as a "psychology of dysfunctional learning." I am not intending here to discount the value of neuropsychological or information-processing approaches to learning disabilities. But I do want to suggest that psychologies that attend to the ways persons construct their experience may be a crucial resource to anyone who wants to relate effectively and helpfully to people who have a learning disability, as opposed to addressing just the disability itself, as if it were a merely inconvenient and complicating fact that the disability happens to reside in whole people. Just like doctors have to resist the tendency to treat broken arms, ulcers, or even manic-depressive illnesses rather than persons who happen to have these maladies, those with a personal or professional interest in learning disabilities have to decide whether they will direct their central loyalty and interest to "learning disabilities," as a detachable phenomenon, or to persons living with learning disabilities. This chapter is an unabashed address to the latter.

A second advantage to the autobiographical sweep of these accounts is the unavoidable fact of psychological development. Anyone holding the misconception that people in their 20s and 30s have not yet lived long enough, or gone through enough qualitative change, to merit autobiographical attention, would surely be disabused of such thinking after reading these accounts. It is a very different thing to be living with a learning disability at age eight than it is at age eighteen. A psychology of self-understanding that also attends to the qualitatively different nature of our meaning-making at different ages might be an especially useful ally to anyone interested in reducing the risk that having a learning disability must mean lifelong captivity in a world of pain.

The third and last of my introductory observations of these autobiographies is that they make clear that children and adolescents are often put at risk not only from a *lack* of adult attention, but also from a *surplus* of self-interested adult attention. The authors show us that one source of our inability as parents, teachers, coaches, and others to hear the voice of a child in pain is that we adults, without even realizing it, can be too tuned in to the script we have authored for the child's voice. If a particular goal or accomplishment is the fulfillment not of the child's dream but the adult's dream for the child (to be a certain kind of student, to operate in the family in a certain way, to have a certain career, to be a professional basketball player, or whatever), it is far less likely, no matter how apparently "involved" and "invested" the adult is, that the adult is actually going to hear the child. The greatest promise of a psychology of self-understanding is that it can be a champion of the child's own voice, a representative of the child's interest that tempers the adult's tendency toward unwitting self-interest (even well-intentioned, hard-working, apparently self-sacrificing self-interest).

The "psychology of self-understanding" to which I refer has its origins in the work of Jean Piaget, whose central passion, interestingly, was actually similar to that of the autobiographers in this book. Like them, Piaget wanted people to stop demeaning the different way a group of learners tended to think, but rather to recognize this different way as composed of a dignity, wholeness, consistency, and power all its own. This group of different learners did not have learning disabilities, but were, rather, children in general. Piaget showed that children utilize a logic that is not a partial or incomplete version of adult thinking, but is rather a distinct species of thought all its own.

Piaget's work has led to a whole branch of psychology, often referred to as "constructive-developmental" psychology, because it attends to developments in the very meaning-constructing systems people use to understand themselves throughout the lifespan—not just in childhood, but in adolescence, and adulthood, as well.

Considering some of these qualitatively different systems of self-understanding—well-reflected in the autobiographers' accounts—we may be helped to new thoughts about the differing risks persons with learning disabilities run at different periods in their lives and the differing nature of supports they need from others to be protected from these risks. I should perhaps be explicit about one point before I begin this discussion of developmentally different systems of self-understanding: I do not regard persons with learning disabilities as likely to lag behind others in the complexity of their self-systems. While many of the autobiographers refer to themselves as "behind" in relation to their age-mates, they are talking about continua such as grade-level norms in language arts abilities. This chapter may represent a new and more interesting way of claiming that people with learning disabilities reflect the same spectrum of "intelligence" as people without diagnosable learning difficulties in its suggestion that persons with learning disabilities should not be expected to reflect a range of self-complexity any different from that of their age-mates (a suggestion that is clearly supported in these accounts).

It is no surprise that most of the autobiographers do not date the origins of their learning disabilities before they are well into the primary grades. Until we are seven or eight none of us (whether we have learning disabilities or not) have a self-system complex enough to construct durable self-properties of any sort, positive or negative. Young children live in the moment, and their "self-understanding" is as mercurial as New England weather ("if you don't like it, wait a minute"). They can be dissolved in a puddle of tears one moment and delighted the next, with no need to "repair," "integrate," or "process" the prior disaster. In Piaget's language, they do not yet "conserve" through time or space any durable mental category. If they are girls, they believe they could become boys. They believe they could become older than an older sibling. Their expressed preference for one kind of fruit juice can be replaced tomorrow by a preference for another. No impulse, desire, or perception at one moment is predictably linked to the next. Naturally, then, young children who notice on any given day that they lag behind another in memorizing nursery rhymes or recognizing letters are unlikely to regard this as a permanent condition or as evidence of an enduring aspect of their own minds.

This is quite different from the system of self-understanding that typically begins to evolve between five and seven, and is usually well-established by eight to ten. The child at this age constructs a self that has become a psychological "container" for properties that not only are true at this moment but also are ongoing. "I don't like liver" no longer means "I don't want it now." It means, "I didn't like it yesterday; I don't like it today; and I can be presumed not to like it tomorrow, thank you very much!" The child with "durable categories" can describe a self with ongoing properties ("I'm a Catholic girl"), ongoing preferences ("I like my hair combed this way!"), ongoing dispositions ("I don't care for Uncle Willy"), and ongoing self-assessment ("I suck at math").

This older child has gained a more powerful grasp of the world and herself, but she has also lost something quite valuable to any child who is likely to encounter repeated forms of frustration and unsuccess, such as those that may come with learning disabilities. What the child with the more complex self-system has lost is the protective effect of having the consequences of one moment count very little for one's ongoing sense of self. The simpler, younger children can fall on their faces, literally and figuratively, at one moment, and pick themselves up and carry on in the next moment with no significant cost to their self-esteem.

Issues of self-esteem begin to be important around age seven or so precisely because a new form of the self has been created—a self that is, for the first time, deciding about its properties ("I'm a fast runner; I'm a bad writer") in an ongoing way. Thus, development—a phenomenon so desired by parents, teachers, and many others in the child's life—can itself be a risk condition for some children, a theme that will recur in this chapter when we consider transformations in self-understanding from late childhood to adolescence.

What risks particularly obtain for children who have learning disabilities once they have constructed this "durable self," and what are the particular forms of support they need as a buffer against these risks? The route to a buoyant sense of self-esteem for the "durable self" comes from the experience of self-efficacy, the sense that "I can." The biggest risk is that children who have learning disabilities will come to the conclusion that they "don't work." The developmental psychologist Erik Erikson referred to this era in the life span as "the age of industry," a time of making and goal-directed doing, the era of the "industrial self." Above all, the self has to "work." This is the earliest world of pain we learn about in the autobiographic accounts, the sense of oneself as a bad machine:

> *"Class clown," "fidgety," "rude," and "a discipline problem" were the standard accusations made against me up until mid-elementary. (Aaron Piziali)*

> *I was constantly told to sit down, to stop talking; if the teacher gave instructions, I was always one step behind everyone; if we were supposed to hang up our coats, I would be easily distracted by something else. I was constantly yelled at for being disruptive, and I remember feeling very guilty, but, also confused: I did not mean to disrupt my class, and I often didn't even realize I was doing anything wrong. (Gretchen O'Connor)*

> *When I was younger, teachers and coaches often accused me of being lazy because of missed or uncompleted responsibilities. This criticism hurt because I knew it was not true, but it did seem that the harder I tried, the more things slipped by me unnoticed. (Joshua Green)*

These words about "standard accusations," being "constantly told," and "often accused" indicate very clearly the beginnings of a durable, ongoing self-perception of behavioral ineffectiveness.

What supports are especially well-suited to children who have learning disabilities, given what we know of their self-understanding? Let us return to the image of children at work, of children who experience themselves as people who work, in both senses of that phrase: They function properly (they "work"), and they produce. The second sense is not meant to invoke the dispirited assembly-line worker, but something more like the craftsman or artisan who "shows his work" and calls on us to attend to the artist's intention; that is, we are called on to take the work seriously. This raises the first question for those who would seek to be supportive to children who have learning disabilities: How wide a range of a child's endeavors are we willing to respect? The child's making can go on in the world of bodily discipline (dance, sport), social production (sustaining a friendship circle), or mental exercise (being a good student, a computer jock, a chess team competitor). It may be solo work (pianist or model builder) or done together (membership in a basketball team or science club). It may be more characterized by its products (coin collection, doll house) or its processes (keeping friends in touch with each other). The question, again, for those who would be supportive is, "How wide a range of being up to something will win our respect and attention?" If we shrink the respectable "industrial" arena down to the one domain in which children who have learning disabilities have most difficulty, we create childhood worlds of pain.

This does not mean we should ignore the arena in which the child has the most difficulty. What it does mean is that effective support must go well beyond providing the aid and special help that can strengthen children's "workability" in the arena of their greatest weakness. We must also look for, welcome in, and celebrate the arenas in which the child already works. "God bless the child who's got his own," the old song says. Yes, a parent of a child who has a learning disability may need to be on the lookout for a good tutor. But are we, with equal fervor, on the lookout for the child's bliss, the child's passion, the activity that fires the child up?

All children (whether they have learning disabilities or not) need and can have spheres of activity or social participation in which they can demonstrate and experience their competence. The child's bliss may run quite contrary to the expectations of the parents, to their own talents, politics, life-style choices, or dreams for their children. It is not even an entirely bad thing when a child chooses an arena in which the parent is a rank amateur. The parent's noviceship or indifference may protect the child from having his or her own passion overrun by that of the parents.

Those persons and environments are maximally supportive that consider the widest range of childhood industry worthy of respect. Any activity ought to be respectable so long as it admits of the following four features:

- It is not harmful or hurtful to the child or to others.
- The child can come to be in charge of it, feel like it is "my own," "my work."
- It allows a building up of skills, competencies, mastery—the acquisition of a discipline.
- It can be displayed, publicly acknowledged, recognized, seen.

Every child needs and can have the opportunity to "show their stuff," to display competencies, even to "show off." (And I do not mean this in the unpleasant sense. The unpleasant child we call "a show-off" has usually had too little opportunity for genuinely acknowledged displays of personally accomplished mastery or competence.)

The fact that some children, such as children who have learning disabilities, will have necessarily frequented spheres of participation in which they will struggle or feel ineffective should in no way sentence them to a pervasive sense of incompetence. It is as outrageous that a child who has a learning disability would not have other arenas for the intense experience of personal mastery and accomplishment as it would be to deprive a good reader who is a poor athlete from the arena of language arts. Nor do I mean to suggest that these other arenas for children who have learning disabilities need to be, or should be, exclusively found outside of school. School is not or should not be a monolithic arena. It is incumbent upon schools that they themselves create as wide a set of respectable, coachable, applaudable arenas for childhood industry as possible. While the good school has every right to insist that children who have learning disabilities participate in arenas they may find unpleasant and frustrating, the parents of these children (and all children) have an equal right to insist their children experience school as a place where their teachers are also seeking to discover the children's interests, are supporting their own learning agendas, and are being helpful to them on behalf of meeting their own goals relative to these interests. This is not an extraordinary thing to ask of the schools. It is dismaying, in reading the autobiographies in this book, to find not a single gradeschool that seemed able to provide this for the child.

Between the ages of 12 and 16, our system of self-understanding undergoes a further, qualitative but gradual transformation. A more complex structure evolves that, rather than being defined by the "durable category," can now hold onto multiple categories and the relationship among them. The concrete thinking of the child is exercised now in the service of the abstract thinking of the adolescent. The self becomes less identified with simply pursuing its own interests, purposes, and plans (the industrial self of late childhood), and more defined by shared feelings, expectations, and agreements with others. This new, more complex mode of self-understanding can internalize the point of view of another and relate to it intrinsically rather than extrinsically, thus creating a new capacity for empathy and mutuality with others. Internal self-perceptions undergo a similar increase in complexity—a shift from the child's registering of outer social or behavioral manifestations (abilities, preferences, habits) to the adolescent's registering of inner psychological manifestations (inner motivations: "I feel conflicted"; self-attributions: "I'm becoming much more self-confident"; biographic sources: "my mother's worrying has influenced the way I think about the future"). This new world of self-understanding constitutes a move from the "industrial self" to the "interpersonal self," a self whose loyalties, identifications, and sense of personal coherence and esteem are oriented to its integration, psychologically and socially, with "the surround," the community beyond itself, which it is prepared to relate to in an entirely different way than in childhood.

When this new system of self-understanding is fully evolved sometime in adolescence, it is a cause for celebration, relief, or self-congratulation among the adults who have lived with a formerly semisocialized creature (the "industrial child" is also "the child on the make," as Erikson pointed out). That child has now become a responsible member of the family, of the community, of society. The "interpersonal self" has become socialized, become more a part of "society" because—society's values and expectations having been internalized—society has become more a part of the self.

However desirable such a transformation may be and however much parents and teachers and other adults surrounding the adolescent seek—without knowing it—exactly this development, it too (like the development that brings on the industrial self) involves a loss as well as an obvious gain. The industrial child loses the protection from past personal failure implicating one's future sense of self. The interpersonal adolescent loses the protection of a merely external, transactive relation with the surround. If the values, messages, and definitions of all our surrounds—which the adolescent now internalizes and identifies with—were completely benign, there would be no need to be protected from them. But they are not.

So while it is true that adolescents who do not make the developmental move to the "interpersonal self" are at risk, it is equally true that adolescents—especially adolescents who may be a part of any marginalized or socially demeaned subgroup—are also at risk if they do! Identifying with the surround (as conveyed by family, peers, school, society-at-large) means taking it inside psychologically, not just strategizing in relation to it to get one's needs met. It means having it "make us up." It means drawing the cultural air into one's psychological lungs (something the younger child does not have complex enough mental development to do). If the cultural air were pure, this would not be a problem. But where is there such a culture? Certainly it is not to be found in the surrounds of a single one of our autobiographers, and they hail from all walks of American life. If the surround has toxins—if it has devaluing, demeaning, disempowering, stigmatizing ways of regarding members of any subgroup—then taking in the surround also means taking in these toxins and to some extent identifying with them, a process of self-poisoning. If a culture is filled with toxins favoring white people, males, thin people, heterosexuals, able-bodied people, people who enter their families biologically, people who learn in the ordinary, expected fashion, then the development of the interpersonal self—growth itself—can be a condition of risk, a danger to an adolescent who is nonwhite, female, heavy, homosexual or bisexual, physically challenged, who joined their family by adoption, or who has a learning disability.

Psychologists seem to rediscover a version of this same risk about every 30 years. In the 1960s, David Elkind wrote about the child with a physical handicap or challenge who is at risk of going from being "a happy, gutty, scrappy kid" to someone with a depressive, self-rejecting experience of self in adolescence. Lyn Brown and Carol Gilligan (1992), in the 1990s, described a transformation they found in girls in very similar terms. At 10, they said, they are spunky, self-assured, resilient, and decisive; at 16, they are ripe for depressive uncertainty, self-deprecatory, and without their big voices. Will it take us another 30 years to notice a particular depressive turn to which certain children—say, children who join their families by adoption, or children with learning disabilities—are vulnerable in adolescence? Adolescence, in general, is a time (or, some would say, a "condition") ripe for depressive self-uncertainty for anyone. But the combination of new psychological equipment permitting an internalization of the surround and membership in any socially demeaned subgroup is a recipe for an especially corrosive turn in self-understanding in adolescence.

We can see exactly this turn in the accounts of our autobiographical informants. While they do not necessarily describe themselves as happy in childhood, they are plucky and embattled. The forces they contend with they see as outside themselves (the people and systems who called them "rude," "fidgety," "class clown," and "a discipline problem"). It is quite a different battle when, by internalizing and identifying with the negative picture of themselves picked up in the surround, they begin to stand against themselves. This is a second and qualitatively different world of pain we hear in the autobiographic accounts:

At 13, I was sad, afraid, isolated. I came to believe I didn't have anything to say. (Nelson Vee)

I struggled to fulfill what I perceived to be my parents' expectations for me. I thought they expected this latest round of testing to verify that I had some learning disability and perhaps would confirm that my difficulties had not been due to their neglect. I desperately wanted to absolve them. I was the faulty one! (Alison L. May)

I thought I was stupid, fat, ugly, and worthless for a long time. So when Mr. Peeps told me I was a "typical blond bimbo," I guess he was confirming my negative view of myself. Then when the principal of the school just sort of swept it under the rug, he made it all seem unimportant. Nobody once said to me that those things were not true, and nothing was done to show me that his actions were wrong. Therefore, I was allowed to accept that kind of treatment from a teacher. A teacher! You know, those people who are smart, intelligent, and highly educated. Yes, that is who confirmed to me that I was worthless. (Kelly Miskell)

I was so tired of disappointing my parents. I knew I was doing poorly in school, but I never expected to be kicked out. I think this was a turning point for me in many ways. I think this is when my parents finally gave up on me, and when I gave up on myself. I was tired of not being understood and of being hurt so much that eventually I stopped caring about myself. I couldn't trust anything I believed, and I became a sponge for other people's opinions. I never told anyone my feelings because I was so embarrassed about myself all the time. (Gretchen O'Connor)

How can we think about the particular kinds of supports needed to ease this very different world of pain? I suggest we return again to the metaphor of toxicity. Internalizing the toxins of our surround leaves us intoxicated in our self-understanding. The protections from, and routes out of, this world of pain may lie in antitoxins and detoxification, in people or processes that fight the poisons we have taken into our system.

When we are intoxicated, we do not see straight or think clearly. When we are intoxicated in our self-understanding, we do not see ourselves clearly or think clearly about ourselves. It is possible to live in this fog for years and years, and the longer we do, the more costly it is.

"Antitoxins" and "detoxification" are meant to suggest two different sources of relief from this particular world of pain. The first, antitoxins, refers to saving counterforces, relationships that live alongside the toxic ones, providing us instead more wholesome psychological air to breathe. As the autobiographic accounts demonstrate over and over again, even a single relationship with one other influential person who holds up a different picture of us can begin to neutralize or counterbalance the poisons that have made our self-understanding sick.

This story of "one warm hand in a freezing world" is a central finding in numerous studies of how people who have overcome traumatic life histories have been able to do so. Sometimes this person is a professional helper such as David to whom Aaron writes:

> The sessions we had were healing moments. What was so important was that you took the time to look into and behind my papers to see how I constructed them both psychologically and cognitively. You not only painted a clearer picture of my work style but also tried to teach me how to paint that picture myself.

Sometimes the person is a peer to whom we risk showing our fullest self, and their acceptance of us allows us better to accept ourselves. Remember Christie Jackson's story:

> The day after the test, I was sitting on a stone bench with a friend of mine. I mentioned I was upset, that I didn't feel smart sometimes. She nodded her head, and I heard something in the way she spoke, a hesitation, that seemed very close to mine. So I went out on a limb.
>
> "Well, I have an LD." I was afraid that I would be branded by my intimate revelation, or worse yet, that it would be totally ignored.
>
> "What? Well, so do I."
>
> Like long-lost family reunited, we understood each other. We spoke about the feeling of failure, about the pain of isolation. Nothing is more comforting than to hear someone else speak the words you are unable to express. She let me talk mostly, yet her eyes told me that she wanted to soak in all I said, as if my words were what she longed to hear another human utter. Then she thanked me, and I will remember this as the only time I have ever been happy to have an LD.
>
> "Christie, you just put my mind so at ease. Your way with words, with expression, they speak of all that I can only try to express but can't. You have a communi-

cation skill to comfort people by saying exactly what they are unable to say, but need to hear themselves. Thank you."

As antitoxic as a single healing relationship can be, nothing may be so beneficial as participation in a "filtered" alternative subcommunity in which the very same dynamics of the interpersonal self-internalization, socialization, and identification, practiced now in "clean air," fight against the poisons with which one has long lived. We need only look, for example, at the shocking statistics on suicide attempts by homosexual adolescents, to consider whether gay and lesbian support groups or gay-straight alliance groups in high schools are an extracurricular frill or a potentially life-saving source of support. How much more would our autobiographers have found their teenage worlds of pain eased had they had regular access to learning disability support groups facilitated by people able to help them feel for once normal about who they were? Such experiences of social integration might have provided profound counterpoint to those all-too-common moments in which they felt that they had to hide who they were, thus relieving them of the burden of those "secrets" that Oliver Queen says folk who have learning disabilities learn to live with like a second skin.

These antitoxic forms of support, clearly, do not ask the "interpersonal self" to operate any differently than it had been operating. The self is still being "made up" by the surround. But this same mode of self-understanding that brought the toxins into the system is now fighting those toxins through the internalization of the more wholesome self-definitions communicated in the more positive relationships. Subject to the opinions of the surround, the interpersonal self is desperately in need of more experience of a more benign surround.

But another way out of this world of pain may occur to the reader: "Become less 'made up' by the surround; learn to stand apart from others' definitions of who you are and decide more for yourself who you are." Such a capacity would leave us less dependent on others to counteract the poisons we take into our system, and put us in a position to cast them out, to separate ourselves from them, to purge ourselves by standing against them. Interestingly, the call for such a capacity—which would permit a more "self-detoxifying" route out of the adolescent world of pain—amounts to a call for a third, qualitatively more complex mode of self-understanding, the development not of "the industrial self" or "the interpersonal self" but "the self-authoring self." The self-authoring self is less "written by" the definitions of the surround—as these are communicated by family, school, friends, and society-at-large—and more able to itself be the author of its self-definition. The self-authoring self has the capacity to critique, or reflect on, the messages and scripts offered by society. Where such scripts are depreciative, this capacity to critique amounts to the capacity for detoxification.

Two things need to be said about this hope or exhortation for people with learning disabilities to secure for themselves this second, detoxifying means of psychological support: one cautionary and one optimistic. The first thing to say is that it is unrealistic and unfair to ask teenagers to be able to lift themselves by their own psychological bootstraps out of their internalized self-definitions. This is so because all the research demonstrates that the self-authoring mode of self-understanding does not develop before young adulthood and often not until well into adulthood. The implication of this cautionary note is that we must not ask teenagers to do this by themselves, but should rather emphasize the abundant provision of nontoxic relationships and subcommunities for adolescents with learning disabilities in order to support their more wholesome self-perceptions.

The optimistic note—and a good way to conclude this chapter—is to point out that there is ample evidence in these autobiographic accounts for the existence of this more complex mode of self-understanding and its salutary effect on one's relationship to oneself as a person who has a learning disability. "Whenever some teacher or parental frustration becomes the mirror of who you think you are," Aaron Piziali says, "you're in danger of being blocked." This is a construction of reality that comes from someplace beyond the interpersonal self, because it is able to look at the workings of the interpersonal self and critique its limits. Aaron's words ring out with the personal responsibility of the self-authoring self. He is making not only a claim against the distortions of a frustrated parent or teacher, but also a claim against the idea that the self must take this definition as its own. The words that follow these signal a different kind of bravery than that of the industrial self and the interpersonal self. This is the courage to be responsible now for the ways one can foster one's own ongoing "disabling"—or refuse to—without letting others out of their responsibility:

> *I am a prisoner, a survivor, a target, and a struggler, continuously defending, negating, and recreating myself. My disability? My disability is that I have been disabled, as well as discouraged and discounted, by a temporarily able-minded, able-bodied general public. My success and failure have been based on an existing value system created by the dominant majority. Although I am now constantly disabling myself though a process of disbelief, exacerbating disabilities already in work, I know that I shouldn't be compared to anyone else. My evolution is the only standard against which to check my progress. That I now struggle as I do for self-acceptance, may, in fact, be my learning disability. Thus, my learning disability is something I must perpetually fight to define and also something I must fight to reject.*

Well enough supported, the process of development itself, it seems, can create another route out of a world of pain.

18

Forging Identities, Tackling Problems, and Arguing with Culture

Psychotherapy with Persons Who Have Learning Disabilities

Pano Rodis

The autobiographies gathered in this volume provide lucid and revealing accounts of what it has been like for their authors to grow up with learning disabilities. Years of life experience are encoded in words and thus made elegantly and movingly visible.

As such, these essays can function as powerful teaching tools for therapists, allowing us to extract learnings about what sufferings and benefits learning disabilities (LDs) seem to engender, how to diminish this suffering (or at least to find meaning in it), how to cultivate and celebrate strengths, how to challenge long-held fears and anxieties, and how to generate the means for a more abundant future. All of these lessons are here—sometimes stated outright, sometimes in need of elaboration, and sometimes gaining force only when placed under a particular theoretical lens.

The published literature on psychotherapy with persons who have learning disabilities is surprisingly scant, especially when compared with the large number of studies that explore the kinds and degrees of psychological difficulties and life problems that can be associated with LDs (Bender & Wall, 1994). This scarcity may be due in part to the fact that, typically, psychologists are charged with the task of *diagnosing* LDs, while *treatment* is usually considered the domain of educators. The logic undergirding educators'—particularly special educators'—involvement in supporting mental health agendas is clear: They spend a great deal of time with students with LDs, and they unquestionably have a powerful influence on their pupils' academic and psychosocial education. But—as the testimonies in this volume make clear—the logic supporting the involvement of psychotherapists is at least as compelling. Nonetheless, there is little evidence to suggest that psychotherapy has been widely and generally engaged in working for the benefit of persons with LDs. As an illustration of this point, it should be noted that only two of the autobiographers (Gretchen O'Connor and Nelson Vee) mention a sustained encounter with mental health treatment. Moreover, in both of these cases, there is no indication that LDs and their impacts were directly addressed by their treatment providers.

In the hopes of making some contribution to changing this state of affairs, the broad purpose of this chapter is to discuss how psychotherapy might be designed to benefit persons who have LDs. Perhaps encouraging therapists to think about how to approach therapy with persons who have LDs will lead to more dialogue—and then more action—in clinics, schools, and other settings. Specifically, then, this chapter aims to access the wisdom of the autobiographers who participated in the *Learning Disabilities and Life Stories* project, to integrate these learnings with data and concepts found in the research literature, and then to apply these learnings to psychotherapy. In so doing, this chapter tries to answer questions such as the following: What issues and problems, resources and capabilities, do persons with LDs commonly bring to psychotherapy? How can therapists be sensitive to—and helpful in supporting—the developmental processes of persons who have LDs? And, what psychotherapeutic values, approaches, and strategies are most congruent with some of the most frequently expressed challenges and aspirations of persons who have LDs? Although this chapter touches on a range of both psychological and philosophical issues, it is primarily oriented toward helping mental health practitioners carry out the actual task demands of doing psychotherapy. All the same, it is also hoped that nonpsychotherapists will find what is written here helpful in expanding their understanding of both the inner and social worlds of persons who have LDs.

Stated simply, psychotherapy is a process designed to assist persons in achieving positive change. Whether this process is conceptualized as "healing," "problem-resolution," or engagement in a special kind of affirmative and empathic fellowship, the fundamental rationale is the same: for clients to experience their lives as palpably *better*. Of course, the right to decide what makes a life "better" (or worse) belongs ultimately to the individual whose life is the subject of the therapeutic dialogue. Recognizing this, the psychotherapeutic strategies described next generally share the aim of bringing the question *How can I live better?* to the fore, thus actively engaging clients in change processes. Moreover, as a key value of the approaches suggested here, change is conceptualized not merely in reference to the world of the self (e.g., the client's emotions, beliefs, or ideas), but just as emphatically in reference to the social and cultural worlds in which clients live. For oftentimes, in order for life to be better, persons must take action to change the practices, attitudes, and ways of talking that define such wider social spaces as the school, the family, and the workplace.

Perspectives from Other Research Studies

Despite the relative sparseness of published research on psychotherapy with persons who have LDs, there is a vigorous and extensive body of literature on the effects that LDs can have on the well-being of the persons who have them. Taken as a whole, this literature suggests that persons with learning disabilities are inclined to suffer more often than the general population from (a) depression (Brumback & Weinberg, 1990), (b) stress and anxiety (Margalit, 1992), (c) poor social interaction skills and lowered social status (Rourke & Fuerst, 1991; Voeller, 1993), (d) external locus of control and learned helplessness (Lewis & Lawrence-Patterson, 1989), (e) conduct disorder and delinquency (Larson, 1988), (f) low self-esteem and feelings of incompetence (Barton & Fuhrmann, 1994), and (g) substance abuse (Spreen, 1988). *The Diagnostic and Statistical Manual of Mental Disorders-IV* (1994) states that "Many individuals (10%–25%) with Conduct Disorder, Oppositional Defiant Disorder, Attention-Deficit/Hyperactivity Disorder, Major Depressive Disorder, or Dysthymic Disorder also have Learning Disorders" (47). Despite the relevance of such broad claims, it is generally recognized that the mental health impact of LDs is influenced and may be mitigated in each individual case by a host of clinical, personality, and environmental variables (Spekman, Goldberg, & Herman, 1993). These include the specific nature and severity of one's LD, the level of support provided by one's family, economic status, the degree to which friendship and other social support is available, the value and goodness-of-fit of one's educational program, the existence of personal competencies that offset areas of impeded performance, and the established ways that persons have for making sense and meaning out of their experiences (Margalit, 1992). The interaction of learning disabilities with these and many other variables—each of them altering the diagnostic and therapeutic picture—is quite evident in each of the essays collected here. The strong parental advocate that Alison May found in her mother, for example, likely played a significant role in helping her to escape some of the bitter experiences reported by writers whose parents were either less able to be supportive or—as in the case of Gretchen O'Connor—might be described as abusive. Similarly, an obvious talent such as Kevin Marshall, Jr. had in athletics or Michael Sanders had in debate not only gave them a basis for evolving positive self-concepts when they were young but also protected them during the period of later adolescence when their LDs finally emerged as significant. There is very little in the research annals, however, to suggest that learning disabilities should be underestimated as a potential source of unhappiness and maladjustment, especially for those persons who must cope with manifold or severe cognitive difficulties, lack of environmental resources, or other life challenges.

Past studies concerning what causes the negative mental health effects associated with LDs may be sorted into three categories. The first—but by no means most widely embraced—of these posits a *biological* explanation; that is, its proponents claim that organic brain differences may be at the root of such symptoms as poor social understanding, diminished or "robotic" affect, impulsivity, hyperactivity, and explosive anger (Rourke & Fuerst, 1991; Brumback & Weinberg, 1990). According to this position, socioemotional symptoms are not peripheral and secondary to neurological differences, but among the first-order and primary expressions of such differences. Perhaps the category to which this line of reasoning is most often applied is Attention-Deficit/Hyperactivity-Disorder (ADHD), a syndrome in which brain differences, cognitive processing differences, and behavioral difficulties appear to be closely correlated. A second LD category for which a neurobiological mechanism is used to explain socio-emotional disturbance is that popularized by Rourke (1989) as Nonverbal Learning Disability (NLD). According to Rourke, the syndrome of cognitive and psychosocial deficits (including problems with social perception, judgment, and problem solving) associated with NLD are the result of the destruction or dysfunction of white matter in the brain. While conceptualizing the psychological challenges associated with LDs as biologically grounded may have benefits in certain cases (e.g., reducing the tendency to blame persons for their difficulties), this approach is limited by (a) the inability of this model to describe the majority of persons with LD, (b) the absence of data to support the model's application to common LD subtypes such as dyslexia, and (c) the danger of leading to the broad prejudice that socio-emotional symptoms may be biologically "given" and thus resistant to intervention.

The second—and probably most widely shared—theory about the causes of socio-emotional disturbance in persons with LDs is grounded in a concept of *developmental vulnerability*. According to advocates of this position, persons with LDs may develop negative self-concept, anxiety, depression, or become frustrated and angry as a result of their difficulty in meeting developmental challenges, such as schooling, earning social esteem, or establishing a career. As persons' efforts to acquire a sense of competence and mastery over their environment are repeatedly thwarted by their LDs, a range of maladaptive and compensatory behaviors may set in, negatively affecting ego-formation, socialization, and other important developmental processes. Certainly, among the virtues of this second theory are not only the large number of studies that support it, but also the suggestions it offers to persons with LDs concerning how their lives can be improved. It follows that if there is a logic of experience that leads to psychosocial dysfunction, then there must also be experiential pathways to psychosocial health. Unfortunately, this approach is also rather susceptible to the tendency to see most problems as fundamentally rooted in the LDs or in the persons who have LDs, and thus may lead clinicians, parents, and educators to be less challenging of the social conditions under which persons with LD must live.

The third and perhaps most radical position on the causes of psychological suffering in persons with LDs differs from the first two in that it locates the source of psychopathology not in the persons who have LDs but in the environments and cultures that surround these persons. According to proponents of this position, many of the negative mental health consequences associated with LDs are effectively created by inappropriately narrow and prejudicial cultural notions of what constitutes intelligence, social attractiveness, and academic excellence. The general grounds for this view are succinctly stated by Ray McDermott and Hervé Varenne (1995) in the following passage:

> Culture, the great enabler, is disabling . . . People use established cultural forms to define what they should work on, work for, in what way, and with what conse-

quences; being in a culture is a great occasion for developing abilities, or at least for having many people think they have abilities. People also use established cultural forms to define those who do not work on the "right" things, for the "right" reason, or in the "right" way. Being in a culture is a great occasion for having many people think that they have disabilities. Being in a culture may be . . . very dangerous. (331–332)

The essence of this position is that there is nothing inherently wrong or deficient or disabled about persons with different cognitive processing styles, but that mainstream culture—especially mainstream educational culture—does a startlingly good job of making such persons *feel* like damaged goods. Even worse, persons who do not measure up to the standards of mainstream culture may be compelled to *live* like second-class citizens, able to access only less desirable educations, less prestigious social status, and less well-paid jobs. The psychological and social effects of being declared "misfit" are poignantly discussed by virtually every contributor to this volume: Oliver Queen, for example, discovers alarming overlaps between racism and the treatment of persons with learning disabilities, while Kelly Miskell paints a disturbing portrait of how her lack of secure social status during childhood made her susceptible to sexual victimization as an adolescent. Works such as Howard Gardner's (1983) theory of multiple intelligences and Mel Levine's *Educational Care* (1994) provide support to the position that the culture of schools in the United States creates misfit status in many children by unfairly refusing to recognize the talents that do not sit squarely within the traditional academic paradigm. Naturally, this theory about the causation of psychological difficulties in persons with LDs suggests the importance of working for meaningful change in cultural settings such as education and the workplace. For clinicians, the central implication of this third view is that psychotherapeutic treatment should exclusively focus neither on "fixing" a person nor on helping the person "adjust" to the LD, but on (a) challenging and reframing the concepts of *abled* and *disabled,* and (b) advocating for enlightened changes in the social worlds in which the client lives.

Optimally, clinicians should consider the potential relevance of all three of these theories when providing psychotherapeutic treatment; every case is, after all, different. However, in diagnosing and treating persons with LDs, care and discretion should be exercised. As the writers included in this text have testified, persons with LDs are frequently subjected to two kinds of misunderstanding. On one hand, the psychological challenges of LDs are too frequently underestimated or denied, leaving persons potentially vulnerable to the ill effects and comorbidities listed at the beginning of this section. On the other hand, however, LDs are frequently overpathologized, resulting in a form of misunderstanding that can be every bit as pernicious as denial; persons with LDs are no strangers to the damage that can be done by the deficit-laden assumptions of others.

As an illustration of the dangers of underestimating or denying the emotional effects of LDs, it might be useful to consider Gretchen O'Connor's case. Despite the fact that she had been diagnosed with ADHD, her emotional suffering went unacknowledged by both her parents and her teachers for many years. As a result, her psychological status went from bad to worse, leading eventually to severe depression and drug abuse. "How come nobody ever saw the fear in me?" she asks. As already noted, mental health practitioners cannot be considered exempt from missing or underestimating the effects of LDs; education about LDs and their effects is simply not emphasized enough in the training and ongoing professional discourse of psychologists and counselors. Additionally, failure to consider one of the three theories discussed may be tantamount to denial; a clinician, for example, attempting to counsel persons of like temperament, education, and worldview as Aaron Piziali without honoring the "culture-as-disability" approach might well run the risk of either having them drop out or—much worse—furthering the social oppression that they already acutely feel.

As for the second kind of misunderstanding—that which is linked to excessively deficit-laden assumptions about persons who have LDs—it is instructive to reflect on Lynn Pelkey's comments. As Lynn makes vivid in her essay, persons with LDs who fall too often under the hammer of negativity may internalize a deep sense of personal deficiency: "As a child, my foundation for hating myself grew out of my much noted shortcomings and lack of any abilities deemed positive." Psychotherapists, then—like parents and teachers—must be careful not to radiate in any fashion the perspective that LDs render those persons who have them *less than* others. Indeed, as has been suggested by contributors to this volume, the very term *disability* should be employed gingerly and critically. Whose province is it to decide what is deficit and what is normal, who is able and who is disabled? Perhaps, in the end, it falls to each person in collaboration with certain chosen others to make this call. Moreover, we might well hope that each person who has undertaken this very important judgment decides—as did many of the contributors to this volume—that their so-called disabilities have been also a source of vital personhood, strength of character, and ethical learning. In the end, clinicians must be open to how clients name, feel, conceptualize, and value the set of aptitudes, experiences, and obstacles we are here grouping under the increasingly problematic rubric of "LD." It may well be that one of the central goals of therapy is to transform the entire construct of LD, allowing what is first called by others and experienced by self as a malady or calamity to become something altogether different. Indeed, to positively revalue one's LD may well have a substantial impact on the revaluation of one's self, one's experience and idea of the world, and the meaning of one's life.

What the Autobiographies Teach Us

It is, then, entirely timely now to shift away from the frames of reference provided by other studies of LDs—studies conducted almost exclusively by professional "experts"—and instead draw directly from the writings offered to us here by persons who have become experts on LDs by way of lived experience. These autobiographical essays are almost bottomless sources of insight and wisdom, and it is impossible—especially within the bounds of a single chapter—to fully harvest their contents. We must, instead, be satisfied with relatively brief discussions of only a few of the most important findings and with presenting them in a form that is most likely to be directly useful to therapists.

Accordingly, I will develop three modes or approaches for the psychotherapist or counselor who has the opportunity to work with persons who have received diagnoses of LD or ADHD. I use the word *mode* (and not *model*) because it is more suggestive of flexibility; a therapist can, even in the course of a single session, enter into several modes of interaction with a client, whereas the employment of a model of treatment typically demands sustained compliance. Indeed, the three modes described next are not independent of each other, but productively overlap and interact with one another, offering in their coexistence increased options for therapeutic healing.

The first of these is the *Self-Psychology* or *Identity Formation Mode.* In this mode, the therapist focuses on helping persons to grapple with core issues in the evolution of personhood. While general theories about identity formation (e.g., Erikson's theory) apply to persons who have LDs, the autobiographical essays in this volume alert us to the possibility that certain developmental issues can become uniquely central to these persons.

The second therapeutic mode—the *Problem-Solving Mode*—necessitates that the therapist actively collaborate with the client to solve problems that he or she may be having at school, in the family, or in other areas of life. In the Problem-Solving Mode, a premium is placed on *pragmatic intervention* or on intervening in a direct, practical way to create more positive conditions for the client. Nonetheless—in contrast to an interventional style often associated with special education—the therapist aims to avoid simply "managing" the client's affairs (for this may only encourage feelings of inefficacy) but rather collaborates with the client in learning the arts—both practical and philosophical—of thoughtful problem solving.

Finally, the *Rhetorical Mode* emphasizes the development of persons' proficiency as social thinkers, actors, and speakers. Because LDs powerfully affect persons' social identity, status, and opportunity, it is important to support their ability to reflect on and influence social processes. Accordingly, in this mode, therapists help clients to discern and refute the arguments embedded in disabling educational and cultural practices, and to evolve and internalize arguments that encourage self-esteem and productive living.

The Self-Psychology or Identity Formation Mode

One of the most powerful contributions of the autobiographers gathered in this volume is the way that they propose a rather radical shift in how learning disabilities can be conceptualized. Whereas the foremost frame in the professional community for understanding LDs is neurological or psycho-educational, the writers collected here suggest that it may be more meaningful to think of LDs primarily as constructs that influence and mediate a person's sense of *being* and *identity,* or of self-in-relation-to-self and self-in-relation-to-others. Certainly, the autobiographers do not dispute the long-established perspective that learning differences impact educational experiences, nor do they deny that these differences warrant searching for what special educators call "compensatory strategies" or ways of coping. But the deepest meaning of having an LD appears to be the way it affects one's sense of personhood. The penetration of LDs to the very center of self-hood is so pronounced that many of the writers refer at some point in their essays to *being LD*. The very notion of learning disabilities as a condition of being may seem curious and even undesirable. Why should any person experience life mainly in terms of what is, at least on the surface, an unasked-for, unwanted facet of identity? It is, however, important to keep in mind that these conceptualizations are not purely self-determined, but rather arise out of lifelong interactions with social forces, both intimate and institutional, benign and destructive, all of which insist on LD status and identity. "LD-ness" is not a chosen condition, but rather one that a minimum of 15 years of education and myriad other experiences is likely to embed deep under one's skin. Once identified as having an LD, the internalization of LD-ness may be all but inevitable in the current educational culture of the United States; and it is open to question whether or not this represents an advance over earlier labels (e.g., uneducable) or a pernicious development that mental health practitioners and others should combat. In any case, the phenomenon of being LD is clearly established by almost every autobiographer, with the exception of the two African Americans (Kevin Marshall Jr. and Michael Sanders), both of whom describe having mild and discrete LDs that were not diagnosed until they were already in college

Psychotherapists have over the years made excellent use of global models of identity formation such as those articulated by Freud (1965), Erikson (1963), and Kohlberg (1969). These models help psychotherapists conceptualize where clients "are" in their thinking and feeling, and they also suggest what clients may need in order to develop further. In a similar fashion, the autobiographies gathered here provide the grounds for a developmental schema that may have general import for persons who grow up with LDs. Certainly, this schema does not stand alone, but should be integrated with broader developmental models (Robert Kegan's chapter in this volume is an excellent example of such an integration). Yet this schema captures some of the unique ways in which *having* an LD may turn into *being* LD; moreover it suggests ways that LD-identity can be transformed (both in life and through therapy) so that (a) it signifies positive or neutral rather than negative attributes and (b) it can be subordinated to more personal, life-affirmative, and freely chosen ideas of self.

It is important to note that the developmental schema presented in Table 1 was not derived from an empirical study of persons with LDs, but from a structural analysis of the life stories authored by persons with LDs. All writing—but perhaps especially autobiographical writing—is, in its very nature, a constructive activity that has the power not only to reflect reality but also to transform it. Writing permits descriptive accuracy, but it also allows the writer to create and invent, to transcend and master, to edit and fabricate. As such, Table 1 shows the stages through which persons with LDs who have attained a certain level of self-awareness and maturity construct their own developmental processes. This is not to say that this schema is not objective, but rather to suggest that it may be also a bit more than objective, for it also functions as a kind of therapeutic meta-narrative, as a kind of

TABLE 1   *Seven Stages of Identity Formation for Persons with LDs*

Stage	Description
1. The Problem-without-a-Name Stage	The person has no definite concept of having an LD, although he or she may be well aware of being somehow different from peers, usually because of greater difficulty in meeting academic demands.
2. Diagnosis	The person is diagnosed with an LD, initiating new inquiry into self-identity.
3. Alienation	The person resents the LD as a source of alienation from others and from desired circumstances.
4. Passing	The person conceals the LD in order to "pass" into the social mainstream.
5. Crisis and Reconfrontation	The person discovers that the denials and evasions involved in "passing" have led to some form of life crisis (e.g., substance abuse).
6. "Owning" & "Outing"	The person deliberately reinstates his or her LD as a central part of self-identity, finding through this process an increase in well-being.
7. Transcendence	The person reverses the original view of the LD as unwanted and comes instead to see it as a "blessing in disguise," because it has led to important discoveries about what matters most in life.

folk story enriched by some of the drives and discoveries of real, alive persons struggling to overcome limitations and fulfill themselves.

Although this schema is organized into seven chronological stages, I do not mean to suggest that persons with LDs will necessarily pass through all of them or that they will necessarily pass through them in the order given here. Instead, it is entirely possible that individuals will bypass some stages entirely or experience them in a somewhat different order. Nonetheless, I suspect that the schema is likely to have at least some relevance for the majority of persons whose LDs have been serious enough to have had a noticeable impact on their lives.

Stage 1: The Problem-without-a-Name Stage (Ages 0–Time of Diagnosis)

During this stage—which tends to be shorter when disabilities are severe, longer when disabilities are subtle—persons have no definite concept of having LDs, but they seem to know that something is wrong. It may be that they have difficulties reading, understanding what is being said to them, meeting teachers' and parents' behavioral demands, or making friends. Even for primary school age children, being "unable" or socially unpopular is usually quite bitter and painful, and this painful awareness of "otherness" only tends to intensify as children enter adolescence. Among the writers gathered here, reactions to such experiences run the gamut from externalization (i.e., acting out behavior, such as that described by Oliver Queen) to internalization (e.g., the anxious set described by Christie Jackson), but because the "problem" has not been clearly named, these reactions may be kept secret or expressed in ways that only elicit stern or character-damning reactions from others. During an individual's growing years (and often for a long time thereafter), the self is constantly under revision, a work in progress, and children quite naturally wonder about such questions as "Who and what am I?" And, "Who and what will I someday become?" Experiences of failure or feelings of being a misfit function like hypotheses about the value of the present and future self: "If I can't read, I might be stupid, and I may turn out quite badly." While in this stage, persons may form quite a number of hypotheses about who they are, and these hypotheses are tried on for size again and again. The very difficulty of this stage is its vagueness. Naturally, one of the foremost tasks of the clinician in this stage is to help replace this vagueness with clarity.

> *Examples:*
> *I was constantly yelled at for being disruptive, and I remember feeling very guilty, but also confused: I did not mean to disrupt my class, and I often didn't even realize I was doing anything wrong. I realize now that I was not a child with a discipline problem, but a child with ADHD. (Gretchen O'Connor)*
>
> *Once in Mrs. Lin's kindergarten class, however, I was still having obvious difficulty understanding what she said to me. When she noticed my anxiety and helplessness, she would gently ask if I understood. But I often felt so overwhelmed that all I could do was hide behind a charming, bewildered smile, or go to the corner and lie down on my mat. (Alison May)*
>
> *I was not diagnosed with an LD until my junior year in high school. Because I had been tested a number of times before without anything being detected, I believed that the only explanation for why I did badly in school was that I was just plain stupid. Perhaps, a better term would be, not intelligent. I mean I knew I was not retarded, but I also knew I was not smart like my friends. Growing up believing that you are not as good as your peers, in any aspect, takes a toll on a person. (Kelly Miskell)*

Stage 2: Diagnosis (Typically Ages 8–Early Adolescence)

When a person is diagnosed as having a learning disability, he or she is typically initiated into a new set of possibilities for self-identity, the diagnosis often serving as the touchstone for a revision of one's sense of self. This phenomenon probably derives in part from the fact that diagnoses—especially when they lead to measurable changes in a person's daily life—may have all the power and status of explanations.

As such, an LD is viewed not just as another characteristic, but as a root cause, a kind of "first fact" that determines the shape of many other features of the self. An LD seems to answer not only questions like "What is going on with me?" but also "Why am I having trouble in school?" and "Why am I the person that I am?"

Often, persons experience diagnosis as a positive and even redemptive event. For Kevin Marshall, Jr. and for Kelly Miskell, diagnosis was a boon, most of all because being told that they had an LD was measurably better than the hypotheses about themselves with which they had been living up until that time. Rather than attributing past difficulties to poor character or stupidity, they could now say, "It's not me; it's my disability." In such cases, diagnosis is liberating because it seems to relieve the self of onus; the problem is not with the self, but with some part of the machinery of the brain: "*It* has the problem, not *me*." Like having poor eyesight or especially large feet, an LD can be viewed as just another one of those things that aren't under one's control and shouldn't be worried about too much. Moreover, special education programming or academic accommodations, together with adjustments made by parents and others, often lead to improvements in learning, a reduction of anxiety, and the discovery of a peer group.

Diagnosis may, on the other hand, be experienced as quite negative, carrying with it a connotation of personal imperfection, social demotion, or a loss of certain future hopes. This is especially true of adolescents, who are in an active process of searching for their place in the world, socially and professionally. For Christie Jackson, who had dreamed of becoming a marine biologist, diagnosis was heartbreaking, for it seemed to portend the end of these dreams. But even younger children— like Velvet Cunningham at age eight—can react to diagnosis with hopelessness, confusion, or grief. For these persons, diagnosis is tantamount to being told that there is a problem with the elemental self, with the I-of-one's-I. The universal childhood fantasy of being whole and complete, able to become whatever one dreams of, is threatened, and not because of some external event, but because a flaw in the very design of the self has been discovered. In such cases, diagnosis is received as a kind of lifelong sentence in the face of which it is natural to begin cutting one's losses: walking away, for example, from such hopeless investments as education. Why bother when you're disabled? Why try when, at the very core of you, there's something wrong or broken?

It should be noted that diagnosis does not always come on with the force of a thunderclap, producing sudden and profound motions toward self-revision. Just as often, the significance of diagnosis dawns slowly, driven by the gradual changes in everyday life and future expectancy that come with being placed in special education, being treated differently by one's parents, or falling behind peers in some area of learning or social skill.

Examples:
When I was first diagnosed with the disability, I felt that a weight had been lifted from my back . . . learning that many of the problems that I encountered were actually not caused by my lack of intelligence or lack of effort, but by a learning problem that I could not control, helped to alleviate some of my fears. (Kevin Marshall, Jr.)

Tears welled up in my eyes, and I heard myself say it for the first time, "I have a learning disability." I began sobbing as my parents hugged me. Others around me must have thought I had just found out I had some fatal disease or had lost something. (Christie Jackson)

After being diagnosed at around age eight with dyslexia, I thought that was it, that was as far as my learning was going to go. I was never going to learn anything again. I felt that I was stupid, dumb, incompetent. The funny thing is that I did not even know what dyslexia was. I think that after that I just shut down, stopped even caring. It was all downhill from there. (Velvet Cunningham)

Stage 3: The Alienation Stage (Typically Early to Middle Adolescence)

Regardless of whether they initially experienced diagnosis as positive or negative, many persons come eventually to resent their learning disability as a source of alienation or estrangement from themselves (for it is easy to dislike or resent oneself for not being more able), from others (especially peers), and from any number of desired circumstances. Typically coming during early adolescence—a period when persons often wish to expand and experiment with their social identities, as well as with their capacities for self-expression—this stage features a reconceptualization of learning disabilities as a significant and much-deplored obstacle to the "good life." Like invisible glass walls—which Lynn Pelkey graphically calls the "LD bubble"—learning disabilities seem to demarcate the inner world from the outer world, the individual from the group, the actual from the desired, yet always in ways that leave one feeling shut out and undervalued.

Persistently comparing themselves to others—especially so-called normal peers—and finding themselves lacking, persons with LDs wish to shed any "special" status (along with the social segregation that often accompanies such status) but have little opportunity to do so, because this status appears to be "fixed." It is fixed, first of all, because it emanates from an unremediable condition of the self; it is anchored in a fact about one's person. Expressions such as "Why do I have to be weird?" "Why am I so stupid?" or, "Why can't I be like everybody else?" are common. But status also appears to be fixed by the exacting rules and operations of social existence, especially among young adolescents, in whose society any kind of difference is apt to be persecuted. Resenting the way that they are often labeled by—as well as educationally and psychologically managed by—others, persons in this stage may demonstrate apathy or noninvolvement in school and established friendships. Their tendency, rather, is to pull away from the familiar environments—like the resource room—that no longer seem to promise security but instead intensify the degree of exposure to social danger and misfit status. Feeling easily insulted, undervalued, or disparaged, behavioral difficulties or anxiety may again come into evidence, even in persons who formerly presented as fairly well adjusted.

One of the most important aspects of this phase is that persons typically do not know what to do with these feelings. They feel oppressed by their surroundings (and able to say so) and alienated from themselves, yet they cannot clearly envision constructive alternatives. The external world seems to render judgment and make decisions concerning their fate, and they seem to have little say in the matter.

> *Examples:*
> *At first, the gap between me and my classmates was small. However, it was not long before I was ashamed of myself. I would compare myself to those around me. My performance was always less, the lowest, the bottom of the class. As the years passed, the gap grew, and the shame turned to deep-rooted self-hate. (Lynn Pelkey)*
>
> *For four years, I attended the learning center daily. Over that time, I learned the most disabling skills ever. The atmosphere was depressed, attributable in part to the others in there who were also on the top ten troubled students list. All the tricks of the LD trade that are supposed to enable us to learn were provided: mind-mapping, better note-taking, comprehension tricks. But there was a lack on the center's behalf to encourage the sense that we were there not to compensate for a disability, but to gain an insight into our learning styles and our relationships to them. A large part of me is angry that this was not provided. (Aaron Piziali)*

Stage 4: The "Passing" Stage (Typically Early to Middle Adolescence)

One way out of the social and intrapsychic discomfort of the Alienation Stage is to try to "pass" as a person who does not have a learning disability (Corbett, 1994). For many minority groups in the United States, "passing" as a member of the straight, white majority culture has been at one time or another either obligatory (e.g., in many states, laws banned homosexuality, thus compelling gays and lesbians to closet themselves) or tempting (e.g., for light-skinned African Americans in the early twentieth century, passing as white could mean a radical expansion of social freedoms and economic opportunity). Where differences between oneself and a majority group are slight, it may seem not only desirable but also rational to hide these differences altogether and blend in among the mainstream.

The comparison between other minority groups in the United States and persons with LDs is quite apt (Corbett, 1994). The great majority of writers gathered in this volume attempted during their adolescence to conceal or deny their disabilities, usually driven by the need to fulfill a wish for self-wholeness and social acceptance.

For the concealment of a feature of self to qualify as "passing," it must meet two criteria: (a) this feature of identity must be somehow socially salient or linked to social status, and (b) the person must be consciously engaged in the concealment. That the "passing" stories told by the autobiographers here generally meet both criteria is provocative. First of all, it suggests that having an LD is perceived (at least by many of those who have LDs) as a social liability or stigma. Secondly, it offers an indication of the degree of difficulty that may be involved in trying to integrate LD-ness into one's own identity. The definition of a learning disability as a neuropsychological entity is hardly relevant here; whatever LDs may be to others, they are experienced by those who have them during this stage as a kind of social marker, a sign of lower caste membership. Consequently, to successfully deny or bury one's LD is potentially to raise one's social stock value; or, at the very least, to give oneself a new social identity to trade on in the open market. Complementarily, to try to willfully shoulder the negative social value of having an LD must conjure numerous fears and conflicts, for to do so—to consciously embrace a social liability—runs counter to the primal longing to achieve affiliation with others. It is in this stage, then, that LD-ness and a viable selfhood are perceived as most diametrically opposed to one another, causing persons with LDs to be most vulnerable to any number of problems, including substance abuse and dropping out of school.

Unfortunate as it may be that persons in this stage want to conceal their LD identity, the narratives in this volume suggest that actually doing so may have bitter consequences. In order to hide an LD, it stands to reason that one must avoid situations in which the LD might be discovered; the result, of course, is that one may lose a precious part of one's formal education or avoid those persons who might have made excellent friends. Intrapsychically, the costs may be greater yet; that is, one may be anxious about being ferreted out, angry and unhappy at having to lie, and yearning for acceptance as one really is.

All the same, it must be remembered that it is any person's right to decide for themselves if they will or will not "come out" as having LDs. Much of life—and much of the process of identity formation—is theater, and each of us has a basic prerogative to experiment until our proper role or vocation can be found.

Examples:
The whole angry world I created around me was to protect me. The clothes and make-up were a disguise: I hoped that people would see me as a freak, instead of stupid. I would have everyone think I had done too many drugs, and that was why I was slow, instead of them knowing the truth. (Velvet Cunningham)

Emma . . . was the person I would do the most self-reflecting about and with. Yet, she never knew that I had an LD or a hearing deficit. No matter how intimate I would get with Emma, I did not let her know that I was a person with disabilities. Since I did not come out to the person I loved, I naturally did not tell the people I met in school. . . . Much like in the gay community, it is not easy deciding whether or not to come out. (Garett Day)

Some know you as LD, and others know you as one of them, but you are not one of them. You are just pretending. You hate yourself for being LD, and you hate yourself for being a fake. And in the end, who are you? (Lynn Pelkey)

Stage 5: Crisis and Reconfrontation: (Typically Late Adolescence–Early Adulthood)

As suggested, "passing" and other forms of denial of an LD rarely bear good fruit. Most often, in fact, these efforts lead eventually to some form of life crisis. For Nelson Vee, this meant substance abuse and addiction; for Joshua Green, the crisis took the form of romantic losses and poor academic performance; and for Oliver Queen, the safe shelter of a fantasy world was bravely abandoned, but with searingly painful consequences.

These crises, however, appear to have had the fortunate effect of allowing the writers to reopen important questions regarding their self-identities. And this time, when asked "Who am I?" their responses included an acknowledgment of their learning disabilities and a willingness to reclaim severed or marginalized portions of their identities.

Whereas the Passing Stage involves experimentation, theater, and efforts at wish fulfillment, the Crisis and Reconfrontation Stage lays the foundation for the evolution of a predominantly realistic and worldly orientation. Often terribly hurt, persons in this stage recognize that they cannot afford illusions or partial solutions. Rather, they more often express the need to "get real" and to more candidly take the measure of their capacities, challenges, and opportunities. However, before such a pragmatic, solution-oriented attitude can fully arise, the majority of persons must first undergo a time of suffering—of acknowledging and grieving past losses and injuries, of confronting past patterns of self-deceit, and of surrendering dreams that cannot be sustained.

Examples:
I had hidden my disabilities, sneered in the face of my handicaps, refused to embrace my shortcomings. My confidence and grades slipped, my girlfriend broke up with me. With nowhere to turn, I turned to myself: Never has introspection been so vengeful. (Joshua Green)

My whole world was turned upside down, and I could put it back together any way I wanted. I had so many options, but the only thing I could think of was going back to school. (Velvet Cunningham)

Not so long ago, it became very clear to me that I would have to come face-to-face with my feelings about being stupid if I was going to find peace within myself. (Lynn Pelkey)

Stage 6: The "Owning" and "Outing" Stage (Typically Late Adolescence, Early Adulthood)

During this stage, persons deliberately reinstate their LDs as visible and even central parts of their self-image and social identity. Unlike the Diagnosis and Alienation stages, when LD identity is typically thrust on persons by an external source, in this phase, persons with LDs are the active agents in assuming such an identity. Persons are no longer reticent about acknowledging their LDs either to themselves or to others; quite to the contrary, being LD is kept at the forefront of self-identity, providing persons with an emporeringly clear marker for their sense of motivation, struggle, socio-political position, and philosophy of life. To *not* acknowledge their LDs—especially in academic and work settings—is now perceived as risky behavior, as behavior that hazards misunderstandings by professors or coworkers, the loss of beneficial accommodations, or—perhaps most importantly—personal disorientation. Persons have learned from their past crises and have no interest in repeating these sufferings. Yet, it also appears that not acknowledging one's LD is tantamount at this stage to not acknowledging one's self, and so might be compared to an act of self-erasure or self-denigration. At this juncture in the process of identity formation, LDs have taken on a range of potent significances; they signify suffering, selfhood, loss, challenge, reality, fear—and the list goes on. Thus, any denial of their existence is experienced as a kind of unwholesome silencing, rife with political, social, and psychological resonances. In fact, social and political frames of reference for situating learning disabilities gain increasing salience and utility, for they allow one to reject the temptation to identify with the cultural practices that persecute differences, and so, as Lynn Pelkey suggests, breed self-hate. These frames of reference also confer dignity upon the struggle and hardship of living in a mainstream culture, in part through their suggestion that LDs are not, in fact, merely personal problems, but are shared by a great number of persons who may well be considered a culturally distinct group, much as persons bound to one another by a common religion or ethnicity. In essence, then, what it means to be LD has been powerfully shifted, for at this stage LD-ness is about belonging (not alienation), about living consciously and deliberately (as opposed to being a victim of "bad" neurology), and about self-pride (not self-denigration). As such, this stage has three major dimensions:

The Pragmatic Dimension.   Persons realize that knowledge about their LDs and avowal of LD status allows them to pursue "real-life" goals such as advanced education, vocational promotion, or the resolution of lingering psychological problems. Accordingly, they seek to understand their own unique learning styles, and they actively access their legal rights and protections in educational and vocational settings.

> *The best way to combat the self-destructive path is to wear your LD badge proudly, to show it off like a Congressional Medal of Honor. Make it work for you, not against you. (Oliver Green)*

The Intrapsychic Dimension.   The avowal of an LD is not just a public act, but even more importantly, a private one. To admit one's LD status to oneself allows the evolution of a more realistic and more accepting self-concept. Instead of hating the self for its deficiencies, the emphasis now is on supporting the self in the accomplishment of life's pursuits.

> *LD is a label and, as a label, stereotypes will always surface. But the label is also part of me. It's as much a part of me as my middle name, as my smile, as my love of lilacs. (Christie Jackson)*

> *ADHD is not merely a part of me or an influence in my life. It is me. It is the main force that controls me mentally, physically, and socially. I cannot separate it from myself or keep it under control. (Gretchen O'Connor)*

The Political/Ideological Dimension.   Often, persons in this stage engage in social, cultural, and political analysis of LDs and LD identity. This process of inquiry leads on one hand to the recognition that LDs are social constructs/fictions (i.e., "invented" disabilities) and on the other hand to the belief that persons with LDs should organize into a conscious political body. In this phase, the person often views him or herself as having much in common with others, especially persons in oppressed or disadvantaged minority groups.

> *I want people to understand that ADHD should not be labeled a disability, that it only becomes a disability when it is not understood and when people fail to see the benefits and the positive aspects of it. (Gretchen O'Connor)*

> *For those with invisible disabilities and those that have configurations that fall into undefined spaces of disability, there is a constant haranguing of them to get it together and figure their problems out. If they can't do this, then the response is usually to ask them to be okay with their difficulties and limitations. After doing a great deal of reading and conducting a general review of my own experiences, my general feeling is to say bullshit to every person who can't take onboard my concern. (Aaron Piziali)*

> *I realized that God may have given me an LD not only to make classes much more challenging but to help others identify and deal with their LDs. (Christie Jackson)*

Stage 7: Transcendence

In this stage, persons fully reverse the original view of their LDs as negative and unwanted, and instead come to see their LDs as "blessings in disguise." Although continuing to acknowledge that their LDs can still cause them significant hardship and so require a continuous pragmatic and socio-political discipline, persons nonetheless feel that these experiences have allowed them to learn important moral truths and to develop estimable personal characteristics, such as self-knowledge, compassion, and internal resourcefulness. In general, during this phase, LDs are not seen as emblematic of the total self (and thus as markers of the self's worth), but as one of many circumstantial factors that helped to shape personhood. LDs are, in essence, both important—for they tell a significant part of the story of the self, bind one to others through empathy and solidarity, and offer continuous instruction about living—and unimportant—for that which is really precious is the whole person, myriad in nature and abilities, complex in design and purpose, and ultimately resistant to enslavement or limitation.

> *Examples:*
> *Sometimes I think what it would be like if I didn't have a learning difference. What would I be like? I know one thing for sure: I would not be as understanding of differences. I probably would have been one of those kids that teased everyone who was different from me and tried to make them feel as bad as possible about themselves, only to make myself feel better. (Velvet Cunningham)*

I always felt so cheated in life, and wondered why I could not be normal. Well, I no longer feel cheated, I honestly feel lucky. I feel like I was faced with difficulties for a reason, and it has ultimately made me stronger . . . Who knows, maybe because of my past experiences, I will be able to help young adolescents like myself, or maybe I will be a speaker about rape, or politics in the school system, or peer pressure. (Kelly Miskell)

Though burdensome, [my LD and my ADHD] are no longer intrusive. Rather, these traits provoke bursts of creativity and mental activity that I could not accomplish otherwise. They make me sensitive to the world and to the people who are important to me. Most importantly, ADHD and my learning disability make me sensitive to myself. . . . I know now that a learning disability does not have to be a handicap, that it can be a window, a weapon, or a support. In sum, I do not think that it has hindered me more than it has helped. (Joshua Green)

Therapeutic Use of the Seven Stages of Identity Formation

Contained in this schema of identity development is much that may help to guide the psychotherapeutic process with persons who have learning disabilities.

First of all, this series of stages suggests that LDs have a potent *mediating* function in the lives of those who have them: They mediate the self's relationship to self, the self's relationship to others, the self's institutional and political identities, and so on. In many cases, whatever a person with an LD does or experiences, it passes through the LD construct. What an LD actually signifies to a person, then, can be tremendously important to that person's self-construct. If an LD signifies stupidity or deficiency, the global self-concept may likewise reflect stupidity and deficiency. If, however, an LD signifies personal uniqueness or a source of learning about the human condition, it is likely to encourage a more positive view of self. It is important, then, for therapists to work with clients to explore what LDs mean, to generate new meanings and associations, and, perhaps, to encourage either more or less identification of self with the LD. Therapists may do this in many ways, including inviting clients to take active roles in constructing and revising their own life stories, finding in the disciplines and demands, losses and challenges that their LDs have thrust on them the path toward maturity, compassion for others, and self-possession.

Fortunately, the life experiences of the autobiographers suggest that the meanings of LDs appear to be neither static nor fixed, but rather quite mutable. Influenced by experience, age, shifts in environment, and countless other factors, LDs are—as a natural consequence of social existence—ever metamorphosing. While this instability in the concept of LDs can be a liability (especially in a culture that persistently urges a negative view of LDs), it can also function as an advantage, for persons who learn how to invest their LDs with positive meaning may gain unique advantages in life. When, for example, an LD signifies not *the thing that is wrong with me*—but rather *the thing that has encouraged me to develop strength and courage, the thing that has taught me compassion and tolerance for others,* or *the thing that has shown me how to be a teacher of myself and of others*—it may have an uplifting and salient effect on a person. Therapy that serves as a site for the discovery and man-ufacture of such significations—that urges clients to explore and reevaluate their LD experiences—can thus be very powerful, especially given how closely linked the meaning of an LD tends to be to a person's sense of self.

Because any attempt to revise the meaning of an LD continuously interacts with and may depend on clients' basic sense of self-value and self-understanding, one of the primary charges of the therapist is to encourage clients—primarily through strategies of *affirmation*—to accept and value themselves as they are, thus undercutting the mythology of the deficit self. While affirmation may take many forms, perhaps basic to them all is a kind of deep, empathic attentiveness to the client, a willingness to acknowledge and explore all that the client has felt, experi-enced, and expressed. The first lesson that clients learn by such affirmation is that they are viable persons, precious and substantial, whose way of seeing and experi-encing the world is not only legitimate, but also valuable to others. Given the severely damaged sense of self-worth that so many of the autobiographers report, such fundamental affirmations are likely to be often needed and much valued by future clients.

While the task of affirming the self of the client at the existential or, if you will, absolute level is likely to be a continuous aspect of therapy, it is equally necessary for therapists to simultaneously nurture a very different philosophical perspective: one, that is, that emphasizes the self as a *construction*, or as the product of various forces and agents, both social and self-directed, accidental and intentional, institu-tional and personal. In encouraging such a perspective (one that is, by the way, quite natural to most persons), the therapist is able to suggest to the client that the self is an ever-changing entity, one whose "shape" is ever being negotiated and revised. Influenced by the particularity of social circumstance and the character of important social relationships, as well as by the evolution and direction of the client's own will, the self's story is not given or prescribed, but is, rather, open and undetermined.

Because the self's story is open to various social forces, it is deeply relevant to study the way these social forces work. Naturally, these studies are more likely to be concrete than philosophical, taking the form of inquiries such as the following: "How did having to repeat first grade affect your sense of self?" "Why is it that having to repeat a grade matters?" "Why does anybody really care?" "How do other people—both your peers and adults in your life—tend to explain why this happened to you?" "How do you explain it to yourself?" Although concrete, such investigations lead also to the gradual learning of more general truths about the ways that we are each continuously subject to the influences of external factors. Which of these factors are beneficial to us? Which tend to be harmful? In being able to discern answers to such questions, the history of the self becomes clearer and the future story of the self somewhat more secure. In grasping more directly the set-tings or contexts that impact the self's experience in the world, the client learns to see that what he or she "is" may change as the social frame changes. And, finally, in discovering that many social conditions—including those that have had some of the most powerful impact on the self—are arbitrary, the client develops the basis for critiquing and challenging those things that have been most harmful and for consciously aligning with those things that have been most beneficial.

Ultimately, however, all discoveries about the self as a construction or subject ought to be used to encourage clients to exercise their own powers of agency and authorship. If the self is a construction—if it is inherently plastic, malleable, open to revision—then why not choose to be the chief genius and architect of its construction? It is in this work of supporting clients in choosing to live actively and willfully that therapy perhaps realizes its essential purpose.

All of this work on fundamental issues of the self's value, nature, and capacities contributes to clients' ability to live with their LDs in a healthy fashion. All the same, there is no reason that a person's identity should be either primarily defined or subsumed by their LDs. Indeed, it appears that acknowledging and positively (yet realistically) valuing an LD may be the best way to assign it a proportionate role in the identity of the person in all of his or her complexity. Therapists, then, may wish to be careful not to peg clients who have LDs as just this; indeed, part of the rationale for treating LDs and their effects is to prevent them from absorbing or engulfing those persons who have them.

In any case, to have an LD is to be set on a long, complex, and unique journey toward selfhood. To have even an approximate sense of what this journey might entail can be tremendously helpful to both therapist and client.

The Problem-Solving Mode

Most readers of the 13 autobiographies gathered in this volume are likely to be struck by how little assistance the writers were given in facing—and learning to solve—many of the life problems that beset them. Learning disabilities are, unfortunately, often a seedbed for difficulties. As described by the autobiographers, these problems may involve not only the intrapsychic realms of thought, feeling, and behavior, but also important social systems, such as school, family, and peer society. These are large and daunting problems for anyone to face, but especially children. Feeling ensnared not only by their LDs but also by some of the so-called solutions (such as the resource room) developed in response to them, many of the writers surrendered early to the conviction that their troubles were unresolvable and so drifted toward depression and the compensatory activities (e.g., substance abuse) often connected with it. Several of the autobiographers offer almost archetypal descriptions of learned helplessness or of the evolution of a psychology of self-disbelief, self-inefficacy, and demoralization. Indeed, in the majority of the essays, we find evidence of wounded or poorly developed agency or sense of authorship over one's own existence.

It follows that therapists working with persons who have LDs should enter often and vigorously into what I call the Problem-Solving Mode, engaging clients in dialogue that features posing, exploring solutions to, and acting to resolve the various problems—emotional, social, educational, familial, and so on—that face them. While the short-term rationale for entering into this mode is to relieve pressures currently acting on the client, the long-term and perhaps more important rationale is to train clients in the empowering skills of problem posing/problem solving. Clients who internalize the belief that they can, with the appropriate efforts, determine the course of their own affairs and attain their goals are likely to be happier and more fulfilled people.

Equally as important to the Problem-Solving Mode, therapists should be willing to accept the role of active advocates for their clients, directly intervening to produce change in the social systems to which clients belong. The autobiographers collected in this volume offer several portraits of parents and professionals who, usually unwittingly, colluded with rather than challenged unhealthy or unjust circumstances. The autobiographers also gratefully profile those rare but important teachers and parents who honored their views and advocated for constructive change at the systemic level. Therapists who appropriately and within the boundaries of their profession follow the example of this latter group are likely to have great value for their clients.

In so doing, the following points should be kept in mind:

1. Clients ought to be encouraged to identify, describe, and explore problems as they see and experience them. Not only does such an approach promote sensitivity to and affirmation of clients' right to evolve their own worldviews, but also clients' problem statements often (a) implicitly contain clues and keys to satisfying solutions, (b) reveal broader or more deeply seated beliefs, both positive and self-defeating, which it may be beneficial to explore, and (c) allow clients and therapists to begin studying how a problem's construction may have much to do with how it may (or may not) be solved. Therapists ought to involve clients in brainstorming solutions to problems, allowing these discussions to take various avenues until a realistic and viable answer is discovered.

2. When it can be instructive, therapists should *model* problem-solving strategies. After exploring with a client how a particular problem might be solved, the therapist may wish to demonstrate how this solution may be implemented. For example, a therapist working with Lynn Pelkey might have placed a call to her teacher while Lynn was in the office. Respectfully engaging the teacher in conversation about Lynn's concern that the "RR" stigmatizes the children who receive a portion of their education there, the therapist might ask the teacher if she or he would be open to working with Lynn and other students on somehow changing public perception of the RR or looking for alternative ways of providing special education instruction. Witnessing this conversation, Lynn is likely to feel cared about and validated, as well as encouraged to work for the changes she wishes to realize.

3. Therapists may also consider working with a client to produce a step-by-step plan for solving a problem and then oblige the client to implement this plan, offering ample coaching and support along the way.

4. Therapists ought to involve clients in exploring how responsibility for a stated problem might fairly be apportioned. Clients (especially young clients) should be shown how some problems—such as, say, getting beat up by school bullies as Oliver Queen was—fall at least partly into other persons' purviews of responsibility. School principals and teachers are obliged to ensure the safety of their pupils. Additionally, a person who aggressively injures another is subject to legal sanction, and it may be the responsibility of parents and the police to take appropriate steps to enforce these sanctions. In short, clients—especially clients who have been victimized—should be helped to see that many problems can be solved by identifying other persons responsible for solving them and collaborating with these natural allies.

Even in such cases where others are involved, however, clients should be encouraged to accept responsibility for their own actions and reactions, for taking a constructive approach to the issues at hand, and for working to find solutions to problematic feelings and cognitions. An important key to increasing agency is accepting and acting on responsibilities.

5. Therapists should familiarize themselves with best practice models for special education as well as with disabilities law, so that they can (a) directly advocate for clients and their families and (b) instruct clients and their families in how they may advocate for themselves. Of all the problems that may afflict persons with LDs, some of the most pernicious stem directly from a failure to acquire essential academic skills. If, for example, a child fails to learn to read while in elementary school, nearly every other developmental task still to be accomplished may be imperiled or made much more difficult. The fact that substantial research has demonstrated that virtually *every* child can learn to read suggests that therapists have not only a right but also an ethical duty to join clients and their families in influencing schools to provide an adequate education. Naturally, therapists can be most effective in their advocacy if they can go beyond calling for change and can also help design changes that will be beneficial.

6. As the autobiographies demonstrate, the experiences of persons growing up with LDs is powerfully influenced by familial factors. Therapists may wish to make psycho-educational sessions with parents, spouses, and other family members a standard part of the therapeutic treatment of clients who have LDs. The goal of such sessions should be to help families better understand LDs and their effects, and to engage families in looking for ways that they can support the positive development of the persons who have LDs. Additionally, therapists should arrange family sessions to work collaboratively on solutions to familial problems that may be impacting the well-being of the client.

While this list of problem-solving strategies is more suggestive than exhaustive, I hope that it somehow manages to convey a fundamental message that is expressed and amplified from autobiography to autobiography: LDs are real-life challenges, and they must be met head-on. Therapists who wish to work in the area of learning disabilities need to function as pragmatic social activists, willing and able to use their offices to engage the various persons and systems positioned to improve the lives of clients. In so doing, they should mentor and support clients to do the same. Therapy is not just a place for talk but also a site for action.

The Rhetorical Mode

Rhetoric is the name given to the discipline concerned with the study and practice of *persuasive communication,* be it in formal settings such as politics and law, or in everyday conversation and relational life. Acts of communication—written or spoken, gestural or symbolic—almost always have a rhetorical dimension: That is, embedded in almost every communicative act is a desire to influence or persuade the audience to whom it is directed. Although the rhetorical dimension is clearly present in statements as common as "I want a glass of milk" or "I love you," it is typically most evident when communication involves *argumentation,* or the articulation and exchange of contestable positions.

In psychotherapy, argumentation is quite common. A therapist may argue with a client's unhelpful beliefs. A client may argue with him or herself, with the therapist, or (albeit usually indirectly) with some person in his or her life. Additionally, both client and therapist may join in formulating an argument that challenges what has been done or said by a third party. In general terms, it may be said that psychotherapy is a process during which clients evolve a series of arguments regarding self, others, problems, and potentialities that are conducive to good mental health. Optimally, they learn to contest the "bad" arguments made by themselves and by others, and to align themselves with those "good" arguments that render life livable, even sweet.

Argumentation is not only especially likely—but also especially critical to the healing process—in cases wherein the client has been the subject of disregard, prejudice, or abuse, particularly if this antipathy is generalized throughout a culture. As nearly every one of the autobiographers has made clear, having a learning disability is a social, cultural, and political liability. They describe being frequently ridiculed and undervalued, humiliated and misunderstood, first by others, and then eventually by themselves. For many of them, life is depicted as a continuous struggle for self-esteem. Having coped since early school days with external oppositions, they have internalized a good deal of negativity. As Aaron Piziali put it, "Most days are hard. What is apparent to me now is that we (myself and my abled self) have so far failed to combine the knowledge needed to monitor my emotional state so as to develop a more resilient head-space" (17).

If we look at these autobiographies in rhetorical terms, we see that they are organized, in the simplest sense, as arguments *against* being held down or undervalued and *for* living with pride and optimism. Each describes a primordial contest in which the voices of criticism and despair square off against the voices of self-affirmation and hope.

As such, these essays constitute, first of all, a nearly encyclopedic review of the negative arguments that have challenged their authors throughout their lives. We find descriptions of the debasing arguments made by peers and schools, the demeaning arguments made by parents and teachers, and, perhaps most striking of all, the self-undermining arguments the authors have made against themselves. Psychotherapists may wish to study these arguments, for it may well be that their own clients wrestle with them.

But even more importantly, these autobiographies illustrate how the writers fought back and what they needed in order to fight back successfully. For many of the writers, crucial to their success in this arena is the evolution of techniques of social critique. While these techniques can be said to exist in embryonic form during the first stages of identity development, they are limited by their focus on concrete events, as well as by the writers' understandably egocentric orientation. However, beginning in the "Owning" and "Outing Stage," the writers start to realize that the "LD problem" is not theirs alone, but is created and sustained by a complex network of persons and social forces. As they externalize the issue of learning disabilities—that is, as they place it within wider frames of reference—they gain in their capacity to challenge the disabling, disempowering, and disconcerting rhetorics of education, popular culture, and others.

The sources of social critique on which the autobiographers drew are various. For Oliver Queen and Aaron Piziali, techniques of social critique were learned in part during the course of studies in the social sciences. For most, however, the most potent source of critical consciousness was affiliation—and thus conversation—with others who have learning disabilities. Just being able to share impressions and experiences—to compare notes, if you will—allowed many of the writers to recognize that their own struggles were not unique, but that they derived from more generalized cultural settings and practices. Even if their formulation of their common predicament was not taken to this level of abstraction, there was a definite awareness of an "us" and a "them," of a cultural divide—one perhaps separating the educational "cans" from the educational "cannots"—which needed to be challenged and bridged. And the manner by which this divide was bridged had to do largely with the formation of a self-affirming, ethically centered, rights-based rhetorical stance. Using social critical skills to determine that they did not want to collude with the negating arguments emanating from the general culture, they began to consciously examine their own internalized patterns of self-denigration, to voice their desires and rights to an education, and to search out lives that fit.

The message to psychotherapists is clear: Encourage the cultivation of social critique, as well as the corrolary formation of an empowering rhetoric. There is no reason why this process should not occur when clients are first diagnosed as very young children. Indeed, there is every reason to support the rhetorical skills of persons with LD throughout the life span. These persons, like many others from minority cultures, are going to need to speak out in defense of themselves.

Even when clients are young or when there is some reason (e.g., a severe verbal processing LD, lack of education, or simply lack of comfort and interest) that an adult is unable to make good use of the more academic socio-critical discourses, rhetorical methods are still both viable and useful. From the time we are very young and first battle with a sibling over a toy, we know how to engage in rhetorical activity: We cry, scream, point fingers, or simply grab the goods. By the time children are in elementary school—especially if they are children with low social status—they have generally had a good deal of experience with tauntings and rebuttals, accusations and defenses, value judgments and criticism. They also generally have a sense of what is right and wrong, and can meaningfully engage in efforts to think, act, and speak in ways that are congruent with their values. Exploring and strategizing answers to these very concrete social dramas, in fact, provides perhaps the best opportunities for the development of rhetorical skills—and through them, for the development of more effective social skills. If, for example, a young client tells in therapy the story of how he or she got into a fight that morning with another student, the rhetorical dimension is directly accessed. In such an instance, the therapist might begin by writing down the words that players in this drama said to one another. Next, the therapist might ask the child if he or she could explain what the intentions of each speaker's words might be. Next the therapist might ask the client to express what his or her real desires and ideals are for social interaction: How should persons treat one another? Why? How are these hopes and expectations either disappointed or fulfilled on any given day? Eventually, the therapist and client might explore rewriting the drama, developing new, better options for the child's "speeches." In many cases, it may even make sense to work with the child to develop certain rote positions and "I statements" that the child can utilize in the future as needed.

In engaging in such concrete rhetorical problem-solving, the ultimate goal is to help clients develop and internalize more global arguments about the value of self, the purposes and practices of education, the rights and prerogatives of persons with disabilities, and other portions of a self-respecting and constructive worldview.

Indeed, if we extract from the autobiographies profiles of emotionally healthy and socially useful worldviews, we find that these are quite multi-faceted, integrating a rhetoric of self with arguments concerning social, political, and cultural values and beliefs.

Naturally, the formation of such positions often takes time: In our group of autobiographers, the average age was probably somewhere in the mid-twenties. But, inasmuch as therapy often follows along with the current of a client's life, focusing on what is most needed, it is more than sufficient to use it to formulate rhetorical solutions for the rhetorical problems occurring in the present. Out of these solutions, then, may develop the global framework that enables persons with LDs to chart a positive course throughout their life spans.

At a minimum, however, therapists should endeavor to help their clients develop a rhetorical position—a set of convictions and arguments—regarding LDs and what is to be done about them. If clients can receive through therapy the means to resist the voices that undermine them and also to strengthen the voices that enable them to take their life challenges in stride, they are much more likely to succeed.

Conclusion

By way of a conclusion, I would like to offer four broad recommendations to psychotherapists who might have the privilege of working with persons who have LDs.

1. First of all, psychotherapists should focus less on managing or remediating LDs per se and much more on supporting persons in their totality. All psychotherapy is by design attentive to problems and psychopathological processes, and, when effective, able to counter and reverse them. But a psychotherapy animated chiefly by sensitivity to the ways that persons' lives are constructed, both from within (i.e., how persons see the world) and from without (i.e., how persons are seen, treated, and valued by others) is apt to be most beneficial. Accordingly, the goal of psychotherapy reaches beyond the common emphasis in many special education programs of "understanding one's LD" to the broader question of understanding one's own self.

2. Learning disabilities typically influence those who have them throughout the life cycle, often exerting a powerful and lasting effect on persons' sense of self or identity. It is, then, appropriate that psychotherapy should assume a developmental lens, taking as one of its major goals that of assisting persons in meeting developmental challenges. As part of this developmental orientation, it is important to accept that treatment may at times legitimately focus on the careful exploration of clients' personal life histories. Understanding the narrative construction of a life—that is, its major plots, themes, characters, and surrounding contexts—can often be crucial to encouraging a person to find new, fulfilling pathways for living.

3. Because LDs are socially meaningful—and thus are at least partly socially constructed—they often have a profound impact on persons' social status, opportunity, roles, and self-identity. In many instances, it is appropriate to consider this impact a palpable form of social oppression, its manifestations as diverse as a schoolmate's jeers, feelings of depression or hopelessness, or exclusion from a desired profession. Accordingly, psychotherapeutic treatment should concern itself with the exploration, analysis, and critique of social and cultural processes, addressing both externalized and internalized manifestations of social oppression. Psychotherapists are wise to employ strategies of treatment that at once emphasize the often underappreciated strengths and competencies of persons who happen to have LDs and that deliberately deconstruct the conditions that have caused them to feel inadequate, depressed, anxious, angry, or, in a word, disabled. Through these means, clients may learn to turn feelings of self-blame or inadequacy outwards, thus establishing the grounds for negotiating new meanings and life pathways.

4. Finally, clients with LDs should be assisted in giving voice to their experiences, their values, and their desires, thereby entering into the process of asserting active authorship over their own lives. The links between language and being are vibrant. If one of the chief dangers of having an LD is that it can result in one's person being labeled, defined, and interpreted by others—all of which have silencing effects—then one of the primary objectives of therapy must be to support clients in restating life in a living tongue of their own.

Appendix

Resource List for Persons with Learning Disabilities

National Center for Learning Disabilities (NCLD)
381 Park Avenue South
Suite 1401
New York, NY 10016
Toll-free information/referral: (888) 575-7373
(212) 545-7510
FAX: (212) 545-9665
http://www.ncld.org

National Clearinghouse on Women and Girls with Disabilities
Educational Equity Concepts, Inc.
114 East 32nd Street, Suite 701
New York, NY 10016
(212) 725-1803

Office of Special Education and Rehabilitation Services (OSERS)
U.S. Department of Education
Switzer Building
330 C Street SW
Suite 3006
Washington, DC 20202
(202) 205-5465
FAX: (202) 205-9252
http://www.ed.gov/office/OSERS/

U.S. Department of Education
600 Independence Avenue, SW
Washington, DC 20202
(800) USA-LEARN
FAX: (202) 401-0689
http://www.ed.gov

Americans with Disabilities Information Hotline
Disability Rights Section
Civil Rights Division
U.S. Department of Justice
Post Office Box 66738
Washington, DC 20035-6738
(800) 514-0301
(202) 514-0301
http://www.usdoj.gov/crt/ada/adahom1.htm

Division for Learning Disabilities (DLD)
The Council for Exceptional Children (CEC)
1920 Association Drive
Reston, VA 22091-1589
(888) CEC-SPED
(703) 620-3660
FAX: (703) 264-9494
http://www.cec.sped.org

International Dyslexia Association
Chester Building, Suite 382
8600 LaSalle Road
Baltimore, MD 21286-2044
(800) 222-3123
(410) 296-0232
FAX: (410) 321-5069
http://www.interdys.org

Learning Disabilities Association of America
4256 Library Road
Pittsburgh, PA 15234-1349
(412) 341-1515
(412) 341-8077
FAX: (412) 344-0224
http://www.ldanatl.org

Children and Adults with Attention Deficit Disorder (CHADD)
8181 Professional Place, Suite 201
Landover, MD 20785
(800) 233-4050
FAX: (301) 306-7070
http://www.chadd.org

SAT Services for Students with Disabilities
Post Office Box 6226
Princeton, NJ 08541-6226
(609) 771-7780

Glossary

Ablism A set of prejudicial assumptions and false beliefs about persons who have some form of disability. Like racism or sexism, ablism can be either overt and pronounced or subtle and unintentional. Ablism may be manifest as overly low/high expectations of a person with disabilities, the belief that people with disabilities are deficient or abnormal, or a refusal to make appropriate accommodations so that a person with a disability can express his or her capabilities and interests.

Attention-Deficit/Hyperactivity Disorder (ADHD) According to the *Diagnostic and Statistical Manual for Mental Disorders,* Fourth Edition (DSM-IV), "The essential feature of ADHD is a persistent pattern of inattention and/or hyperactivity-impulsivity that is more frequent and severe than is typically observed in individuals at a comparable level of development." There are at least three subtypes of ADHD: *ADHD, Combined Type* (both inattention and hyperactivity-impulsivity); *ADHD, Predominantly Inattentive Type* (high levels of inattention); and *ADHD, Predominantly Hyperactive Type* (mainly hyperactivity-impulsivity). Various estimates have been given of the prevalence of the disorder, with 3–5 percent of school-age children constituting a conservative estimate.

Cranial-sacral Therapy A form of therapy used in the treatment of various musculoskeletal disorders. The treatment involves forms of manipulation and pressure techniques in an effort to initiate muscular control. A variety of passive movements and pressure are applied to areas of the body, including the head and neck, in different positions. The efficacy of this technique for improving cognitive functioning for persons with LDs is at present neither sufficiently documented nor scientifically proven.

Dyslexia Plainly speaking, dyslexia refers to unexpected difficulty in learning to read. A more precise definition of dyslexia by the Orton Dyslexia Society is as follows: "Dyslexia is one of several distinct learning disabilities. It is a specific language-based disorder of constitutional origin characterized by difficulties in single-word decoding, usually reflecting insufficient phonological processing. These difficulties in single-word decoding are often unexpected in relation to age and other cognitive and academic abilities; they are not the result of generalized developmental disability or sensory impairment. Dyslexia is manifest by variable difficulty with different forms of language, often including, in addition to problems with reading, a conspicuous problem with acquiring proficiency in writing and spelling."

IDEA '97 The acronym for the Individuals with Disabilities Education Act Amendments of 1997, Public Law 105-17, the fifth set of amendments to the Education for All Handicapped Children Act passed by Congress in 1975. IDEA '97 mandates a free appropriate public education in the least restrictive environment for all children with disabilities living in the United States. It is the legislation which effectively shapes the way that special education services are provided to children with learning disabilities, regardless of where they go to school. Information on IDEA '97 may be obtained from the United States Department of Education or the National Information Center for Children and Youth with Disabilities.

Phonological Awareness (also known as **phonemic awareness**)   The ability to attend to and decipher the speech-sound structure of words. Phonemes are the basic speech sounds that are represented by the letters of the alphabet. Phonological awareness involves understanding that words are sequences or groupings of phonemes. Phonological awareness is measured by tasks, such as phonemic counting, dividing words into syllables, and word recognition. Excellent phonological awareness in preschool or kindergarten is a predictor of high reading ability. Many persons with dyslexia, on the other hand, have developmentally unexpected difficulties with phonological processing.

The Rassias Method   An approach to teaching foreign language that emphasizes having students "listen to and speak the language to learn it instead of learning the language to speak it." This approach—which demands efficient auditory and phonological processing capacities and strong verbal memory skills—can be inordinately challenging for students with deficits in these areas.

Bibliography

Adelman, H. S., & Taylor, L. (1984). Ethical concerns and identification of psychoeducational problems. *Journal of Clinical Child Psychology, 13*, 16–23.

Adelman, H. S., & Taylor, L. (1994). *On understanding intervention in psychology and education.* Westport, CT: Praeger.

American Psychiatric Association. (1994). *Diagnostic and statistical manual of mental disorders* (4th ed.). Washington, DC: American Psychiatric Association.

Anderson, K. G. (1997). Gender bias and special education referrals. *Annual of Dyslexia, 47*, 151–162.

Armstrong, T. (1994). *Multiple intelligences in the classroom.* Alexandria, VA: Association for Supervision and Curriculum Development.

Artiles, A., & Trent, S. (1994). Overrepresentation of minority students in special education: A continuing debate. *Journal of Special Education, 27*, 410–437.

Atwell, N. (1988). A Special Writer at Work. In Thomas Newkirk (Ed.), *Understanding writing: Ways of observing, learning, and teaching K–8* (2nd ed.). Portsmouth, NH: Heinemann.

Barton, S., & Fuhrmann, B. (1994). Counseling and psychotherapy for adults with learning disabilities. In P. Gerber & H. Reiff (Eds.), *Learning disabilities in adulthood: Persisting problems and evolving issues* (pp. 82–92). Boston: Andover Medical Publishers.

Bateson, M. C. (1994). *Peripheral visions: Learning along the way.* New York: Harper Perennial.

Bender, W., & Wall, M. (1994). Social–emotional development of students with learning disabilities. *Learning Disabilities Quarterly, 17*, 323–341.

Boscardin, M. L., & Jacobson, S. (1997). The "inclusive" school: Integrating diversity and solidarity through community-based management. *Journal of Educational Administration, 35*, 466–476.

Brown, L., & Gilligan, C. (1992). *Meeting at the crossroads: Women's psychology and girls' development.* Cambridge: Harvard University Press.

Brumback, R., & Weinberg, W. (1990). Pediatric behavioral neurology: An update on the neurologic aspects of depression, hyperactivity, and learning disabilities. *Pediatric Neurology, 8*(3), 677–703.

Carew, J., & Lightfoot, S. L. (1979). *Beyond bias.* Cambridge: Harvard University Press.

Chandler, L. (1994). Emotional aspects of learning problems: Implications for assessment. *Special Services in the Schools, 8*(2), 161–165.

Corbett, J. (1994). A proud label: Exploring the relationship between disability politics and gay pride. *Disability & Society, 9*(3), 343–357.

Delpit, L. (1988). The silenced dialogue: Power and pedagogy in educating other people's children. *Harvard Educational Review, 58*(3), 280–298.

Duckworth, E. (1994). *The having of wonderful ideas. Essays on Piaget and other theories.* New York: Teachers College Press.

Erikson, E. H. (1963). *Childhood and society.* New York: W.W. Norton.

Five, C. L. (1992). *Special voices.* Portsmouth, NH: Heinemann.

Freire, P. (1970, 1992). *Pedagogy of the oppressed.* M. B. Ramos (Trans.). New York: Continuum.

Freud, S. (1965). *New introductory lectures on psychoanalysis.* New York: W.W. Norton.

Garcia, S., & Malkin, D. (1995). Toward defining programs and services for culturally and linguistically diverse learners in special education. *Annual Editions: Educating Exceptional Children,* 8th Ed., pp. 109–114.

Gardner, H. (1983). *Frames of mind: The theory of multiple intelligences.* New York: Basic Books.

Gardner, H. (1991). *The unschooled mind: How children think and how schools should teach.* New York: Basic Books.

Gardner, H. (1993). *Multiple intelligences: The theory in practice.* New York: Basic Books.

Gould, S. J. (1981). *The mismeasure of man.* New York: Norton.

Hammill, D., & Bartel, N. (1995). *Teaching students with learning and behavior problems.* Austin, TX: Pro-Ed.

Heath, S. B., & Branscombe, A. (1985). "Intelligent writing" in an audience community: Teacher, students, and researcher. In S. W. Freedman (Ed.), *The acquisition of written language: Response and revision* (pp. 16–34). Norwood, NJ: Ablex.

Heller, K., Holzman, W., & Messick, S. (Eds.). (1982). *Placing children in special education.* Washington, DC: National Academy Press.

Hubbard, R. (1995). *Workshop of the possible: Nurturing children's creativity.* Portsmouth, NH: Stenhouse.

Huntington, D., & Bender, W. (1993). Adolescents with learning disabilities at risk: Emotional well-being, depression, suicide. *Journal of Learning Disabilities, 26,* 159–166.

Jacobson, S., & Boscardin, M. L. (1996). Learning to lead inclusive schools in the U.S. *International Studies in Educational Administration, 24,* 10–16.

Kaye, H. S., LaPlante, M. P., Carlson, D., & Wenger, B. L. (1994). Trends in disability rates in the United States, 1970–1994. *Disability Statistics Abstract, 17.* Washington, DC: National Institute on Disability & Rehabilitation Research.

Kazdin, A. E., & Kagan, J. (1994). Models of dysfunction in developmental psychopathology. *Clinical Psychology: Science and Practice, 1,* 35–52.

Keefe, C. H. (1996). *Label-free learning: Supporting learners with disabilities.* York, ME: Stenhouse.

Kohlberg, L. (1969). Stage and sequence: The cognitive-developmental approach to socialization. In D. Goslin (Ed.), *Handbook of socialization theory and research.* Chicago: Rand McNally.

Larson, K. A. (1988). A research review and alternative hypothesis explaining the link between learning disability and delinquency. *Journal of Learning Disabilities, 21,* 357–369.

Lerner, J., Lowenthal, B., & Egan, R. (1998). *Preschool children with special needs: Children at-risk and children with disabilities.* Boston: Allyn & Bacon.

Lerner, J. W. (1993). *Learning disabilities.* Boston: Houghton Mifflin.

Levine, M. (1994). *All kinds of minds.* Cambridge, MA: Educators Publishing Service.

Levine, M. (1994). *Educational Care: A system for understanding and helping children with learning problems at home and in school.* Cambridge, MA: Educators Publishing Service.

Lewis, S., & Lawrence-Patterson, E. (1989). Locus of control of children with learning disabilities and perceived locus of control by significant others. *Journal of Learning Disabilities, 22,* 255–257.

Luria, A. R. (1973). *The working brain: An introduction to neuropsychology.* New York: Basic Books.

Maag, J. (1997). Managing resistance: Looking beyond the child and into the mirror. In Paul Zionts (Ed.), *Inclusion strategies for students with learning and behavior problems* (pp. 229–271). Austin, TX: Pro-Ed.

Margalit, M. (1992). Sense of coherence and families with a learning-disabled child. In B. Wong (Ed.), *Contemporary intervention research in learning disabilities* (pp. 134–145). New York: Springer-Verlag.

Maxwell, J. (1994). *Diversity and solidarity.* Paper presented at the Annual Meeting of the American Educational Research Association, New Orleans.

McDermott, R., & Varenne, H. (1995). Culture as disability. *Anthropology & Education Quarterly, 3*(26): 324–348.

McGrady, H. (1983). Adolescents with learning and behavior problems. In B. J. D'Alonzo (Ed.), *Educating adolescents with learning and behavior problems* (pp. 37–66). Rockville, MD: Aspen.

McKinney, J. (1990). Longitudinal research on the behavioral characteristics of children with learning disabilities. In J. Torgesen (Ed.), *Cognitive and behavioral characteristics of children with learning disabilities* (pp. 115–138). Austin, TX: Pro-Ed.

McLesky, J. (1997). Students with learning disabilities at primary, intermediate, and secondary grade levels: Identification and characteristics. *Learning Disability Quarterly, 15,* 13–19.

Mercer, J. (1972). Sociocultural factors in the educational evaluation of black and chicano children. Paper presented at the Tenth Annual Conference on Civil Rights Educators and Students.

Mishna, F. (1996a). Finding their voice: Group therapy for adolescents with learning disabilities. *Learning Disabilities Research & Practice, 11*(4), 249–258.

Mishna, F. (1996b). In their own words: Therapeutic factors for adolescents who have learning disabilities. *International Journal of Group Psychotherapy, 46*(2), 265–273.

National Joint Committee on Learning Disabilities. (1988). *Collective perspectives on issues affecting learning disabilities: Position papers and statements.* Austin, TX: Pro-Ed.

Neruda, P. (1988). *Late and posthumous poems: 1968–1974.* New York: Grove Press.

Noddings, N. (1992). *The challenge to care in schools: An alternative approach to education.* New York: Teachers College Press.

Olivier, C., & Bowler, R. (1996). *Learning to learn.* New York: Fireside.

Ostrow, J. (1995). *Room with a different view: First-through-third graders construct curriculum.* Portsmouth, NH: Stenhouse.

Overton, T. (1996). *Assessment in special education: An applied approach.* Englewood Cliffs, NJ: Prentice-Hall.

Patton, J. R., Blackbourn, J., & Fad, K. (1996). *Exceptional lives in focus.* Englewood Cliffs, NJ: Merrill/Prentice-Hall.

Reid, D. K., Hresko, W. P., & Swanson, H. L. (1996). *Cognitive approaches to learning disabilities.* Austin, TX: Pro-Ed.

Reiff, H., & Gerber, P. (1994). Social/emotional and daily living issues for adults with learning disabilities. In P. Gerber & H. Reiff (Eds.), *Learning disabilities in adulthood: Persisting problems and evolving issues* (pp. 72–81). Boston: Andover Medical Publishers.

Reynolds, M. C. (1984). Classification of students with handicaps. In E. W. Gordon (Ed.), *Review of Research in Education, 11,* 63–92. Washington, DC: American Education Research Association.

Reynolds, M. C. (1991). Classification and labeling. In J. W. Lloyd, N. N. Singh, & A. C. Repp (Eds.), *The regular education initiative: Alternative perspectives on concepts, issues, and models* (pp. 29–41). Sycamore, IL: Sycamore Press.

Rhodes, L., & Dudley-Marling, C. (1988). *Readers and writers with a difference: A holistic approach to teaching learning disabled and remedial students.* Portsmouth, NH: Heinemann.

Roller, C. (1996). *Variability not disability: Struggling readers in a workshop classroom*. Newark, DE: International Reading Association.

Rosaldo, R. (1989, 1993). *Culture & truth: The remaking of social analysis*. Boston: Beacon Press.

Roth, L., & Weller, C. (1985). Education/counseling models for parents of LD children. *Academic Therapy, 20*(4), 487–495.

Rourke, B. (1989). *Nonverbal learning disabilities: The syndrome and the model*. New York: Guilford Press.

Rourke, B., & Fuerst, D. (1991). *Learning disabilities and psychosocial functioning: A neuropsychological perspective*. New York: Guilford Press.

Schulz, J., & Carpenter, C. D. (1995). *Mainstreaming exceptional students: A guide for classroom teachers*. Boston: Allyn & Bacon.

Sergiovanni, T. (1993). *Organizations or communities? Changing the metaphor changes the theory*. Invited address, Division A, American Education Research Association, Annual Meeting, Atlanta, Georgia.

Shaywitz, S., & Shaywitz, B. (1988). Attention deficit disorder: Current perspectives. In J. Kavanaugh & J. Truss (Eds.), *Learning disabilities: Proceedings of the national conference* (pp. 369–567). Parkton, MD: York Press.

Spekman, N., Goldberg, R., & Herman, K. (1993). An exploration of risk and resilience in the lives of individuals with learning disabilities. *Learning Disabilities Research & Practice 8*(1), 11–18.

Spreen, O. (1988). *Learning disabled children growing up: A follow-up into adulthood*. New York: Oxford University Press.

Standing, E. M. (1998). *Maria Montessori. Her life and work*. New York: NAL Dutton.

Steele, C. M. (1992). Race and the schooling of black Americans, *The Atlantic Monthly*, April, 68–78.

Stein, M., Dixon, R., & Isaacson, S. (1994). Effective writing instruction for diverse learners. *School Psychology Review, 23*(3), 392–405.

Stires, S. (Ed.). (1991). *With promise: Redefining reading and writing for "special" students*. Portsmouth, NH: Heinemann.

Sustein, B. (1991). Notes from the kitchen table: Disabilities and disconnections. In Susan Stires (Ed.), *With promise: Redefining reading and writing for "special" students*. Portsmouth, NH: Heinemann.

Swadener, B. B., & Lubeck, S. (Eds.). (1995). *Children and families "at promise": Deconstructing the discourse of risk*. Albany, NY: SUNY.

Treisman, U. (1992). Studying students studying calculus: A look at the lives of minority mathematics students in college. *The College Mathematics Journal, 23*, 362–372.

U.S. Department of Education. (1997). *To assure the free appropriate public education of all children with disabilities: Nineteenth annual report to Congress on the implementation of The Individuals with Disabilities Education Act*.

U.S. General Accounting Office. (1981). *Disparities still exist in who gets special education*. Washington, DC: U.S. General Accounting Office.

Voeller, K. (1993). Techniques for measuring social competence in children. In G. Lyon (Ed.), *Frames of reference for the assessment of learning disabilities* (pp. 523–554). Baltimore: Paul H. Brookes.

Vogel, S., & Reder, S. (1998). Educational attainment of adults with learning disabilities. In S. Vogel & S. Reder (Eds.), *Learning disabilities, literacy, and adult education* (pp. 43–68). Baltimore: Paul H. Brookes.

Vogel, S. A. (1990). Gender differences in intelligence, language, visual-motor abilities, and academic achievement in students with learning disabilities: A review of the literature. *Journal of Learning Disabilities, 23*, 44–52.

Wang, M., Reynolds, M., & Walberg, H. (December 1994/January 1995). Serving Students at the Margin. *Educational Leadership, 52*(4), 12–17.

Webber, J. (1997). Responsible inclusion: Key components of success. In Paul Zionts (Ed.), *Inclusion strategies for students with learning and behavior problems* (pp. 27–55). Austin, TX: Pro-Ed.

Wiig, E. H., & Semel, E. (1984). *Language assessment and intervention for the learning disabled.* Columbus, OH: Merrill.

Winebrenner, S. (1996). *Teaching kids with learning difficulties in the regular classroom: Strategies and techniques every teacher can use to challenge and motivate struggling students.* Minneapolis, MN: Free Spirit.

Witherell, C., & Noddings, N. (Eds.). (1991). *Stories lives tell: Narrative and dialogue in education.* New York: Teachers College Press.

Ysseldyke, J., Algozzine, B., & Thurlowe, M. (1992). *Critical issues in special education.* Boston: Houghton Mifflin.

About the Editors and Contributors

MARY LYNN BOSCARDIN is Associate Professor and Chair of the Special Education Program in the School of Education at the University of Massachusetts at Amherst, where she teaches classes on language intervention strategies for children and youth with disabilities. She has published numerous journal articles, reports, abstracts, and book chapters in the areas of service delivery, finance, and assessment of special education. Currently, she is a member of the CASE Executive Committee and editor of the *Journal of Special Education Leadership,* the journal of research, policy, and practice for the Council of Administrators of Special Education. In addition to her experience in higher education, she has served as a speech and language pathologist, classroom teacher, and special education administrator.

LISA DELPIT is the holder of the Benjamin E. Mays Chair of Urban Educational Excellence at Georgia State University in Atlanta. Her publications include *Other People's Children: Cultural Conflict in the Classroom* and the coedited volume *The Real Ebonics Debate: Power, Language, and the Education of African-American Children.* Dr. Delpit describes her strongest focus as "finding ways and means to best educate urban students, particularly African-American, and other students of color." She is a former MacArthur fellow and recipient of the Award for Outstanding Contribution to Education in 1993 from the Harvard Graduate School of Education, which hailed her as a "visionary scholar and woman of courage."

ANDREW GARROD is Associate Professor of Education and Chair of the Department of Education at Dartmouth College, Hanover, New Hampshire, where he teaches courses in adolescence, moral development, and educational psychology. His recent publications include *Preparing for Citizenship: Teaching Youth to Live Democratically* (written with Ralph Mosher and Robert Kenny) and the coedited volumes *Souls Looking Back: Life Stories of Growing Up Black* (with Janie Ward, Tracy Robinson, and Robert Kilkenny) and *Crossing Customs: International Students Write on U.S. College Life and Culture* (with Jay Davis). In 1991 he was awarded Dartmouth College's Distinguished Teaching Award.

ROBERT KEGAN is a senior lecturer on education and the Chair of Learning and Teaching at Harvard University, Cambridge, Massachusetts. He is also the Educational Chair of the Institute for the Management of Lifelong Education and codirector of a joint program with the Harvard Medical School to bring principles of adult learning to the reform of medical education. He has explored the topic of adult development in his books *The Evolving Self: Problem and Process in Human Development* and *Over Our Heads: The Mental Demands of Modern Life.* A licensed psychologist and practicing therapist, he is also a faculty member at the Massachusetts School of Professional Psychology and a fellow at the Clinical Developmental Institute.

JANET LERNER is a professor at Northeastern Illinois University in Chicago. She is the author of the book *Learning Disabilities: Theories, Diagnosis, and Teaching Strategies,* now going into its eighth edition. The topic of successful adults with severe learning and reading disabilities has long been of interest to her. She is intrigued with the traits of these successful adults and how these individuals manage to overcome the odds. Dr. Lerner serves as Editor in Chief of the Learning Disabilities Association's journal, *Learning Disabilities: A Multidisciplinary Journal.*

HAROLD J. (HAL) McGRADY is currently the Executive Director of the Division for Learning Disabilities (DLD) in the Council for Exceptional Children (CEC). He has previously worked in both public schools and universities as a speech pathologist, special education administrator and professor of special education. He served as professor and head of the graduate program in learning disabilities at Northwestern University and headed the doctoral program in special education administration at Virginia Tech. His publications focus on speech/language pathology, learning disabilities, and the administration of special education programs.

PANO RODIS is a psychotherapist and psychological evaluator at Upper Valley Associates in Psychology & Education of East Thetford, Vermont. His clinical practice is primarily focused on supporting the psychological well-being of children, adolescents, and adults with learning differences. Additionally, Dr. Rodis is the school psychologist for a public high school and middle school in western New Hampshire, and a visiting assistant professor in the Department of Education at Dartmouth College.

CAROL WITHERELL, Professor of Education at Lewis and Clark College, teaches in the fields of moral development and ethics; child, adolescent, and life-span development; and the uses of narrative and dialogue in education. She is the editor and contributing author, with Nel Noddings, of *Stories Lives Tell: Narrative and Dialogue in Education,* published by Teachers College Press of Columbia University. Dr. Witherell serves on the editorial board of the *Journal of Moral Education* and as an editorial advisor for Learning Communities Narratives. She is a member of the Oregon Ethics Commons and the Association for Moral Education, and she serves as cochair of the Education and Human Development Committee of the City Club of Portland. She is active within the arts community as a singer and board member of the Oregon Repertory Singers, where she serves as chair of the artistic committee.

Index

Note: A page number followed by a t indicates a table.